CHURCH AND CHAMBER BARREL-ORGANS

IN MEMORIAM

J. T. N. B.

" Quis desiderio sit pudor aut modus tam cari capitis ? "

Horace : Odes, Bk. I. 24.

A Barrel-organ builder's workshop in 1775 (from Père Engramelle:
La Tonotechnie, Paris 1775).

Church and Chamber Barrel-Organs

Their Origin, Makers, Music and Location

A CHAPTER IN ENGLISH CHURCH MUSIC

BY

LYNDESAY G. LANGWILL,

O.B.E., HON.M.A., HON.F.T.C.L.

AND

THE LATE

CANON NOEL BOSTON

M.A., F.S.A., M.M.C.M., HON.F.A.M.S.

Second Edition, revised and enlarged

PUBLISHED BY

LYNDESAY G. LANGWILL

7 DICK PLACE, EDINBURGH, 9.

February 1970

First Published 1967.
Second Edition 1970.

PRINTED IN GREAT BRITAIN BY LINDSAY & CO. LTD., EDINBURGH

FOREWORD

By W. L. SUMNER, PH.D., B.SC., F.L.S., A.K.C.
Fellow of the Royal School of Church Music
Fellow of the Institute of Musical Instrument Technology.

It is splendid news that a second edition of this book is called for so soon, since it testifies both to its value and the interest that there is in its subject. The " Music that goeth with a wheel " is of great antiquity. " The organ which plays by itself " (as long as a head of water was maintained to raise the wind and turn the barrel) was known in Byzantium in the seventh and eighth centuries of our era. Moreover, I suspect that most of that which was known to the Arabs was recorded centuries before, in the great Alexandrian Library, sacked and destroyed by fire. It is a far cry from these Graeco-Arabian instruments, with their noisy modal tunes, to the lengthy and highly sophisticated works, composed by Mozart, towards the end of his short life, for the self-playing organs and musical clocks in Count Deym's wax-work museum on the Danube canal in Vienna. Indeed, so remarkable are these compositions, that when they are transcribed to be played by hands and feet on the organ, they appear as major works, which will stand up unashamedly in the company of J. S. Bach! The self-playing organ has attracted composers for centuries; and Handel, Haydn and Beethoven together with many lesser composers, produced significant music for it. A magnificent early nineteenth century example was the Apollonicon, built by Flight and Robson, in their factory in St. Martin's Lane, London. This was so large and had so many barrels that it was intended to replace a whole orchestra. A smaller example, built first in 1501, in the side of the Castle above Salzburg, and known as the Bull organ, because it finishes its thrice-daily performances by a roar caused by making its pipes sound all together, still plays as it did in Mozart's time, though in the noisy city of today it is not easy to hear it. Another automatic organ, driven by water power, plays in the Archbishop's pleasure gardens, not far away. Examples of old pinned barrels, such as those set out in Dom Bedos's monumental book on organ-building, which appeared a few years before the French Revolution, have been useful to musicologists to inform them exactly how ornaments were played at the time when the barrels were pinned.

The history of the church barrel-organ in England throws an interesting light on the sociology of organ-playing in the period when the church " orchestra ", in the gallery, had been displaced by the organ, whether " barrel " or " finger " or a combination of both. There must have been a shortage of male organists in the earlier decades of the nineteenth century because many of the notable London churches had women organists, and the smaller churches and village churches had barrel organs. In the second half of the century, owing to the influence of J. Stainer, W. T. Best, H. J. Gauntlett, G. Cooper, the organists and a galaxy of organ-builders, such as Hill, Willis, Lewis, Walker, Bryceson, Bishop and Bevington, there was a plentiful supply of male organists and barrel organs were converted to finger organs, were " junked " or left in dark corners and galleries as museum pieces. A few still ground out their tunes Sunday by Sunday. The Fair-organ, the Dutch " dray-organ ", the Musical Box, the German clock and automatic organs have been considered already in competent books. With the present work the authors have at last, provided an account of the English barrel organ, and thereby dealt with an interesting aspect of the history of the organ. The late Canon Noel Boston, an example of the ideal Anglican priest, and a member of the Organ Committee of the Central Council for the Care of Churches, has contributed in Chapters I, III and IV (in part) the results of a life-time of interest in barrel organs and the music they provided. His co-author, Lyndesay Langwill, a well-known authority on orchestral instruments and their makers, has been a worthy collaborator on whom devolved the completion of the book. Without him the book could not have appeared. Arthur Ord Hume's chapter on the barrel mechanism provides an invaluable contribution.

A pathetic interest attaches to this foreword, which I am honoured to write. This pleasant task was undertaken by Dr. Wilfrid Greenhouse Allt, C.B.E., a former Principal of Trinity College of Music, London, when his death prevented it. May this note be a tribute to him.

W. L. SUMNER.

The University,
  Nottingham,
    January 1970.

CONTENTS

LIST OF PLATES

Frontispiece: A BARREL-ORGAN BUILDER'S WORKSHOP IN 1775.

PREFACE TO THE FIRST EDITION

When in March 1965 the late Canon Noel Boston invited me to collaborate with him in writing a book on Church Barrel-Organs, I little thought that his participation in the work was to be cut short with such untimely suddenness by his death in July 1966. He had completed Chapters 1, 3 and 4—the latter including only the list of sacred tunes, but so much remained to be written that publication was inevitably delayed.

The survey of barrel-organs, past or present, in English and Welsh churches and chapels involved prolonged and extensive correspondence with vicars, rectors, church-wardens to all of whom the surviving author records his gratitude. It was to be expected that after the lapse of a century or more, information, if any, would normally be meagre and this certainly proved to be the case. In only two cases was a privately printed barrel-organ tune-book found to exist, *viz*. Milton Abbot, Devon (where alas, the barrel-organ no longer exists) and Cardeston, Shropshire. Tune-lists, however, survive in many cases as these, invariably written in a flowing hand between c. 1780 and c. 1850, are to be found pasted on the back or inside a panel of original organ-cases even where the organ has been converted to manual and the barrel mechanism removed in whole or in part.

It was decided to include chamber barrel-organs in the survey and lists of secular tunes on the barrels. Private owners and museum curators readily supplied lists of chamber barrel-organs in their possession and soon the titles of over a thousand secular tunes had been card-indexed for inclusion in Chapter 4. It is hoped that this feature may afford an interesting side-light on the " home music " of our ancestors in Georgian and early Victorian days.

The compilation of a list of all known barrel-organ makers proceeded simultaneously with the list of churches known to have had or have still a barrel-organ. Naturally the makers in Chapter 5 grew in number as the list of churches recorded in Chapter 6 became longer. Finally, over 120 makers were recorded and some four hundred churches which for convenience have been listed under their respective counties. It will be observed that barrel-organs were most numerous in East Anglia and the West Country. The record of over fifty in Sussex is exceptional due to the researches of the late Canon K. H. MacDermott whose charming books " Sussex Church Music in the Past " and " The Old Church Gallery Minstrels " afford fascinating reading for all interested in this period of English Church Music. The final Chapter consists of a list of barrel-organs of all kinds—chamber, Church, table, bird-organs etc, in private collections and public museums, surely the first such list to be compiled. The ready assistance received is gratefully acknowledged.

Such a pioneer work might well have had a very restricted appeal and the authors were encouraged by receiving a generous guarantee from the Marc Fitch Fund. The circulation of a prospectus resulted in nearly four hundred pre-publication orders.

Finally, to add interest to a book so largely composed of tabular matter, a score of illustrations of surviving and, in most cases workable, barrel-organs has been included.

The surviving author wishes to express his gratitude for much help and encourage-ment, in particular to F. L. Balmforth, John Budgen (of Messrs. Bishop, Ipswich), Rev. B. B. Edmonds, H. W. Geary, F. F. Hill, John Holmes (Eire), Noel Mander,

Roy Mickleburgh, Arthur Ord-Hume, Miss Barbara Owen (U.S.A.), F. W. Steer, John Wilson, and to Mr. Brims and his staff of Messrs. Lorimer & Chalmers Ltd. for care and attention in the printing of this book.

L. G. LANGWILL.

7 DICK PLACE,
EDINBURGH.
April 1967.

PREFACE TO THE SECOND EDITION

The gratifying reception accorded to the first edition of this book in 1967 was followed by a succession of letters from readers at home and abroad reporting examples of surviving barrel organs, in some cases for church use, but mainly chamber instruments. Besides adding these, it has also been possible to bring up to date information about organs merely recorded in the first edition, and a few additional illustrations have been included.

Indicative of the growing interest in the subject, to which this is the first book to be exclusively devoted, is the restoration of a number of church barrel organs: viz. Sutton, (Beds.): Avington, (Hants.): Newchurch (I.O.W.) (Dumb-Organist): Raithby, (Lincs.): Bettws Cedewen (Montgom.) (Dumb-Organist): Trelystan, Montgom.): Bressingham, (Nflk.) Letheringsett, (Nflk.): Mattishall Burgh, (Nflk.): Witton, (Nflk.): Wood Rising, (Nflk.): Cranford Chapel, (Northants.): Easton-on-the-Hill, (Northants.) (Dumb-Organist): Sutton, (Northants.): Winwick, (Northants.): Ossington, (Notts.): Staunton, (Notts.): Brightwell Baldwin, (Oxon.): Hampton Gay, (Oxon.): Wardley, (Rutland): Cardeston, (Salop.): Isle Abbots, (Som.): Muchelney, (Som.): Shelland, (Suffolk): Wiston, (Suffolk): Brightling, (Sussex.): Liddington, (Wilts.): Compton Wynyates, (Warws.): Blacktoft, (Yorks.).

In conclusion, it is a pleasure to express my indebtedness afresh to those who helped me with the first edition and to Mr John Budgen and the Rev. B. B. Edmonds in particular for their continued help. Much assistance in the present edition has been received from Mr Laurence Elvin, author of *Forster & Andrews* the Hull Organ builders, and from Mr Leslie Morgan.

LYNDESAY G. LANGWILL

7 DICK PLACE,
Edinburgh. EH9 2JS.
December 1969.

CHAPTER 1

THE HISTORY OF THE BARREL ORGAN.

By the late CANON NOEL BOSTON

Automation tends to come as the latest development of a machine. Whatever that machine may be, the normal pattern of its evolution tends to be years of manual control gradually lessening as the machine becomes more and more complicated, levers giving way to press buttons and then, finally, the controls are reduced to a single switch which sets in motion the fully automatic machine.

But this was not at all the pattern of the barrel organ. In organ history there exists a sort of twilight period. This twilight period of organ history goes back to Ctesibius of Alexandria (BC 250) and both he and Banu-Musa in " Muristus," Bagdhad, 813-833, seem to describe a primitive barrel organ. Dr. Sumner in his book *The Organ* (Macdonald) devotes some space to this very early period and prints a translation of a description of a hydraulic organ by Anathasius Kircher, a Jesuit archaeologist who lived 1601 to 1680 and had access to an early Latin translation of an Arabian MS which may well have been Bana Musa's work. A 14th century MS at Stamboul describes a mechanical organ built by Tagi al Dini Farabi (813-33). The evidence of this is examined in H. G. Farmer's " *The Organ of the Ancients,*" and in Hopkins and Rimbault's " *The Organ, Its History and Construction* " and, in Clutton and Niland's excellent book " *The British Organ,*" the statement is positively made: " The organ dates from the third century B.C., at latest." And, from the very first, it seems there were self-operating organs just as there were Aeolian harps.

So much for the " twilight " period. What we term the modern history of the barrel organ really begins with a statement by William of Malmesbury, the monastic chronicler, who died in 1142. On page 175 of the Bohn edition of the *Chronicle* he describes a barrel organ built by Pope Silvester II (c. 1003) when a young man, and states that the organ was still existing at Rheims.

It is difficult to think that the mediaeval skills which could produce such wonders of mechanical intricacy as the Wells Cathedral and other great clocks would not have produced some self-playing organs, just as they produced self-playing carillons and chimes. Indeed, such may well exist in some remote corner of a little-frequented continental church. But no such instances are known to us. When, however, the barrel organ does occur again in known history it does so in so complicated and marvellous a form that it is quite impossible to believe that it is anything but the culmination of years of experience and building of such instruments.

It was in the year 1597 that the English merchants, whose trade lay in the Near East, persuaded Queen Elizabeth the First to send a present to the Sultan of Turkey and thus improve relations between the two countries. At first, it was thought that this present might well take the form of an elaborate chiming clock, more especially as it was known that the Queen possessed just such a clock which she could well spare.

But perhaps Elizabeth had other ideas. We do not know, but we do know that it was decided that the present should take the form of an organ and Thomas Dallam, the famous organ builder who was to build the organ at King's College, Cambridge around 1605, was commissioned to do the work. Thomas Dallam was a great character as well as a great organ builder and happily kept a diary for, to his consternation, he discovered that Elizabeth not only required him to build the organ but also to accompany it out to Turkey and erect it safely in the Sultan's Palace. Stanley Mayes, in 1956, published a splendid edition of Dallam's Diary under the title *An Organ for the Sultan* (Putnam). This book is very well worth reading from many aspects such as Elizabethan travel, Elizabethan life and a rollicking sea story; but is with the evidence concerning the organ itself that we are concerned, for the organ was both a keyboard organ and a barrel organ. But let Thomas Dallam himself describe what he made:

"in the tope of the orgon, being 16 foute hie, did stande a holly busche full of blacke birds and thrushis, which at the end of the musick did sing and shake theire wynges . . . . tow personagis . . . stood upon to corners of the seconde storie, houldinge two silver trumpets in their handes." There were in addition " 7 planets everie one to appear at this minat houldinge in his hande what he did signifie."

Dallam himself, though he built and assembled the organ, did not make the mechanical and clockwork parts. These were the work of Randolph Bull, the famous Elizabethan horologist. What immediately concerns us obout this organ is that " it would goo of itse'f but 4 times in 24 hours." Although there was also a keyboard yet "There shall be placed in the lower part of the instrument three several strong, forcible and artificial bellows, with a very strong sufficient motion of wheels and pinions, very well wrought, and sufficient to drive and move the bellows at all times from time to time for the space of six hours together, whensoever the wheels and pinions shall be applied to such purposes; and that there shall be contained within the said instrument a board called a sound-board, with certain instruments or engines called the barrels and keys, and five whose stops of pipes, viz., one open principal, unison recorder, octavo principal, and a flute, besides a shaking stop, a drum and a nightingale."

It was all carefully packed and crated and, in February, 1599, this wonderful instrument accompanied by its builder, Thomas Dallam, set out for Turkey in the good ship " Hector."

We can hardly think that the art of barrel organ building, having reached such a height, was discontinued in the 17th century for a time. But no 17th century barrel organs are known to me. The only evidence of mechanical organs in that period comes from an article contributed by Lady Susi Jeans and Guy Oldham to *The Organ* in January, 1959, entitled *Water Blown Organs in the 17th Century*. They reprint illustrations of such organs at Rome (1650) and Wurzburg (1657) which show very clearly that these were in fact barrel organs.

The year 1700 is a most important one in the history of the barrel organ if we are to believe that it was in that year that a barrel organ was installed in the Church of King Charles the Martyr, Peak Forest, Derbyshire. A number of English parish churches may well have possessed barrel organs by that date, but we know nothing about them. Yet, between the building of the Peak Forest organ in 1700 (it is said that it was still there in 1870) and the erection of the Ash Priors (Somerset) barrel organ in 1879, we know of the existence of something like 500 barrel organs in English Churches. Often our knowledge is no more than a mention of the existence, at some period, of a long lost and destroyed instrument; but something like 80 survive of which we have examined some fifty.

Often the church barrel organ was quite a small instrument. The one in Plate 25 is small but typical. It possesses only two stops, Principal and Diapason. It is 2 feet 6 inches wide, 4 feet high and 16 inches deep. One of the features in many small barrel organs which led to their eventual destruction, rather than adaptation to keyboard organs, was the fact that they were not chromatic. In order to save pipes, and hence size and expense, all the tunes were in two or three keys, usually G or D. Normally there were three barrels, but any number could be purchased. The fascination and the historical usefulness of the barrel organ lies in the fact that, alone of musical instruments, it not only shows us what tunes were used and where, but it also shows us the contemporary fashion of organ playing. We can learn a tremendous lot about the history of the tunes if we know on what organs they occur and the dates of the organs. This book represents the first serious attempt to set out the available material. The lists will show, beyond all doubt, just which tunes were most popular with our forbears and at what part of the country during the hundred and fifty years or so that barrel organs were to be found in many of our smaller churches. Today there is, we believe, only one parish church which regularly depends upon a barrel organ for the accompaniment of its hymn tunes, namely Shelland in Suffolk. The organ was built by Bryceson about 1810 and the following directions, printed by Bryceson, are still to be read pasted on to the organ case: —

"Directions for the Management of Bryceson's Barrel Organs. To change the tunes and shift the barrels: observe on the right hand of the Organ there are two brass sliding plates, one crosses the other, the top plate draws towards you, and that raises the keys from the barrel and prevents the keys and pins from touching each other while you change your tune: the upright sliding plate is for fixing the tune in the round pin that comes through the panel, on which is cut ten notches for the tunes on the barrels; while the keys are free from the barrel you may shift it backwards or forwards by the brass pin, and set it to any tune you would play, counting the outside notch for the first, push down the outside plate into the notch and the cross plate from you, that lets the keys on the barrel in order for playing. When you change a barrel pull across the bolt towards you and raise the upright one that sets the barrel at liberty, pull it out and let the two sliding plates remain until you put in the other barrel, and then set your tunes as above directed."

These directions may become rather clearer after the next chapter and especially if read in conjunction with Plate 2.

But the final portion of Bryceson's directions help us to see the contemporary picture in the early 19th century: —

" Advice to churchwardens on Bryceson's Organs. Built on a peculiar Construction adapted to the Services and Dimensions of any Church. To those wishful to promote decent Psalmody in their Congregations, they are a certain guide; the Tunes are so correctly set, as to be equal in performance to a Finger Organ, and will entirely supercede (sic) the use of other instruments. In consequence of the great Expence of a Finger Organ, and the Salary of an Organist, many serious People are deprived of the means of joining in that pleasing part of Divine Worship, while it is not generally known that an able substitute may be had in one of his Barrel Organs, and at an Expence which almost any Congregation can afford—The Prices are from 40 Guineas to 100 upwards."

Whilst in the smaller organ, one barrel had to be withdrawn and another slid into position by hand, a number of the large barrel organs including those at Wissington, Mattishall Burgh, Staunton and Raithby had a sort of revolving magazine (see plate 16) which enable the organs to hold three barrels of some 30 tunes. Some organs, but very few church instruments, worked like Dallam's famous Turkish Organ, by clockwork so that the mechanism, actuated by great weights, was wound up like a church tower clock and the organ then played entirely on its own, the change of stops being the only function that required hand manipulation. We shall see about the mechanism of the instruments in the next chapter. But the barrel organ must be treated seriously from a musical point of view. After all, the fingers of an organist are ten, even if, today, his control is hugely extended by all manner of couplers and " octaves." But the only limit to the number of notes that the barrel organ can play is the number of its keys. Handel wrote music specially for the third Earl of Bute's barrel organ and his secretary, John Christopher Smith, seems to have arranged it and John Langshaw " pinned " the tunes.*

Indeed, well may the great Dr. Burney write in his *General History of Music* (1776),

" Of all the instruments the barrel organ is the most easy of performance, as it merely requires a regular motion given to it by a handle. On this account it is an instrument of very general use; and the recent improvements of some English artists have rendered the barrel capable of an effect equal to the fingers of the first rate performers."

* "Lord Bute's Barrel Organs " by M. I. Wilson, in *Musical Opinion*, February, 1966, p 289.

PLATE 1

'Dumb Organist' by Bevington, London. Early 19th century.
Newchurch Church, Isle of Wight. Restored by R. Mickleburgh,
Bristol, 1961.

Chapter II

THE ENGLISH BARREL ORGAN — A DESCRIPTION

By Arthur W. J. G. Ord-Hume,
Editor: Journal of the Musical Box Society of Great Britain.

The mechanism of the barrel-organ is one of simplicity and extreme effectiveness. That some instruments are still in playing order after over 150 years with little or no attention is evidence of the practical design and durability of the basic organ component assemblies.

The barrel organ may be said to be divided into four basic parts—the pallet chest combining soundboard and pipe-rack with pipes; the key frame and action parts; the bellows and reservoir complete with operating mechanism and finally the barrel which is intended to be removable. The whole is fixed into a case often combining with or standing on a base designed to contain spare barrels of tunes.

In operation, these four parts integrate to produce music from the pins on the barrel which represent the tune to be played. The whole mechanism is shown diagrammatically in Plate 2.

The barrel is a wooden cylinder comprising an arbor mounting two or more formers upon the periphery of which is a continuous casing formed of wood strips glued on. The barrel is lathe-turned to present a smooth outer surface which is then covered with paper. One end of the barrel (the right end when viewed in the organ) is turned to a smaller diameter and formed into a drive pinion by the provision of longitudinal teeth cut into the wood. The barrel was frequently constructed of beech or ash with a softwood exterior such as straight pine. The tune is represented on the barrel by pins and bridges formed from flat-section brass wire. Whilst short notes are catered for with one pin of flat wire, sustained notes are created by forming the wire into staple-like bridges of requisite length. These are shown in Plate 2.

More than one tune can be pinned to a barrel. Nine, ten, eleven or even twelve tunes are often to be found pinned to one. The barrel is supported for playing in the organ by a wooden carrier which is mounted in guide rails which traverse the organ frame. This allows the barrel (a) to be slid in and out of the organ easily when changing barrels, and (b) to allow the slight adjustment needed to play different tunes by bringing another set of pins under the key frame. The location of the barrel into the organ and the tune-changing adjustment is achieved by a long brass stud screwed to the right end of the carrier. This stud is cut with grooves or notches corresponding in number to the tunes on the barrel and in pitch to the spacing of the sets of pins to produce each tune.

This stud protrudes through the right side of the organ case where it can be locked into any tune position by a sliding bolt or 'knife' which engages in a suitable notch.

The pins on the barrel serve to raise metal keys contained in a frame which is held above the barrel and is supported at each end by the sides of the case. This key frame comprises a wooden member carrying beneath it the pivot (usually a long piece of wire) for the keys which are formed from steel sheet. The keys are kept at the correct lateral spacing by being held in a slot in a brass strip in front (and often behind as well) of the frame member. The whole frame is fixed on pivots in the organ frame so that it can be raised *in toto* to enable the keys to clear the barrel pins when moving the barrel. A linkage is provided so that it is impossible to unlock the knife from the tune notch in the barrel stud until the key frame is raised by the action of a cross bolt.

Next to be examined is the organ proper which can be said to comprise the direct speaking mechanism.

This is built up on the pallet chest which is a long, narrow and shallow box containing along its front edge one soft-leather faced pallet for each key on the key-frame. The pallet, when opened, uncovers a windway through to the pipes which are mounted in line along the top of this box—the soundboard. The pallet chest is sealed with a leather-faced front board and the pallets are held normally closed with small brass springs. On instruments having more than one rank of pipes, the soundboard is separated from the pallet chest by an intermediate board drilled with windways for extra rows of pipes. These windways can be closed off by means of a sliding wooden strip. Each sliding strip opens or closes the windway to the soundboard for one rank of pipes and each slider is called a stop and is controlled at will via a draw-stop or knob protruding at the front or side of the case.

The pallets which control the speaking of the pipes are linked to the keys with stickers made of thin wood with wire extensions at their lower ends which pass through small holes in the pallet chest to open the pallets. The stickers are normally hinged to the tails of the keys with soft leather or are supported at their top ends in a guide so that the key tails push them down. Adjustment is usually provided to take up any slack in this action which would delay the speech of the pipe and create mechanical noise in performing.

The pipes of the barrel organ operated on a very low wind pressure usually in the region of two inches pressure. There are four basic types of pipe used; (a) stopped wood; (b) open wood (both of these being either square or rectangular in section; (c) open metal; (d) closed metal (both these being circular in section). Stopped wood pipes provide the stopped diapason and tuning is by movable wooden stoppers with leather seals in the tops of the pipes. Open wood is often used for Principal and Flute, tuning being by shaving or by adjustment of length. Twelfth and Fifteenth stops are of open metal flue pipes. Closed metal pipes, operating on slightly higher pressure, have soldered metal caps and are frequently found on showman's organs (so-called ' grinder organs ') to produce a brash, almost reedy tone. These were tuned by large ears on each side of the pipe mouth. They are also used in the serinette or bird-organ.

Whilst the wood pipes of English organs were of the normal mouthed type, Continental organs often used the Vienna flute form with semi-circular inverted mouths.

Barrel organs seldom possessed a chromatic compass of notes and the majority comprised 8, 14, 17, 19, 27, 28, 29 or, in some instances, up to 56 notes. On the smaller organs having 14 keys, two diatonic scales would be provided, these being G and D. All the barrel tunes would have to be transposed into these two abbreviated scales, supplemented by a few bass pipes at large intervals such as D and G. The majority of barrel organ music was either adapted directly from that played by the earlier church orchestras or capable of optional accompaniment usually played by the violin and since the violin is best in the key of A, most organs of more than 14 keys would incorporate the G♮ to enable this key to be used. Larger organs still would use the D♯ to bring in the scale of E. This enlargement of compass was of course hand in hand with the larger number of keys and the large organs of Forster & Andrews, for example, would carry one, two or even more chromatic octaves.

The fourth item of the barrel organ is the method of providing wind. This comprises a set of bellows, either single or double acting feeders or rocking feeders pumping air into a reservoir, use being made of leather flap valves. The pressure of wind in the reservoir is maintained normally by springs but sometimes by lead or iron weights.

Soft white skin was invariably used for bellows and reservoir, stiffened on the inside with cardboard, to aid in folding.

The feeders are driven by reciprocators connected to a crankshaft at one end of which is a removable handle.

By turning the handle, two separate functions are achieved. Firstly, a worm gear on the shaft engages in the barrel cog and turns the barrel. Secondly, one or more cranks on the shaft serve to move the reciprocators which inflate the reservoir.

Some larger instruments were fitted with percussion—a drum and triangle normally, although tabor and castagnette are sometimes to be found and one notable organ examined by the writer also contained a 12-note spinet! On most large organs, percussion was represented on separate barrel pins and a special stop knob was provided to disengage the percussion if required.

Barrel organ cases tended to follow strictly traditional lines. The majority of early ones were beautifully made in mahogany, often veneered and inlaid with boxwood and rosewood and overlaid with fretted designs. The front, made to slide upwards to gain access to the works, contained one or more panels of gilded wooden imitation pipes on a background of green or red silk.

Comprising a bottom built up of mahogany framing, the case was built around four corner posts, morticed into the bottom. Cross members morticed into these posts provided an extremely robust structure. The corner posts were grooved to take the sides and back panelling. The right hand side panel is always screwed to the frame to determine rigidity for the tune change mechanism which it carries on its outside. Both back and left side panels are free to be slid out as well as the front.

Some chamber and church organs were made with arched fronts of imitation pipes whilst others were made with perfectly flat tops, the imitation pipes being wholly encompassed by the front panelling.

It was usual for the left side panel to contain a small door to permit access to the barrel for changing and the tunes which the barrel or barrels played were written on paper and stuck either to this door or (in the case of flat-top organs) on the inside of the lid. Organs built expressly for church use were often made to be played from the rear, the " organist " remaining out of sight of the congregation. This was accomplished by the simple expedient of making the case back to front. The mechanism remained in precisely the same juxtaposition but the decorative side of the case was behind the organ and the plain side faced the performer.

Later, organs were built in oak, deal and other woods but the rich patina of mahogany is perhaps the most beautiful to behold.

In playing the barrel organ, a skilful performer can induce much colour into the music by the use of the stops and the sympathetic turning of the handle. As any experienced barrel organist knows, there is more to playing the organ than just mechanically turning the crank. Performance calls for rehearsal to obtain the very best and any tendency towards *rallentando* in excess can result in the embarrassing experience of losing wind in the middle of a performance.

THE ORCHESTRION, THE BARREL PIANO, THE ORGANETTE AND THE PLAYER ORGAN.

The English Barrel Organ enjoyed a somewhat unique position in the history of mechanical music. In no other country was the instrument accorded such respect as in Great Britain and even in France and Germany (from whence the barrel organ largely originated) church barrel organs were almost unheard of. Their use outside the church was similarly limited.

Inasmuch as the English Barrel Organ enjoyed a unique position within the British Isles, the Orchestrion can be said to have been the prerogative of the Germans.

Basically, the Orchestrion comprised a Barrel Organ mechanism arranged to play not only flue-type organ pipes, but reed stops and percussion with the aim of imitating the various instruments of the orchestra. These instruments were of necessity very large and perhaps the most famous maker was the Black Forest firm of Imhof & Mukle

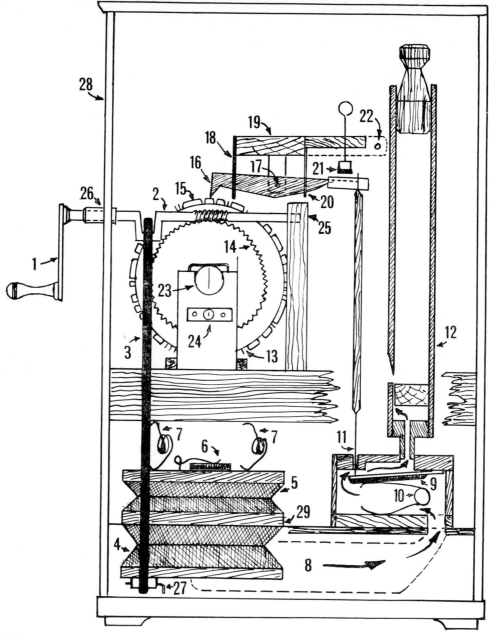

KEY

1. Detachable crank handle.
2. Crankshaft incorporating worm drive gear engaging in (14).
3. Reciprocator between Crank and Feeders.
4. Feeders, (generally termed Bellows).
5. Air reservoir fed through non-return flap valves by Feeders.
6. Spring loaded spill valve to Reservoir (5).
7. Steel springs to maintain air pressure in Reservoir (5).
8. Windway in organ frame between Reservoir and actual organ windchest.
9. Pallet in windchest controlling passage of air into Pipe (pallet shown open).

10. Spring (normally of brass) to keep Pallet (9) closed when Key (16) is at rest.
11. Sticker or operating rod between Key (16) and Pallet (9).
12. Pipe (shown in section) of typical stopped diapason wood flue type.
13. Barrel.
14. Cog carved in end of Barrel (13).
15. Wire bridges and pins on surface of Barrel (13) to lift key (16).
16. Key which controls one Pallet (9) to one note on organ.
17. Key pivot.
18. Slotted brass guide for forward end of Key (16).
19. Key Frame.

20. Slotted brass guide for rear end of Key (16).
21. Adjustment to remove slack movement in key action.
22. Pivot for Key Frame (19).
23. Axis of Barrel (13) resting at each end in carrier frame.
24. Notched stud on barrel carrier to bring different sets of pins under keys to change the tunes.
25. Wooden bearing to support rear end of Crankshaft (2).
26. Bearing to support forward end of Crankshaft (2) where it passes through Case (28).
27. Pin connecting Reciprocator (3) to Feeders (4).
28. Organ Case.
29. Fixed board of bellows assembly.

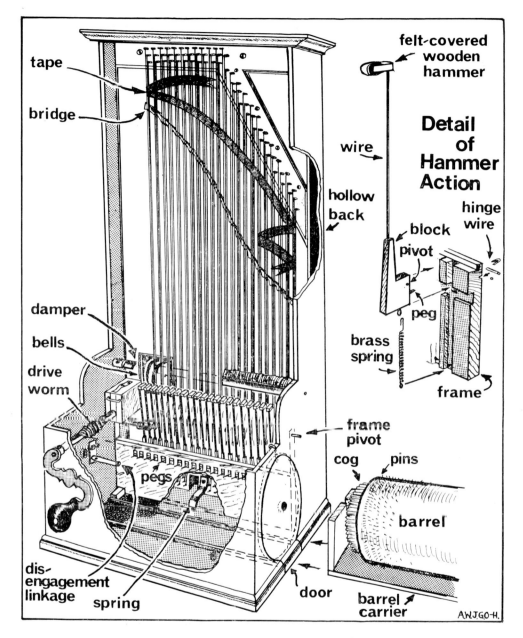

tape

bridge

felt-covered
wooden
hammer

wire

**Detail
of
Hammer
Action**

hollow
back

hinge
wire

block

pivot

damper

bells

drive
worm

peg

brass
spring

frame

frame
pivot

cog   pins

pegs

barrel

dis-
engagement
linkage   spring

door   barrel
carrier

A.W.J.GO-H.

The basic mechanism of the Barrel Piano is illustrated in this cut-away drawing of a
typical portable street piano of the 1800's. Such instruments were the contemporary of
the street barrel organ and provided the accessory of the wandering street musician. As
with street barrel organs, these barrel pianos were intended to be carried by a leather
shoulder strap. Pianos, however, tended to be heavier than portable organs and thus,
as a further support whilst playing, a single vertical pole could be fixed from a socket
in the back of the case upon which to rest the instrument.

Larger pianos resembling an ordinary piano but with no keyboard and with a suitably
corpulent case front to contain the barrel, were made which were both hand turned and
clockwork-operated. These latter were invariably intended for use in public-houses and
were coin-operated.

which later established offices in London (*s.v.* Imhof & Mukle). These instruments ranged from large-compass 'straight' barrel organs playing two stops of all-wood flue pipes to fully orchestral examples having as many as eight or more mixed stops of pipes, reeds and percussion and often complete with swell box. None of these was made in this country although a large number was imported, among these being the famous Blackpool Tower Orchestrion now on permanent exhibition at the Birmingham City Museum.

Whilst it can be claimed that the first Orchestrion-type of instrument was that conceived by Thomas Dallam and presented to the Sultan of Turkey in 1599, no English maker appears to have given serious thought to this type of mechanical organ. Although Orchestrions were being made in Germany late in the eighteenth century, the first true Orchestrion to be seen in England was that designed and built by the Dresden organ builder Frederick Theodore Kaufmann. This was demonstrated at Buckingham Palace and elsewhere in London during the spring and summer of 1851. The nearest British attempt was Messrs. Flight & Robson's Apollonicon, first shown in 1817. Messrs. Forster & Andrews also built large semi-orchestral Barrel Organs which might possibly come into the Orchestrion class.

Many were the early attempts to automate keyboard instruments by the mechanical operation of the keys. Clementi, Collard & Co., the firm which developed from Clementi & Co. (*q.v.*) produced their 'Self-Acting Pianoforte' during the 1820's. This was essentially a barrel organ without the organ part, and the hand-cranked barrel worked keys in the usual way, the keys depressing stickers which acted directly on the piano keys. Courcell (*q.v.*) produced around the same time his 'Cylindrichord' which was most probably an identical principle capable of being pushed up to play any type of keyboard instrument. It is interesting to note that in spite of this logical development, A. F. Debain's 'Antiphonel' appeared in France in 1842 using wooden planchettes with steel pegs which, when moved by a crank, pushed down the keys.

It was left, reputedly, to John Hicks (*q.v.*) at one time of London and Bristol, to develop the Barrel Piano in the early part of the nineteenth century. The date of this invention is not determined. In fact, a French barrel piano with percussion accompaniment and driven, in the same manner as the Orchestrion, by a descending weight, is in the de Vere Green collection, London, and seems to date from the middle of the eighteenth century.

Hicks is best known as a maker of portable street pianos of the type illustrated in Plate 3. Subsequent development of the Barrel Piano principle resulted in much larger instruments, more of the size of the conventional upright piano, which were played either by turning a handle or by a clockwork motor. The itinerant street musicians, their pianos mounted on a hand-cart, favoured the hand-turned variant as, presumably, by this means they could be seen to justify the coppers thrown into the caps which the inevitable monkey held out to the passers-by. The more sophisticated clockwork pianos, operated by a coin-in-the-slot mechanism, found favour in public houses, cafés, amusement arcades and dance halls. The wide use of street music was severely curtailed by the Act of 1898 which made it an offence to cause annoyance by music in a public place. Many instruments were lost then and later when, in 1922, Mussolini recalled all the Italian street musicians — and most of the street musicians were Italian! See Plate 7.

Towards the end of the nineteenth century, the pneumatic mechanism for musical instruments devised early in the 1850's was perfected and this brought about the introduction of the Organette. The Organette comprised, in its simplest form, a set of free reeds mounted in a wooden box open at one end to the atmosphere and connected at the other to a pair of exhausters or bellows. By turning a handle, the exhausting bellows would draw out the air from the reed box. A strip of paper was placed across the open end of the reed box and in this paper roll were punched various holes to represent the tune to be played. When a hole passed over the top of the reed box, it would admit air into the partial vacuum beneath and thereby cause the reed to speak. Many were the variants of the Organette principle and their development continued apace until the end of the nineteenth century. Organettes were made which played paper rolls, endless paper bands, cardboard and metal discs and one American type even played small pinned wooden rollers which directly opened pallets over the reeds. These instruments provided a very cheap form of portable mechanical music at a time when the musical box was in vogue.

No account of the Barrel Organ, the Barrel Piano or the Organette can be considered complete without a brief reference to two popular misnomers—the lay terms 'Hurdy Gurdy' and 'Barrel Organ.' The vast majority of people believe the Barrel Organ and Organette to belong to a mythical genus 'Hurdy Gurdy.' The Hurdy Gurdy (Fr. *Vielle*: Ger. *Drehleier*) was, in fact, a stringed instrument played by turning a handle to sound drone strings and stopping off notes by means of key-operated tangents. Thus the Hurdy Gurdy bears no relationship whatsoever to any of these instruments. The second misnomer arises from the mistaken belief that the Street Piano, typified as being mounted on a hand-cart, played by a tramp and with the frequent addition of a colourfully-dressed monkey, is a Barrel Organ. It goes without saying that this is completely erroneous.

With the development of the Organette which could play, in the more popular styles, from fourteen to twenty-four notes, came the perfection of the pneumatic action which gave us the Player-Piano. Commonly termed 'Pianola' (which is a registered trade-name referring to one make of player-piano only), the self-acting piano industry began with the start of the twentieth century and, in spite of increasing competition from more sophisticated forms of entertainment, continued until the late nineteen-thirties. Indeed, to this day there is still a thriving, albeit small, industry both in England and Australia providing music-rolls to be played on these instruments.

From the development of the Player-Piano and the Organette came the logical step of the Player-Organ. These instruments ranged from full-compass reed organs which played a variety of stops contrived by numerous ingeniously-arranged boxes of different reeds each voiced to imitate a particular orchestral tone, to full-compass pipe-organs playing, much in the same way as a conventional pipe-organ, on a variety of stops. Both the Player-Reed-Organ and the Player-Pipe-Organ operated pneumatically from paper rolls of music. They were produced between 1900 and 1930 and the best-known manufacturer was the Aeolian Company of America which assembled and distributed large numbers of these instruments from their factory at Hayes, Middlesex, later to be destroyed by fire.

The fairground organ, by comparison, plays its music from a folded 'book' of music, the London firm of Chiappa still making music today. Some of the Dutch street-organs still retain the barrel principle of operation. 'Book' fair-organ music was invented by Gavioli in Paris during the first half of the nineteenth century to replace the barrel but many showmen preferred the continuous music available only from the barrel.

For further information on all these instruments, which are fundamentally but kinfolk to the Barrel Organ, the interested reader is recommended to refer to the various articles contained in the Journal of the *Musical Box Society of Great Britain*.

PLATE 4

Wissington Church, Suffolk. Barrel Organ by John Gray, London (1839).

Chapter III

THE PERIOD OF THE CHURCH BARREL ORGAN. ITS PRECURSOR THE CHURCH BAND. THE RISE IN POPULARITY OF THE BARREL ORGAN

" Barrel Organs . . . will entirely supercede (sic) the use of other instruments." So wrote the organ builder, Bryceson, in his Directions which he had printed and stuck into his barrel organs. He was, of course, only partly right. But what were these instruments he thought the barrel organ would supersede and why were they used?

The English scene which witnessed the introduction of the barrel organ was the end of the 18th century and the first half of the 19th, more especially the first half of the 19th. We shall probably be right if we say that the highest number of barrel organs would have been found in churches between 1840 and 1850.

Except for the Commonwealth period, the Cathedrals and great town churches have possessed organs for a very long period, much longer than most people think, and a study of the inventories drawn up at the Reformation will include " a pair of organs " in very many churches including a surprising number of village churches as well. After the Reformation, parish church music was almost entirely confined to the singing of the metrical Psalms concocted by Thomas Sternhold, Henry VIII's Groom of the Wardrobe, with the assistance later of John Hopkins, and published in 1551. In 1696, Nahum Tate and Nicholas Brady produced their revised or New Version. From the time of the Reformation then, right down to the middle of the 19th century, the singing of these metrical psalms was the only music heard in the village church. Of course, the larger parish churches would sing anthems and the Cathedrals both anthem and Setting to the Canticles, and the Psalms, too, would be chanted. Sometimes the villages would attempt a canticle but for the most part everything was said, the Psalms in the Prayer Book being recited, one verse by the Parish Clerk and the other by the congregation, or by the Parson and the Clerk. It is important not to confuse the Prayer Book Psalms with the Metrical Psalms. Both were used, but the Metrical Psalm was always sung. After the Third Collect the Clerk would say, " Brethren let us sing to the praise and glory of God Psalm number . . . " Then followed the sermon. During the singing of the Metrical Psalm the Parson would retire to the vestry and change his surplice for a black gown and in this he would preach his hour-long sermon. Then would follow another sung Metrical Psalm. It was to these words that our incomparable body of Hymn or Psalm Tune music grew up. What these tunes were will concern us in the next chapter. The problem now is how they were sung in the small parish church. I am thinking now of the church which did not possess an organ, and the reason for supposing that a very large number of village churches did not is the absence of any mention of an organ and the fact that in the late 18th century bands were introduced to accompany the singing. In the de Coverley Papers Addison speaks of the clerk " Sounding off the tune on a pitch-pipe." A pitch-pipe is a tiny wooden organ pipe whose note can be varied by the pulling out or pushing in of the stopper. It would be used only for unaccompanied singing. Now we know that the Covenanters were great unaccompanied singers and I think we may take it that many, perhaps most, small country churches tended to sing unaccompanied in the 17th and early eighteenth centuries. But from the Restoration it would seem that church bands gradually gained ground. It may well be that those churches which formerly possessed little organs had them destroyed during the Commonwealth and then, at the Restoration, there just were not enough organ-builders to cope with the mass of work required. Anyhow, Canon K. H. MacDermott in his book *The Old Church*

PLATE 5

Photo: I. G. Howell, Pinner.

Brightling Church, Sussex. Barrel organ by W. A. A. Nicholls c. 1820 ?
Restored by Harrison & Harrison.

Gallery Minstrels (S.P.C.K., London, 1948) lists some 266 church orchestras between 1660 and 1860 and certainly those that he lists are only a fraction of those that existed. Recently I bought the clarinet which had led the singing in Sporle Church, Norfolk, in the the 1780's just after Admiral Nelson's father had ceased to be incumbent. Generally speaking, towards the end of the 18th and during the 19th century, anyone who played an instrument would bring it along to church on Sunday. Thus the instruments Bryceson thought his barrel organs would supersede showed no especial pattern in their grouping. Strings were the most popular, violins, cellos or " bass viols." Clarinets were also popular and the serpent, a splendid bass instrument invented by Canon Guillaume of Auxerre in 1590, was often used. It is played with a cup mouthpiece and is made of wood covered with black leather and really does resemble a serpent. It was George III's favourite instrument, Handel scored for it and, indeed it appears in many great scores until ousted by the Ophicleide in the 1840's. But all sorts of combinations were used. Brightling is said to have possessed nine bassoons and Brierley Hill in Staffordshire, in 1830, had singing led by violins, flute, flageolet and ' bass viol ' (i.e. 'cello). They also had a trumpeter and a drummer; and at Eydon, near Daventry, an Ophicleide led the singing till an organ was installed in 1868. The chronicler of the village band is Thomas Hardy and " *Under the Greenwood Tree* " is largely the story of such a group of players. The same theme occurs in some of his short stories. Mellstock is Stinsford, near Dorchester, though the famous musicians' gallery has been " improved " away. Such were the instruments that came to be accepted as the norm in the small country church. Usually the musicians occupied a gallery in the West of the church and, once the Metrical Psalm had been announced, the entire congregation would turn and face West. During the 17th century the practice arose of "Lining Out " the Metrical Psalms for the benefit of those who could not read. This meant that the words were recited first. An ordinance of 1644 rules: " for the present, it is convenient that the Minister, or some person appointed by him, and the other ruling officers, do read the psalm line by line before the singing thereof." Sometimes the name of the tune would be written on a blackboard which would be hung over the front of the Gallery. The instruments would play a little overture, or introduction, or just three chords, and then the Psalm would begin. After each verse the band would play a few bars by itself which was known as the interlude.

Why did such bands give up? Mr. Mail in *Under the Greenwood Tree* delivered himself on the subject: " Times have changed from the times they used to be . . . People don't care much about us now! I've been thinking, we must be almost the last left in the county of the old string players. Barrel-organs, and they next door to 'em that you blow wi' your foot, have come in terribly of late years." Both musically and pastorally we may deplore the passing of the old church band. Thirty years later the village churches were to ape the Cathedrals and introduce surpliced choirs. It was all part of the process, of the change that was coming over the Church. Why do reforms and forward movements inevitably seem to involve tragedies which are quite unnecessary? One hundred and fifty years after passing of the Church band we have the Parish and People movement and the Liturgical Movement both demanding that the people should take a far fuller part in worship. So they did in those old days. Indeed, it was the sturdy independence of the singing gallery that made it unpopular with the clergy. It was intrenched in the past, in a way of doing things which had to be changed. The Oxford Movement could see little good in the magnificent heritage of English Psalm tune music. It was all part of the bad old days, and so we had the 1860 *Hymns Ancient and Modern*. The clergy looked to the Cathedrals, and so the little parish church was transformed. The box pews in the chancel were uprooted and choir stalls were placed there and, later, filled with boys in surplices. The band had to go, for only organ music would do and, since it was unlikely that anyone in the village could be found to play an organ or, for that matter, sufficient money raised, the Barrel organ was the answer. In fact we may quote, once more, Bryceson's advertisement: " In consequence of the great Expence of a Finger Organ, and the

Salary of an Organist, many serious People are deprived of the means of joining in that pleasing part of Divine Worship, whilst it is not generally known that an able Substitute may be had in one of his Barrel Organs."

The bands were the first to go and then the music, this was lucky since, before the music of the old church tunes went, it was transferred to the barrels of the barrel organs and there it lay till the fashions changed once more and, in our own century, we have seen a great resurgence of the strong and wonderful English tune tradition and the desuetude of the weak mass-produced tunes of the last century.

But there are some tunes that still lie in the barrels of barrel organs, so we must now address ourselves to the repertoire of the barrel organ.

PLATE 6

Photo by Surrey Advertiser Group, Guildford.

Barrel organ by John Walden (c. 1810), in Aldro School, Shackleford, Surrey.
Restored by F. F. Hill.

CHAPTER IV

THE TUNES PLAYED

In considering the tunes played by the barrel organs, a considerable difficulty, or rather limitation, arises. Obviously we shall have to refer to the tunes by their Tune Names rather than print them out in full. From the 16th century names were given to tunes. This was not so at first. The earliest Metrical Psalters had tunes printed by the words, rather like a modern hymn book. When the new Version was published, people would refer to the tunes of the older book as " The Old 100th " or " Old 148th " etc. It is said that Thomas Est, the printer of " *The Whole Book of Psalms* " (1592), was the first man to start giving tunes names with " Cheshire," " Kentish " and " Glassenburie." The practice soon grew and, whereas, in Germany, the tune was usually known by the first line of the words, (just as we might talk of singing " When I survey " instead of its tune name " Rockingham ") in England every tune had its name. No register of names exists and there is a great deal of overlapping. The writer has card-indexed the tunes appearing in his own collection of 17th, 18th and early 19th century tune-books and the list already runs to some 2000 names of tunes written before 1860. What makes it all the more confusing is that one tune can appear in different books under a variety of names. The famous " Tallis's Canon " which we sing to Ken's words " Glory to Thee my God this night," is usually called " Tallis's Canon " but also appears under the names " Evening Hymn," " Brentwood," "Magdalen," and another deservedly popular barrel organ tune, " Surrey," is sometimes called " Careys," " Yarmouth " or " St Olave's, Hart Street."

That is one side of the picture; but an even more confusing factor arises in that often the same name is given to quite different tunes. The name " Norwich " is, for instance, borne by no less than seven entirely different tunes. This chapter is based on the list of Barrel Organ tunes which follows and since some of the organs whose tune-lists survive are no longer in existence and others are no longer playable and yet others the authors have not been able to hear personally, it cannot always be assumed that the tunes bearing the same names are invariably the same tunes. But, with this caution, we may proceed on the assumption that they usually are. Yet, before we actually examine the incidence of tunes, it may be well to remember that it is just here that the barrel organ makes its greatest contribution to musical history, and this it does in two ways. First, it shows us just what was popular with contemporary congregations and how this popularity varied in different parts of the country. Next, where actual barrel organs survive in working order, it shows us just how the tunes were played at the period in which the organ was built. Hence, all sorts of textual variations are revealed by the barrel organ and all sorts of ornaments in the way of trills, passing notes, grace notes and " gathering " notes. Obviously it is out of the question in a book of this size to give details of all the tunes (and, in any case, such details rightly belong to the history of hymn tunes rather than barrel organs). Before taking a long journey to visit a barrel organ, it is always advisable to write to the incumbent of the church concerned and to enquire whether the barrel organ is still in working condition and to ask permission to use it. Handles are often hidden away as a precaution against misuse by children and others.

One other caution is necessary and it is this: Presuming that the date of an organ is established (see Chapter VI), it might be safe to say that the tune must be at least as old as the organ. This presumption is usually correct, yet it must be borne in mind that congregations frequently purchased additional barrels and added, so to speak,

PLATE 7

The last barrel-piano in Edinburgh and probably the last in Scotland. On the death of the owner in 1966, the instrument was placed in the Museum of Childhood, Edinburgh. Probably made in London, the piano was restored by the late Canon Wintle, Suffolk.

to their organ's repertoire in this manner. The big firms of barrel organ makers like Bryceson, Flight and Robson and Gray would certainly have stocks of barrels which would be, to a large extent, standard and could be supplied quickly to any of their organs. Hence the inclusion of a tune on a barrel need not always mean that the tune is as old as the organ: it may be only as old as the barrel. And the same applies, *vice versa,* to the dating of organs by their tunes. Wood Rising, Norfolk, is an obvious instance of barrels being added long after the organ was built.

But now to the tunes themselves. The instances quoted are taken from the List appended to this chapter. This list represents years of investigation and listing, and having been created yields some very interesting information.

In the first edition the places where tunes appeared in tune-lists were given after each tune. It was found, however, that so few of the barrel organs were in working order, if indeed they existed any longer, it has been thought better to include a selection of actual tune-lists, indicating the location of the organ and whether or not it is playable today.

Here are thirty-two tunes, listed in order of frequency, which occur twelve times or more on the tune-lists of 73 barrel organs:

Old Hundredth	Morning Hymn	Wareham	Oxford
Evening Hymn	Shirland	Devizes	St. James
Hanover	St. Stephen's	Cambridge New	German Hymn
Christmas Hymn	Aldridge	Yarmouth	Abingdon
Easter Hymn	Irish	Manchester	Luther's Hymn
Sicilian Mariners	Helmsley	Vienna	Islington
Bedford	London New	Rockingham	Angels
Mount Ephraim	St. Anne	New York	Warwick
(From 73 to 23 cases)		(From 23 to 14 cases)	

Tunes are listed above by the main title given in the list which follows. Many of the tunes have alternative titles which are given after the main title.

It will be seen that the tunes survive in working order, or the written tune-lists are preserved for relatively few of the hundreds of barrel organs that will be found named below. But these organs, whose tunes are listed, are of widely differing dates and are scattered all over the country. We may, therefore, take them as typical . What a fine repertoire they represent! There is hardly a bad or weak tune among the lot.

Now, let us turn to another matter. Was chanting, in the sense that we chant a psalm or canticle, ever attempted on a barrel organ, and if so, how was it done bearing in mind that the barrel went round and therefore had to repeat itself exactly? At Shorne, in Kent, for instance, a parishioner complained that the barrel organ did not play the Amen, so an Amen was duly pinned on the barrel after each tune. The result, of course, was that every single verse, each time it was repeated, an Amen was solemnly played after it!

Since a barrel turns at relatively unvarying speed, and since the essence of chanting is to vary the length of note according to the number of words to be recited, it may be imagined that chanting was not possible to the accompaniment of a barrel organ. On many, perhaps most, barrel organs this was true; but there were larger barrel organs, as, for instance, Mattishall Burgh, Raithby, Staunton and Maxstoke (now at Aston Hall) where there were two handles, or more precisely, a normal organ-blowing handle or pedal for blowing the organ, and a small handle which turned round for rotating the barrel. In such cases chanting was possible for the wind was maintained in the organ by the blowing handle or pedal and a note could be held by the turning handle for any length of time during the " reciting note "; then when the chanting notes came the little handle would have to be simply whirled round. It can be done, for I have done it, and, most certainly, it was done. This is evidenced by more than seventeen barrel organs which include chants on their barrels. Chant Mornington, for instance is found at Bodfearn, Sutton, Boston Collection (2 organs), Winwick, Dorchester, Stratfieldsaye and Burtle. Battishill's and Robinson's Chants, too, were favourites e.g. Letheringsett, Norfolk (see Appendix of Tune Lists), and sometimes the list just mentions " Double Chant." At Bressingham in Norfolk is a whole barrel of chants, Dupuis, Crotch, Jones, Mornington, Dr. Buck, Dr Beckwith (the two latter being composed by organists of Norwich Cathedral), Winwick (1864) even had " Gregorian Chant." At Avington we find Chants by Soaper, Jones, Trent and Norris (see Appendix). Sometimes indeed the Ante Communion Service must have had music. I will discount the " Kyrie Eleison " at Bebington and the " Kyrie from Haydn's 1st Mass " which was once on a barrel on the Aldridge Church organ now in the Boston Collection. These may well have been adapted to a hymn tune as was, for instance, Haydn's Chorus from " Creation," " The Heavens are telling." But the Wardley Organ contains " Response for the 9th Commandment " and " Response for the 10th Commandment " to which is added " The Gospels "—presumably the " Glory be to Thee O God " and " Thanks be to Thee, Oh Christ, for this Thy Holy Gospel." This is clear evidence that, towards the end of their time, the barrel organs were made to accompany the Prayer Book Psalms as distinct from the Metrical Psalms, or rather some few of the larger ones were. And no doubt the same was true of the Canticles. Indeed, there is a glorious story told of Manthorpe in Lincolnshire where they had a barrel organ that could accompany chanting. It was decided that the Te Deum was to be sung, but the principle of the thing had not been explained to the old clerk who turned the handle. " The performer," states an eye-witness of the occurrence, " had been taught that the great point in playing a barrel organ was to maintain perfectly a uniform pace so that he applied this principle to the Te Deum without any regard to the length of the different verses, the singers getting in the words as best they could." (See article " *Notes and Queries* " ser. 12, 1922 p. 353.)

Did the Barrel Organ ever play a voluntary before and after the service? Most certainly, (indeed some are still so used); and this practice alone could account for the inclusion in church barrel organs of such items as " March in Bluebeard " and " Lord Hardwick's March." I discount the many barrel organs which have whole barrels entirely devoted to secular tunes. In many cases the organs were small enough to have been lifted bodily from the church and taken to the local inn or Assembly Room to do duty there. But, when marches appear on the same barrel as Psalm Tunes it is hard to think they were never used in church. " Carnival of Venice " and " Rule Britannia " share a barrel on the Astor organ in my own collection with such tunes as Old 100th, Sicilian Mariners and Compassion.

I cannot feel that the voluntary was a usual custom in the eighteenth century village services, but no doubt the increasing desire to copy the cathedral services often led to the introduction of a voluntary.

It is difficult, in printed words, to do more than call attention to the amazing degree of musical ornamentation in the way of trills, grace notes, passing notes and gathering notes which are to be found in profusion growing around even the most austere tunes as they are pinned on many a barrel. Such was the fashion of the period but these accretions were regarded with horror by the Victorians who mercilessly pruned them, often robbing a tune of much of its strength. Here for example is Tallis's Canon—

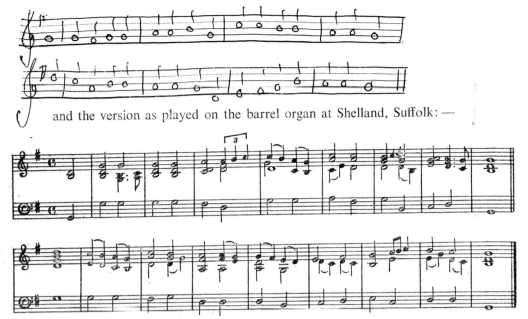

and the version as played on the barrel organ at Shelland, Suffolk:—

SACRED TUNES: HYMNS, PSALMS, CHANTS, ETC.

The following list is compiled from tune-lists of the barrel organs in churches or private or public collections. As, however, different tunes were sometimes named alike, and as only relatively few of the barrel organs are in playable condition, it cannot be stated with certainty that the tune under any one name would be the same in every case.

Abingdon or Heighington or Wakefield:—Dr. Heighington, 1679-1774.
Abridge:—Isaac Smith, c. 1770.
Acton or Eaton:—Beethoven, 1807.
Adeste Fideles:—See **Portuguese Hymn.**
Advent Hymn:—See **Helmsley.**
Airlie Street:—See **Hanover.**
Aisthorpe:
Aldrich or Aldrige:—Henry Aldrich, 1647-1710.
Alfred:
All Saints:—Dr. Howard, 1762.
Alma:—Samuel Webbe, 1792.
Almici:—?
Almidon:—?
Ambrose or St. Ambrose:—? T. Attwood, 1765-1838.
America:—Isaac Smith, 1736-1807.
Angels' Song or Song 34:—Orlando Gibbons, 1583-1625.
Anniversary:—T. Walker ?
Antioch:
Arabia or Arlington:—? Cole, 1800.
Archangel:—See **Vesper Hymn.**
Arne:—Dr. Arne, 1710-1778.
Arnold's:—J. Smith.
Artaxerxes:—Dr. Arne, 1710-1778.
Ashley:—1774.
Aston:
Athens:
Auburn:—Rev. J. Lawson, 1723-1770.
Aurelia:—S. S. Wesley, 1864.

Austria:—See **Vienna.**
Axbridge:—?

Babylon or Babylon's Streams:—T. Campion, 1576-1620.
Bakewell—?
Barnby:—T. Clark, c. 1828.
Batavia:—See **Batty.**
Bath or Lansdown:—H. Harrington, 1727-1816.
Bath Auricula:—Addington, 1788.
Battishill's Chant:—J. Battishill, 1738-1801.
Batty or Batavia:—Chorale "Ringe recht," 1784.
Beckwith's Chant:—J. C. Beckwith, 1750-1809.
Bedford:—Dr. Wheall, c. 1723. Short metre. A long metre version is entitled **Liverpool** (*q.v*).
Beethoven or Germany or Trinity Chapel:—W. Gardiner, 1815.
Belgrave:—W. Horsley, (1774-1858), 1817.
Bellevue:—?
Benediction:—S. Webbe, 1792.
Bennets:—J. Bennet ?
Bermondsey:—B. Milgrove, c. 1731-1810.
Berwick, see **Evening Hymn:**—Long Metre. There is also a Common Metre tune by M. Madan.
Bexley or Colchester:—W. Tans'ur, Harmony of Zion, 1735.
Bethany:—There are nine tunes named **Bethany**—six of the barrel organ period.
Bishopthorpe or **St. Paul's:**—Gardner's Psalms, c. 1786.
Bolton:—John Fawcett, 1789-1867.
Bourne:
Boyce's Chant:—Dr. Boyce, 1710-1779.
Bradley Church:—Mortimer.
Brentwood:—see **Evening Hymn.**
Bridehead:
Bristol or Hermon:—T. Ravenscroft, 1621.
Broadworth (Broadsworth):—Dr. Arne, 1778.
Bromley:—? J. Broderip, 1764.
Bromsgrove:—T. Collins, 1789.
Brunswick:—Handel, 1739 adapted 1760.
Buck's Chant:—Z. Buck, 1789-1879.
Burford:—Chetham's Psalmody, 1718.
Burnham:—T. Clark, 1775-1859.
Bury:
Byzantium:—T. Jackson, c. 1780? See **Mansfield.**

Calvary:—S. Stanley, 1767-1822.
Camberwell:—G. Dixon ?
Cambridge:—R. Harrison, 1749-1810.
Cambridge New:—Dr. Randall, 1799.
Canterbury:—? Adapted from *Este's Psalter*, 1592.
Careys or Pastoral or Surrey or Yarmouth:—H. Carey, 1690-1743.
Carlisle:—C. Lockhart, 1769.
Carton or Kildare:—T. A. Geary, 1783-1806.
Ceylon:—Anon. In T. Clark's *Congregational Harmonist*, 1828.
Charmouth or Manchester:—Dr. Wainwright, 1723-1768.
Chelsea, see **Oxford.**
Chester:—Three tunes of this name were by (1) Kelly, c. 1836: (2) Adapted from Beethoven: and (3) In Wesley's *Sacred Harmony*, c. 1781. There is also the tune Cheshire in Este, 1593.
China:—B. Cuzens, 1787.
Christmas Hymn:—see **Portuguese Hymn.**
Clifford:—?
Colchester:—see **Bexley.**
Comfort:—? Anon. in T. Clark's *Congregational Harmonist*, 1828.
Conway:—see **Mount Ephraim.**
Compassion:—A. Radiger, 1749-1817.
Condescension:—I. Tucker, 1761-1825.
Coronation:—T. Clark, 1775-1859.
Cottenham:—1830.
Cranbrook:—T. Clark, 1775-1859.
Crasselius or Frankfort, *q.v.*
Creation:—Haydn, 1798.

22

Crotch's Chant:—Dr. Crotch, 1775-1847.
Curtis:
Cyrenia:

Darwall's 148th Psalm:—J. Darwall, 1770.
Davey's:
David's Tune:—Ravenscroft, 1621.
Denmark:—M. Madan, c. 1791.
Departure:—Dr. Thompson? or T. Clark, 1775-1859.
Derby or Derbe:—1780?
Devine—?
Devizes:—I. Tucker, 1761-1825.
Devonshire:—J. F. Lampe, 1746.
Doncaster:—Dr. Miller, 1790.
Dorchester:—see **Stockport.**
Doversdale:—S. Stanley, 1767-1822.
Drydens:—not traced.
Dublin:—see Irish.
Duke Street:—J. Hatton, 1793.
Dundee *or French:*—*Scottish Psalter*, 1615.
Dupuis's Chant:—Dupuis, 1733-1796.
Durham:—? Ravenscroft's Psalter, 1621 or ? Hawes' Collection, 1836.

Eagle Street, New:—see **New Eagle Street.**
Easter Hymn:—Lyra Davidica 1708 and present form 1741. *c.p.* **Salisbury.**
Eaton or Acton:—Z. Wyvill, 1763-1837. See also **Acton.**
Emanuel:—Emanuel Bach, 1714-1788.
Emperor's Hymn:—see **Vienna.**
Essex:
Eudoxia:—S. Baring Gould, 1834-1924.
Evans:—Anon. In T. Clark's *Congregational Harmonist*, 1828.
Evening Hymn or Suffolk or Berwick or Magdalen or Tallis or Brentwood:—T. Tallis, c. 1567, corrupt version, mid 18th century. *c.p.* **Glory be to Thee, O Lord.**
Eventide:—W. H. Monk, 1823-1889.
Ewing:—A. Ewing, 1855.
Exeter:—see **London, New.**
Exeter:—W. Jackson, 1730-1803.

Falcon Street:—Isaac Smith, c. 1770.
Farrant in A:—R Farrant. died 1580.
Fonthill Abbey:—W. J. White, 1792-1832.
Foundling:—?
Franconia:—W. H. Havergal, 1847, from König's Choralbuch, 1738.
Frankfort or Crasselius or winchester New:—Musicalische Handbuch, 1690.
French:— see **Dundee.**
Froom:—H. Bond, 1791.

Gabriel New:—W. Arnold, 1768-1832.
Gainsborough:—Isaac Smith, c. 1770.
Galway:—Dr. E. Miller, 1790. See **Lebanon.**
German Hymn or Pleyel's Hymn:—I. J. Pleyel, 1757-1831.
Germany:—See **Beethoven.**
Gibbons Sanctus:—Orlando Gibbons, 1583-1625.
Gladness:—T. Clark, 1775-1859.
Glory be to Thee O Lord:—This title appears in the tune-list at Shelland, Suffolk. (See Appendix). It may be an alternative version of Evening Hymn (*q.v.*).
Gloucester:—B. Milgrove, c. 1731-1810.
God Save The King:—Anon., c. 1745.
Greek Air:—See **Trichinopoly.**
Greene:

Hallelujah Chorus:—G. F. Handel, 1742.
Handel:—G. F. Handel, 1740.
Handel's March or Jericho Tune:—G. F. Handel, 1727.
Hanover or Airlie Street:—Dr. W. Croft, 1678-1727.
   Most confusingly Hanover is often listed in the barrel organs as " Old 104th." The " Old 104th " is a tune set to the Metrical Version of Psalm 104 in Ravenscroft's Psalter, 1621. No doubt " Hanover " was, at the time of the barrel organs, usually sung to those words,

PLATE 8

Photo by courtesy of E. E. Kirby, Kettering.

Letheringsett Church, Holt, Norfolk. Barrel Organ No.
2964 by T. C. Bates, London. *Ex* Hindringham Church
and thereafter in a private house till 1955. 6 stops:
Bourdon, Open Diapason, Stopped Diapason, Principal,
Twelfth and Fifteenth. 3 barrels each of 10 tunes (26
hymns and 4 chants). Pedal for bellows. The instrument
is played only to interest visitors.

hence the duplication of the name. Where the name list survives and not the barrel it is impossible to be sure which tune is meant. Sometimes the list reads "Or 104th." Only in one instance are both Hanover and 104th listed. At Shelland the tune-list includes "**Hanover (Old) Proper, 149th.**"

Happy The Day:
Hardwick's March:
Harington:—M. Harington, 1727-1816.
Hart's:—B. Milgrove, c. 1731-1810.
Hart Street:—See **St. Olave's.**
Hatfield:—Dr. Miller, 1777.
Haughton:—B. Milgrove, c. 1731-1810.
Haydn's Hymn or Austria or Emperor's or Vienna:—F. J. Haydn, 1797. See **Vienna.**
Heber:—See **Missionary Hymn.**
Heighington:—See **Abingdon.**
Helmsley or Advent Hymn or Shopwick:—1765.
Hensbury:—? Matthews, 1836.
Hermon:—See **Bristol.**
Hollingside:—J. B. Dykes, 1860.
Horncastle:—Anonymous.
Hotham:—M. Madan, 1726-1790.
Howard or St. Bride's:—Wilson's Collection, 1825.
Hullah:
Hume's:
Hundred and Fourth:—See **Hanover** and note.
Hursley:—German, c. 1775.
Hymn of Eve or Uxbridge:—Dr. Arne, 1755.
Hymn to the Emperor:—See **Vienna.**

Innocents or Old 113th or Stepney:—Old Strasbourg Psalter, 1525.
Intercession:—*Easy Music for Church Choir,* 1853.
Irish or Dublin:—Dublin *Collection,* 1749.
Irwin Street:—
Islington:—1760.

Jackson's:—See **Mansfield.**
Jacob:—? S. Mather, 1831.
James see St. James.
Jericho Tune:—See **Handel's March.**
Jersey:—W. Aldis, 1844.
Islington:—1760
Jewin Street:—? Rippon's *Selection,* c. 1791.
Job:—W. Arnold, 1763-1832.
Jones Chant:—John Jones, 1770.
Justification:—J. Eagleton, 1816.

Kemsey:—J. Moreton, c. 1802.
Kent:—J. F. Lampe, 1746 or S. Stanley, c. 1800.
Kildare:—See **Carton.**
King David's Pastoral:—Z. Wyvill, 1763-1837.
King Street:—J. Moreton, c. 1802.
Kyrie Eleison:

Lancaster:—Dr. Howard, 1710-1782.
Langdon Chant:—R. Langdon, 1760.
Lansdown or Bath:—See **Bath.**
Layer de la Haye:
Leach:—J. Leach, 1762-1798.
Lebanon:—See **Galway.**
Leeds:—See **St. Anne.**
Leighton:—? Miller's *Sacred Music,* c. 1800.
Lichfield:—1621.
Lincoln:—See **Oxford.**
Lisbon:—1780 ?
Liverpool:—Dr. Wainwright, 1748-1782, Common metre: or Richard Wainwright, 1758-1825.
     A version in the long metre is an alternative title of **Bedford** (*q.v.*)
London:—J. Sheeles, c. 1740.
London New or New Toun or Magdalen or Exeter:—"Playford," 1671.
Lonsdale:—arr. from Corelli.
Lord, Dismiss Us, or St. Werbergh's:—

Lord My Pasture:—*c.p.* **Careys.**
Luke's Hymn:—?
Luther's Hymn:—M. Luther, 1485-1546.
Lydia:—W. Cole, or Phillips, late 18th c.
Lyneham:—See **York Street.**

Maccabees:—G. F. Handel, 1747.
Magdalen:—See **Evening Hymn or London New.**
Manchester or Charmouth:—R. Wainwright, 1774.
Mansfield or Jacksons or Byzantium:—T. Jackson, 1715-1781.
Marina:
Mariners:—See **Sicilian Mariners.**
Marseilles Hymn:—? " Mr. Beaumont " in Miller's *Sacred Music,* c. 1802.
Martin's Lane:—Rippon's Selection, c. 1791.
Martyrdom:—H. Wilson, 1766-1824
Masbury:—See **Tiverton.**
Melcombe:—S. Webbe, 1740-1816
Melita:—J. B. Dykes, 1860.
Messiah:—G. F. Handel, 1742.
Miles Lane or Scarborough:—W. Shrubsole, 1779.
Mington:—?
Missionary Hymn or Herber:—L. Macer, 1792-1872.
Monmouth:—? G. Davis, c. 1800.
Montgomery:—W. Champness, 1772.
Morning Hymn:—F. W. Barthélemon, c. 1785.
Mornington Chant:—Lord Mornington, 1735-1781.
Moscow or Russian Vesper Hymn:—
Mottram:—See **Stockport.**
Mount Ephraim or St. Helena or Conway:—B. Milgrove, c. 1769.
Mount Pleasant:—J. Leach, 1762-1798.
Mount Sinai:—?
Mount Tabor:—See **Tabor.**
Munich:—J. Schop, 1641.
My Rest is in Heaven:—
My God, My Father, or Troyte:—A. H. D. Troyte, 1848.

Nares:—? J. Nares, 1715-1783.
Nayland:—See **St Stephens.**
New Castle:—W. Knapp, 1698-1768.
New Eagle Street:—Isaac Smith, c. 1770.
New 148th:—? Dr. E. Miller in his *David's Harp,* c. 1803
Newington:—B. Milgrove, c. 1731-1810.
Newport:—B. Cuzens.
New Sabbath:—H. Phillips, c. 1800. At Cardeston, Salop, entitled " New Sabbath or Stockport."
New St. David's:—D. Wilson, pre-1844.
New Toun:—See **London New.**
New York or Sheldon or Witton:—J. Whitton, late 18th c.
Norris Chant:—Thomas Norris, 1790.
Norwich:—Playford ? 1701 ?
    Seven tunes bear the name **Norwich.**
Nottingham or St. Magnus:—J. Clark, c. 1659-1707.

Old Hundredth or Savoy:—*Genevan Psalter,* 1551.
Old 104th:—See **Hanover.**
Old 113th:—See **Innocents.**
Old 134th:—See **St. Michael.**
Oldhams:—S. Webbe, jnr., 1770-1843.
Oswestry:—S. Stanley, 1767-1822.
Overton or Resurrection:—c. 1791.
Oxford or Lincoln or Chelsea:—T. Ravenscroft, 1621.

Palmyra:—?
Paris:—E. Everest, 1843.
Pastoral Symphony:—G. F. Handel, 1742.
Peckham:—Isaac Smith, c. 1770.
Pembroke:—T. Clark, 1777-1859.
Peru:—J. Leach, 1762-1798.

Peterborough:—Dr. Boyce, 1710-1779.
Petra:—See **Rock of Ages.**
Piety:—J. Marson, 1800 ?
Pleyel's Hymn:—See **German Hymn.**
Portsmouth Old:—1740 ?
Portugal:—T. Thorley.
Portuguese Hymn or Portugal New or Adeste Fideles or Christmas Hymn:—arranged J. F. Wade, 1711-1786.
Prague:—Latrobe's Selection, 1806-1825.
Praise:—A. Radiger, 1749-1817.
Psalm 8, 9, 47, 66, 92, 93, 121, 147:
Psalm 40:—
Psalm 104:—
Psalm 104 and 109 (Old) occurs in the Letheringsett list.
Psalm 110:—
Psalm 113:—W. Hayes, 1706-1777.
Psalm 148:—See **Darwall's 148th,** but both " **Darwall** " and " **148 Ps** " occur in Draughton list and at Shelland there is " **Burnham 148th.**"
Psalm 150:
Psalm Bond:—? H. Bond, died 1792.
Purcell's:—Attrib. Henry Purcell, 1658-1695.

Ranelagh:—1800.
Ranmore:
Redhead:— R. Redhead, 1853. See **Rock of Ages.**
Regent's Square:—H. Smart, 1866.
Responses and Commandments:
Resurrection:— See **Overton.**
Reuben:—S. Wakeley.
Richmond:—T. Haweis, 1792.
Ringe Recht:—See **Batty.**
Robinson's Double Chant:—J. Robinson, 1740.
Rochford:—Anon., in Rippon's Selection, c. 1791.
Rockingham:—Dr. Miller, 1790.
Rock of Ages or Petra or Redhead:—R. Redhead, 1853.
Rousseau or Rousseau's Dream:—c. 1818-1825, adapted from Rousseau.

St. Alphege:—H. J. Gauntlett, 1852.
St. Ambrose, see Ambrose.
St. Anne or Leeds:—Dr. Croft, 1708.
St. Barnabas:
St. Bernard's:—Beaumont, c. 1828.
St. Bride's or All Saints:—S. Howard, c. 1710-1782. In Riley's Parochial Harmony, 1762.
St. Clement Danes:—A tune **St. Clement or Hilderstone** is by P. Hart, c. 1713.
St. Constantia:
St. Cuthbert:—J. B. Dykes, 1860.
St. David:—Ravenscroft's Psalms, 1621.
St. George:—G. J. Elvey, 1858.
St. George Old:—J. Stanley ? 1762: or from the German.
St. Helena:—See **Mount Ephraim.**
St. James:—R. Courtville, 1697.
St. John:—R. Cecil, 1751: or J. Leach, 1762-1798.
St. Luke:—1746.
St. Magnus:—See **Nottingham.**
St. Mark:—? W. Crowfoot, 1755 or S. Arnold, 1791.
St. Martin:—
St. Mary:—Prys' Psalter, 1621.
St. Matthew:—Dr. W. Croft, 1708.
St. Matthias:—O. Gibbons, 1583-1625.
St. Michael, Old 134th:—Anglo-Genevan Psalter, 1551.
St. Olave's or Hart Street:—R. Hudson, 1732-1815. See **Carey's.**
St. Paul:—See **Bishopthorpe.**
St. Peter:—A. R. Reinagle, c. 1836.
St. Stephen's or Stephens or Nayland:—W. Jones, 1789.
St. Thomas:—Ashworth's Collection, 1760(?).
St. Werbergh's or Lord Dismiss Us:—
Salem:—Rippon's Selection, c. 1791.
Salisbury:—John Playford, 1671. *c.p.* **Easter Hymn.**
Salvation:—?

PLATE 9

Wardley Church, Rutland: Barrel-organ No. 2633 by
T. C. Bates & Son, London. In need of restoration.
3 stops: Open Diapason, Stopped Diapason, Principal.
3 barrels each of 10 tunes: 2 of hymns and psalms,
1 including 4 single and 4 double chants. *Vide Musical
Opinion*, August 1928.

Samson:—?
Sarah:—W. Arnold, 1768-1832.
Savoy, see Old Hundredth:
Saxony:—Adapted from Handel.
Scarborough, see Miles Lane:
Sheffield:—G. Breillat.
Sheldon:—See **New York.**
Shillers:
Shirland:—S. Stanley, 1767-1822.
Shopwick, see Helmsley.
Shore's Cottage:—Rippon's Selection, 1808 edition.
Sicilian Mariners or Mariners or Mariners Hymn:—Herder's Collection, 1776.
Silver Street or Falcon Street or Southern:—Isaac Smith, c. 1770.
Simeon:—? S. Stanley, 1767-1822.
Sion Church:—?
Smyrna:—?
Soaper's Chant:—John Soaper, 1743-1794.
Song 34:—See **Angels.**
Song 67:—See **St. Matthias.**
Spanish Chant:—Burgoyne's Collection, 1827.
Sprowston:—W. J. White, 1792-1832.
Staughton:—J. H. Walker's Collection, 1815: ? Collins.
Stephen's:—See **St. Stephen's.**
Stepney:—See **Innocents.**
Stockport or Yorkshire or Mottram or Dorchester, cp. New Sabbath:—J. Wainwright, 1749.
Stonefield:—S. Stanley, 1767-1822.
Stowey:
Stratfieldsaye:—? Lord Mornington, 1735-1781.
Stuart's Morning:
Stutgard: (*sic*)—If Stuttgart; C. F. Witt (1660-1716) in *Psalmodia Sacra,* 1715.
Suffolk:—See **Evening Hymn.**
Sure Guide:—Anton Radiger, c. 1800.
Surrey:—See **Carey's.**
Sutton:—? J. Whitton.
Sutton Coldfield:—S. Stanley, 1767-1822.
Swiss Cottage:—?
Sylvanus:—?

Tabor:—Rayson, 1853 (or perhaps **Mount Tabor** by J. Leach, 1798).
Tallis's Canon:—See **Evening Hymn.**
Tallis's Chant:—T. Tallis, c. 1505-1585.
Tarporley:—
Tell Me The Old Old Story:—W. H. Doane, 1832-1916.
This must have been added to the barrel of sacred tunes at Alvechurch.
Theodore:—?
Titchfield:—J. Richardson, 1815-1879.
Tiverton, or Masbury:—Rippon's Selection, c. 1791.
Tranquillity:—W. Matthews, 1800 ?
Travers:
Trent's Chant:—?
Trichinopoly:—or " Greek Air."—W. Hawes' Collection, 1836.
Trinity:—J. Goodman, in T. Clark's *Congregational Harmonist,* 1828.
Trinity Chapel:—See **Beethoven.**
Triumphs New:
Troyte Chant:—A. H. D. Troyte, 1848.
Troyte or My God, My Father:—A. H. D. Troyte, 1848.
Truro:—Anon. *Psalmodia Evangelica,* 1790.
Tucker's:—Isaac Tucker, 1761-1825.
Turle:—J. Turle, 1802-1882.

Union:—
University:—Dr. Collignon, 1794.

Uxbridge or Hymn of Eve:—Dr. Arne, 1710-1778.

Vesper Hymn or Archangel:—Russian Air adapted Sir J. A. Stevenson, 1761-1883. cp.
     Moscow.
Vienna or Austria or Haydn's Hymn or Emperor's (not Knecht's Vienna):—F. J. Haydn,
     1797.
Wakefield, see Abingdon:

Walworth:—See **Stockport.**
Wareham:—W. Knapp, 1738.
Warsaw:—T. Clark, 1775-1859.
Warwick:—S. Stanley, 1767-1822.
Watchman:—J. Leach, 1762-1798.
Wells:—Thomas Shoel, 1759-1823.
Westbury Leigh:—Isaac Tucker, 1761-1825.
Westminster:—James Turle, 1802-1882.
Weston Favell:—W. Knapp, 1738.
Weymouth New:—Dr. Randall, 1715-1799.
Wilton:—S. Stanley, 1767-1822: or **Wilton, Old,** by F. Giardini, 1716-1796.
Wiltshire:—G. Smart, c. 1795.
Winchester New:—1690.
Windsor or Dundee:—Damon's Psalter, 1591.
Witton's New York:—See **New York.**
Wokingham:
Woodside:—?
Woodward (Chant in D)?:—R. Woodward, 1744-1777.
Worcester:—?
Worship Street:—?

Yarmouth:—See **Carey's.**
Yorkshire:—See **Stockport.**
York Street or Lyneham:—T. Jarman, 1788-1862.

LIST OF TUNES ON SECULAR ORGANS

The following is a list of tunes, mainly secular, found on tune-lists of barrel-organs in public and private possession. The organs date from c. 1760 to c. 1840 and are all included in the list of non-church instruments. Only a few of the organs are in working order while, in some cases, only the tune-lists survive. It will be noted that a number of sacred tunes are included. Very few of the secular tunes appear to have survived to the present day, but it has been thought worth while to detail them all as an indication of popular music during the period stated. As tune-lists were invariably hand-written in ink on paper pasted to the organ case, some have become barely legible, hence the interrogation marks at some titles.

Abercrombie, Sir R : March.
Abingdon Fair.
Abridge.
Abroad and at Home.
Adeste Fideles.
Advent Hymn.
African Dance.
Agreeable Surprise.
Ah Well a Day My Poor Mary.
Air Balloon.
Air by Dr. Arnold.
Air by Handel.
Air by Rousseau.
Air by Weideman.
Airy Dreams.
Alexander.
Alfred.
Alice Gray.
All away to Bantry.
All Will Hail Him.
Allegrante.
Allemande.
Amelie.
Angels Hymn.
Anglaise.
Ann Nancy.
Anna.
Antigua.
Ar Hyd Y Nos.
As Fate decreed.

Astley's Hornpipe.
Astley's Ride.
A sure Guide.
As You Mean to Set Sail.
Assassination.
Athol House Reel.
Atholl Slow March.
Audrin, La.
Auld Lang Syne.
Auld Robin Gray.
Aurelli's Minuet.
Aurora Waltz.
Austin, Miss J : Reel.
Austria's Retreat.
Autumn Bird Waltz.
Away With Melancholy.

Back of the Change House.
Baird, Sir D : March.
Baker, Mrs : Hornpipe.
Ball, The.
Bamah Droog.
Bandean.
Banks of the Doon.
Banks of the Shannon.
Banks of the Slaney.
Banquo.
Barcarolle.
Barbara Allan.
Bard of Doon.

Bargo.
Bartholoman's Fancy. Jig.
Bateuse.
Bastien et Bastienne.
Bath Minuet.
Bath Waltz.
Battle of Prague.
Bay of Biscay Oh !
Bayne, Mrs: Reel.
Beautiful Maid.
Beautiful Rhine
Because He was a Coming.
Because he was a Bonny Lad.
Bed of Roses.
Bedford: 84th Psalm.
Be Gone Dull Care.
Bee Proffers Honey.
Beggar Girl.
Belgravia Waltz.
Believe Me, if all These . .
Belle Catherine: Dance.
Belle Isle March.
Belle Laitiere.
Belle Levant.
Bellevue Dance.
Beloudi 2nd March.
Be Mine Dear Maud.
Benediction.
Bennets.
Bentinck, Miss: Reel
Beware of Love.
Bewildered Maid.
Bickers Hornpipe.
Bid me to live.
Big Boat of Erdware (?).
Birds Suite.
Bird Waltz.
Birks of Aberfeldy: Reel.
Birks of Invermay.
Bishop, Reel.
Blair, Mrs. D. H.
Blair, Sir David Hunter.
Blaize et Babet.
Blue Bells of Scotland.
Blue Bonnets Over the Border.
Blue Stocking.
Bob of Fettercairn.
Bohemian Lancer.
Bonja Song.
Bonnie Dundee.
Bonnie Wee Wife.
Bonny Lass.
Boulanger, Le.
Bower, The.
Boy, The, That Once . . .
Boyd, Capt: Waltz.
Boyne, Mrs: Reel.
Braes of Auchentyre.
Braw Lads of Gala Water.
Breastknot.
Brechin Castle.
Brian Boru March.
Bridesmaid's Song (Chorus).
Brigans Waltz.
Bright Chanticleer.
Brighton Camp.
Brighton Races.
Brindisi-Traviata.
British Liberty.

British Fair with Three Times Three.
Britons Strike Home.
Broad Sword Hornpipe.
Broken Bridge.
Bromsgrove.
Broom of the Cowdenknowes.
Broom of Lowden Moor.
Brunswick.
Buenos Aires.
Bugle Horn.
Busby, Mr: Reel.

Cachucha.
Calabria.
Calder Fair.
Caledonian Hunts Delight.
Caledonian Reel.
Calypso.
Cambridge, New.
Came Ye by Atholl.
Cameronian Rant.
Cameronian Reel.
Cameronian March.
Cameron's Got His Wife Again.
Camble, Miss: Waltz.
Camp, The.
Campbell, Lucia: Reel.
Campbell, Miss.
Campbells are Coming.
Canock, The (?).
Cape Trafalgar.
Caper Fey.
Captain Glove.
Captain Wyke.
Carey, Mrs.
Carlisle: Hymn.
Carlisle Minuet.
Carnaval de Venice.
Caro Dolce.
Cortina, La.
Castanet.
Castilian Maid.
Cavalier.
Cease Your Funning.
Chamber, The.
Chanteuse, The.
Charles Hornpipe.
Charles, Sir: Minuet.
Charlie is My Darling.
Charming Fellow.
Charms of the Fair.
Chartreuse.
Chase, The, by Burton.
Chatsworth House.
Cheap Meal.
Chelmsford Races: Jig.
Cherry Ripe.
Chorus Jig.
Christmas Hymn.
Christmas Tales.
Christ's Love.
Cinderella, La.
Claremont House.
Clarinet March.
Clayton, Mrs.
Cloches de Corneville.
Clydesdale Lassies: Reel.
Clyene Rippe (on French Serinette).
Coldstream March.

PLATE 10

Photo by Dr G. D. Parkes, Hampton Poyle, Oxon.

Hampton Gay Church, Oxon.
Barrel-organ by H. Bryceson, 38 Long Acre, London.
5 stops. 22 pipes. 3 barrels each of 10 tunes, pre-1823.

Colinett.
College Hornpipe.
Come Gentil—Don Pasquale.
Come under My Plaidie.
Comet, The.
Coming Thro' the Rye.
Compassion.
Concerto by Mr. Hook.
Confederation.
Coolun, The.
Copenhagen Waltz.
Corelli's Psalm Tune.
Corelli's 9th Concerto (part).
Corn Rigs.
Coronation Anthem (Handel).
Coronation Waltz.
Coudrillon.
Count Almadonen's Minuet.
Count, The: Minuet.
Count Zembacari's Reel.
Countess of Louden (sic): Reel.
Countess of Stafford.
Countess of Sutherland's Reel.
Country Bumpkin.
Court Minuet.
Cranbrook.
Crazy Jane.
Cri, Cri: Polka.
Croppies.
Crosthwaite, Peter: March: Fancy: Air:
    Song Tune.
Crown Prince's Reel.
Culver Lodge.
Cupid Benighted.
Cramer's Grand March.

Dainty Davie.
Danish Waltz.
Dans Votre Lit.
Dandy, The.
Dashing White Sergeant.
Dawson's Hornpipe, Miss.
Dawson, Nancy.
Days When Went Gips (?).
Dear Tom, This Brown Jug.
Death of Nelson.
Death of Robin Gray.
Deep Nine.
Del Caras: Hornpipe.
Del conte—Norma.
Delonia's Hornpipe.
Delvin Side.
Dent's Miss. Waltz.
Deserter's March.
Devil or no Devil—Good !
Devil's Dream.
Devine, La.
Devizes.
Devon, Miss: Reel.
Devonshire Minuet.
Dick of Perth.
Dick the Welchman.
Diel Among the Taylors
Dolly's Fancy.
Dominique Von Esch.
Don Alphulia.
Donald Dhu.
Don Pedro.

Don Sampson.
Dorset, La.
Dorsetshire March.
Downfall of Paris.
Drink to Me Only With Thine Eyes.
Drops of Brandy.
Drummond.
Duchess of Buccleugh.
Duchess of Gloucester's Waltz.
Duchess of York's Waltz.
Duett Jig.
Duetto, Mira e Norma.
Duke of Brunswick's March.
Duke of Gloster's March.
Duke of Gordon's Birthday.
Duke of Perth.
Duke of Tuscany March.
Duke of Wellington's Waltz.
Duke of York's Jigg.
Duke of York's March.
Duke of York's Waltz.
Duncan Davidson.
Duncan Gray.
Duns Castle.
Dusky Night.
Dusty Miller.
Dutch Minuet.
Dutch Skipper.

Earl of Balgonie's March.
East India Volunteers' March.
Easter Hymn.
Echo, La. Finale.
Echoing Horn.
Eight men of Moidart.
Elizabethan No. 5.
Emperor's Waltz.
Emsta, L'.
Englishman, The.
Enira, L'.
Eremita, Le.
Erin.
Ernica.
Escape Dance.
Essex.
Eté, L'
Etoile, L'.
Evelin's Bow.
Evening Hymn (Suffolk).

Fair Ellen.
Fair Lisette.
Fairy Dance.
Fairy Queen.
Faithful Emma.
Fandango Dance.
Fal Lal La.
Fanfare.
Farewell to the Mountains.
Farewell to Whisky.
Farquharson, Miss.
Favoroy (?) March.
Favourite Cottillion.
Favourite Minuet.
Favourite New Minuet.
Favourite Song in the Fleives (?)
Fern Hill.
Fields were Gay.

Fife Hunt.
Fight About the Fireside.
Finale, La.
Finale de Freischütz.
Fisher's Hornpipe.
Fisher's Minuet.
Fisherman's Chorus.
Flora, La.
Flowers of Edinburgh.
Flowers of Masons' Court Jig.
Flowers of the Field.
Flowers of the Forest.
Fly by Night.
Fly Not Yet.
For Tender Lip Formed.
Ford's Waltz.
Foundling.
Freemasons' March.
Freischütz Waltz.
French Horn Air by Dubourg.
French Horn Air by Handel.
French King's Minuet.
Friend and Pitcher Song.
Frisky Waltz.
From Egypt lately come.
From Night to Morn.
Froome.
Funicular, La.

Gainsborough.
Gallopade.
Galopourie.
Garland of Love.
Garry Owen.
Gavot in Correlli's 10th Solo.
Gavotte by Dr. Boyce.
Gavotte in Otho.
Gavotte by Dubourg.
Gayton, Miss.
Gayton, Mrs. or Miss: Hornpipe.
General Toast.
General Washington's March.
Generous Present.
German Air.
German Hymn, Pleyel.
German Spa Dance.
German Waltz.
Gibraltar March.
Giordani's Minuet.
Gist, Miss, Fancy.
Glory to Thee, My God, This Night.
God Save The King/Queen.
Golden Fair.
Goodnight An' Joy be Wi' you A'.
Gordon's Minuet.
Grinder, The.
Go to Berwick, Johnny.
Go to the Devil and Shake Yourself.
Gramachree.
Great God of Hosts.
Green Grow the Rashes.
Greig's Pipes.
Grove, The.
Guillaume, La.
Guild Hall Squabble.
Gunning, Miss.
Gustavus.
Guy Mannering.

Habilinus Minuet.
Hackney Assembly
Had I a Heart.
Hainoult Waltz.
Hall, Miss ? Kate
Hampton.
Handel's Clarinet Air.
Handel's Favourite Air.
Handel's Water Music.
Hanover (sacred).
Happy Land.
Happy Meeting: Jig.
Happy Returns.
Happy the Heart. Hymn.
Hark, Hark, Ye Joy Inspiring Horn.
Harlequin Amelet.
Haymakers' Dance.
He Comes: The Hero Comes.
He was famed.
Heave On, My Boys.
Heavens are Telling.
Heaving the Lead.
Hedley (sacred).
Helmsley (Advent Hymn).
Hero, The.
Hessian Dance.
Highland Cottage.
Highland Laddie.
Highland Plaid.
Highlandman Kissed His Mother.
Home Sweet Home.
Honeymoon.
Hope, Thou Lovely Nymph.
Hope Told a Flattering Tale.
Horace.
House That Jack Built.
How broke the light.
How Cheerful Along Ye . . .
How Imperfect.
How Oft Louisa.
How Sweet in the Woodlands. Song.
How Sweet is the Pleasure.
How Sweet is Your Hand.
How Sweet is Love. Song.
Howthen's, Mrs. Waltz.
Hungarian Waltz.
Hunting Song in Apollo & Daphnis.
Huntsmen's Chorus.
Huntsman Song.
Hymn for the Lord's Day.
Hymn on Y'r Sacrament.

I ask not Beauty Quite Compleat.
I'd be a Butterfly.
If a Body Meet a Body.
If It's Joy to be Loved.
If you can caper in Midas.
Ilustrous (?) Miss: Reel.
I'll Gang Nae Mair to Yonder Town.
I'll Hae a Wife of My Ain.
I'll Make Fun of You.
I ne'er lo'ed a laddie but ane.
In My Cottage Near the Wood.
In the Dead of the Night.
Infantry.
Irish.
Irish Emigrant.
Irish Quadrilles.
Isabel Waltz.

Irish Washerwoman.
Irish Waterman.
Isle of France.
Isle of Skye.
Italian Air.
I w'd mourn the hopes.
Jackson.
Jack Latten.
Janizaries March.
Jarchou, La Vielleuse.
Jean de Paris.
Je Pense à Vous.
Jenny Dang the Weaver.
Jenny Jones.
Jenny's Bawbee.
Jenny Nettles.
Jenny Sutton.
Jessie the Flower of Dunblane.
Jeptha Chorus.
Jigg *by* Signor Cramer.
Jigg *by* Vento.
Jim of Aberdeen.
Jimmie & Jenny's Farewell.
Job.
Job, Miss, Minuet.
Jockey to the Fair.
Jock's Alive.
John of Paris (*cp.* Jean de Paris *supra*).
Johnny Hunsdon.
Johnny Sutton (*cp.* Jenny Sutton *supra*).
Johnny's Grey Brecks.
Johnson's, Miss: Reel.
Johnston, Miss, of Houghton.
Johnstone, Miss.
Jolies Dames, Les.
Jubilee Dance.
Juheims Polka.
Julia, La.
Juliana.

Kate of Aberdeen.
Keep the Country, Bonny Lassie.
Kelvin Grove.
Kempshott Hunt.
Kidderminster.
Kind Robin lo'es me.
King in the Zoo Valse.
King of Prussia's Minuet.
Kinloch of Kinloch.
Kirriemuir.
Kitty Hall.
Kitty o' the Clyde.
Kitty of Coleraine.
Kitty o' Lynch.
Kitty's Favourite.
Knickerbocker Quadrille.

Labories Name.
Labyrinth.
Ladoniska.
Lads and Lasses.
Lads of Bonny Town.
Lads of Dundee.
Lady Abingdon's Fancy.
Lady Amelia Stewart.
Lady Ann Howard.
Lady Betty.
Lady Billingcroft's Waltz.
Lady Campbell's Waltz.

Lady Campbell's Reel.
Lady C. Campbell's Strathspey.
Lady Caroline Lee's Waltz.
Lady Caroline's Reel.
Lady Cathcart.
Lady Catherine Polett's Minuet.
Lady Charlotte Campbell.
Lady Cholmondley.
Lady Coventry's Minuet.
Lady Dawn Storey.
Lady Denbigh's Minuet.
Lady Derby's Minuet.
Lady Eliz. Burrel's Minuet.
Lady Errington's Minuet.
Lady Gordon.
Lady Harold Campbell.
Lady Harriet Hope.
Lady Harriet Napier's Reel.
Lady Harriet Spencer's Delight.
Lady Jean Hume.
Lady Lindsay.
Lady Lucy Ramsay.
Lady McDonald's Dream.
Lady Madelina Sinclair.
Lady Maria Carter.
Lady Mary Parker.
Lady Mary Douglas.
Lady Mary Ramsay.
Lady Metcalfe.
Lady Montgomery's Reel.
Lady Mary Stopford.
Lady Nellie Wemyss.
Lady Shaftesbury.
Lady Spencer's Fancy.
Lady Sutherland.
Lady Townsend's Fancy.
Lady of the Lake.
Lady's Delight.
La mia letizia Lombardi.
Lancers Quadrille.
Lancers: 1st Figure.
Lanciers, Les.
Land of the Leal.
Largo Lee.
Lass o' Gowrie.
Lass of Richmond Hill.
Lassie wi' the Yellow Coatie.
Last Rose of Summer.
Laura & Louisa.
Laurette.
Leanere? Muir.
Lea Rig.
Legacy, The.
Le Portrait.
Let Erin remember.
Lewie Gordon.
Lieber Augustine's Waltz.
Life Let Us Cherish.
Lightly Trip.
Light Little Island.
Lilling Hall.
Limerick Lasses.
Lincoln or Oxford (sacred).
Lisette, La.
Little Fanny's Love.
Little Jenny.
Little Peggy's Love.
Liverpool.

Church of King Charles the Martyr, Shelland, Suffolk: Barrel-organ by Bryceson, London, pre-1823. 6 stops of 31 notes. 3 barrels of 12 tunes each. Cleaned and restored by Messrs. Mander, London, in 1956 and in regular use since. Broadcast on radio, 28th December, 1957.

Sydney Armstrong, son of Robert Armstrong (right), who succeeded his father in 1935 as "organist" of Shelland Church. He died in 1967.

Robert Armstrong, Parish Clerk, at the Shelland Barrel-organ which he played from 1885 till his death in 1935 aged 79.

Logan's Strathspey.
Lo, He Cometh. Hymn.
Lochiel's March.
Lochrannoch Side.
Lodiska March.
Logie o' Buchan.
London Military Dance.
London.
Long's Miss Tilney, Favourite.
Lonsdale.
Lord Beauchamp's March.
Lord Berkeley's March.
Lord Cathcart's Reel.
Lord Clive's New Trumpet Minuet.
Lord Cornwallis' March.
Lord Cuthbert.
Lord Eglinton.
Lord Granby's March.
Lord Hardwick's March.
Lord Howe's Hornpipe.
Lord How's Reel.
Lord Macdonald: Reel.
Lord Milton's Hornpipe.
Lord Moira's Welcome.
Lord Mornington's Chaunt.
Lord Murray.
Lord, My Pasture. Hymn.
Lord Nelson's Hornpipe.
Lord Nelson's Waltz.
Lord Saniva?
Lord Wellington.
Lord Wellington's Reel.
Lordeski, La. (cp. Ladoniska supra).
Lost in My Quest.
Louisa, La.
Love Among the Roses.
Love and Glory.
Love From the Heart.
Love let us cherish.
Love Song, Valse.
Lovers' Mistake.
Lover's Petition.
Love's a Tyrant.
Low Down in the Broom.
Lowland Willy.
Lowther, Mrs: Waltz.
Lullaby.
Lunardi's March.
Lyre, The.

McBean's Hornpipe.
Macbeth.
McDonald, Sir Alexander: Reel.
Macduff.
Mackintosh, Capt.
McLean's, Miss, Reel.
McLeod, Captain.
McLeod, Miss, of Ross.
McLeod, Mrs. of Raasay.
McLeod's Reel.
McCloud, Mrs (sic).
McLeod, Mrs. of Eyod (?).
McPharson (sic).
Ma Chère Amie. Song.
Madrigal, The.
Magdalen Evening Hymn.
Maggie Lauder.
Maid of Athens.

Maid of Isla.
Maid of the Mill. Song.
Maid of Lodi.
Malbrook. Song.
Maltese Dance.
Manchester.
Manila Waltz.
Mapher (?) March.
Marcello.
March, Sir R. Abercrombie.
March, Abingdon.
March, Dr. Arnold.
March, Battle of Prague.
March, Berkshire Militia.
March in Blue Beard.
March, Bolducca's.
March in the Cateract of the Ganges.
March by Mr. Griffin.
March in Miltozomer.
March, New Coldstream.
March, Puritain.
March, 3rd Regiment.
March, 13th Regiment.
March in Rinaldo.
March in Tara.
March, Turkish.
March in the Caravan.
March in Pizarro.
March by Signor Fiorini.
March in Judas Maccabeus.
March in La Virgine del Sole.
March, Westminster.
Marchini's Minuet.
Marchioness of Wellington.
Marchion's Buckingham's Allemande.
Margaretta, La: Dance.
Margate Assembly.
Mariners' Hymn.
Mariono.
Marionette.
Market Chorus.
Martyrdom.
Marlbroug s'en va t'en Guerre.
Marquis of Huntly.
Marquis of Lorne's Reel.
Marriage Day.
Marshal Sax's Minuet.
Marseillaise.
Martin Luther's Hymn.
Martin's Minuet.
Mary & Kitty.
Masked Ball.
Mason's Apron.
Maud of Ladie.
Maxwell, Miss: Reel.
Mayquielo Quadrille.
Medley.
Meeting of the Waters.
Melbourne Port.
Melrose, Col.
Men of Harlech.
Menage's, Miss: Hornpipe.
Mercurio, El. Valse.
Merrily danced the Quaker's wife.
Merry Lads of Ayr.
Merry Dance.
Merry Swabbois.
Micklenburgh.

Mick Wiggins.
Miles Lane.
Mill, The, Mill O'.
Miller of Drone (?).
Minuet by Haydn.
Minuet—Fischer.
Minuet de la Cour.
Minuet by Signor Eidelman.
Minuet by Signor Fiorini.
Minuet by Vaudiniere.
Mirance, Miss B.
Mirror, The.
Miss Billingcroft.
Miss Billington's Air.
Miss Hankey's Return.
Misses, The.
Mitchell, Mrs.
My Mither's Ay Glouren Ou'r Me.
Mol in the Wad.
Molly Hopkins.
Molly a Store (?).
Money in Both Pockets.
Moneymusk.
Monk, The.
Montreal.
Montrice.
Monzie, Miss Campbell: Reel.
Morgan Ratler.
Morgiana.
Morgiana in Ireland.
Morgiana in the Park.
Morgiana in Portugal.
Morgiana in Spain.
Morning Hymn (Suffolk).
Morpeth Reel.
Mother Goose.
Mount Pleasant.
Mount Ephraim.
Mount Sinai.
Moyes Delight.
Muchachas, Los Americanas.
Mug, Mr.
Mullomeney's Jigg.
Murphy Delaney.
Murray, Miss, of Ochtertyre.
Muses, The.
My Heart's My Own.
My Lodging is on the cold ground.
My Love is Like a Red Red Rose.
My Love, where but . . .
My Native Highland Home.
My pretty Page.

Nameless, The.
Nancy of the Dale.
Nancy's Delight.
National Waltz.
Native, La.
Neapolitan Mariners.
Neapolitan Waltz.
Neil Gow's Fancy.
Neil Gow's Strathspey.
Nelson's Jig.
New Claret.
New Forest Hunt.
New Galop.
New German Waltz.
New Hornpipe.

New May Moon.
New Mountfield.
New Sabbath.
New Spa Minuet.
New Wakefield.
New Waltz.
New way of wooing.
New Year's Day.
New York Minuet.
Nightingale.
No, My Love, No.
Nobody's Coming to Woo.
Nocturne by Moonlight.
Noel Park (?).
Non Vash (?).
Nouvelle Anglaise.
Nouvelle Fantasie.
Nymph, The.

October Meeting.
O'er the Moor Amongst the Heather.
Off She Goes.
Oh, had I Jubal's Lyre.
Oh, had I the wings of a dove.
O, Listen to the Voice of Love.
Oh, My Kitten.
Oh! Nannie, wilt thou gang wi' me?
Oh, No, We never mention her.
Oh, Rest the Babe.
O, Stay Bonny Lass.
Oh, Thou Dearest Ellen.
Oh, Wouldn't Thou Know.
Old English Gentlemen.
Oldgaty House.
Old House at Home.
Old Jowler.
Old Song, The.
Oldest Couple's Polka
O Nanny, cp. Oh! Nannie. . .
One Hour Waltz.
Opera Dance.
Opera Hat.
Opera Jigg.
Opera Reel.
Orange & Blue.
Orange Tree.
Organ Waltz.
Original Polka.
Orphan Mary.
Oscar.
Oswald, Mrs.
Oswald's, Mr. Stab.
Oswestry.
Over the Water.
Owen's March.

Paddy Carey.
Paddy O'Connell.
Paddy O'Rafferty.
Paddy Whack.
Pandean Dance.
Pantaloon.
Pantheon, Le.
Parisian Dance.
Parisols Hornpipe (sic).
Parson in Boots (and his boots).
Parson's Jig.
Pasame, La.

Pastorale, La.
Patriote, La.
Paul et Virginia.
Peckham.
Peggy Brown.
Persian Dance.
Perth Reel.
Perthshire Hunt.
Peruvian Boy.
Petit Duc, Le.
Petite Chaise.
Petit Matelot, Le.
Petit Tambour, Le.
Philida Adieu Love.
Philly McCue.
Philurian Waltz.
Pie Valaise, La.
Piety.
Pierfitiore, La.
Pipe de Tabac, Le.
Pirate, The.
Plaisirs des Dames.
Pleasures of Sproughton Jig.
Pleyel's Dance.
Pleyel's German Hymn (s.v. German Hymn).
Plough Boy.
Point du Jour, Le.
Polacca.
Pollacio.
Polly Put The Kettle On.
Polonaise.
Pompiers, Les.
Poor Jack.
Poor Mary Ann.
Poor Soldier, The.
Pop goes the weasel.
Pope's Foe, The.
Portuguese Hymn.
Poule, La.
Powis's Miss, Reel.
Praise.
Pray Goody.
Preston Races.
Pretty Lanie's Love.
Prima Donna-Valse.
Prince of Brunswick Minuet.
Prince of Brunswick March.
Prince Charles of Austria March.
Prince Eugen's March.
Prince of Orange's Waltz.
Prince Regent's Waltz.
Prince Regent's Favourite.
Prince of Wales' Delight.
Prince of Wales Minuet.
Prince of Wales Waltz.
Prince of Water ?
Princes' Favourite.
Princess Dulkominski.
Princess of Wales' Waltz.
Prussian Waltz.
Prussian Dance.
Psalm 15.
Psalm 18 (London New Tune).
Psalm 23.
Psalm 84 (or Bedford).
Psalm 95.
Psalm 96.
Psalm 100 (Savoy).

Psalm 104.
Psalm 105.
Psalm 115 (Abingdon).
Psalm 117 (St. James).
Psalm 149.
Pulleys Fancy, Le.

Quaker's Wife.
Quanista.
Quaton, Miss: Reel.
Queen of Prussia's Waltz.
Queen's March.
Queen's Minuet.
Quentin, La.
Qui Vive Galop.
Quick March.

Rachel Rae: Reel.
Radicate, Signor, Allemande.
Rakes of Mallow.
Ranelagh Garden.
Rara Mahles (?) Waltz.
Read, Col.: Minuet.
Recovery, The.
Reichstadt (sic.) Waltz.
Repose, La.
Request, The.
Résolute, La.
Return, The.
Richer's Hornpipe.
Rob Roy.
Robin Adair.
Robinson's Chant.
Robinson Crusoe Jig.
Rockingham.
Roger de Coverley, Sir.
Romance Adouilar (?).
Romanella, La.
Rophens (?).
Rorey O' More.
Rosalie, La.
Rosanna's Dream.
Rose, The
Rose Will Cease to Bloom
Rosebud of Summer.
Roselny (?) Castle.
Rosenburgh, Ella.
Roses Waltz: Strauss.
Rothwell Castle.
Rousseau, Le.
Royal Galop.
Royal Quick Step.
Roy's Wife of Aldivalloch.
Rule Britannia.
Rush About the Farm (?).
Russian Dance.
Russian Rant.
Russian Retreat.
Rustic Dance.

Said a smile to a tear.
St. Anne.
St. Bride's Bells.
St. Clement Dane's.
St. George's.
St. James's.
St. Matthias.

St. Patrick's Day. Jig.
St. Paul's.
St. Stephen's.
Sallie's Fancy.
Sally in Our Alley.
Salvation ! Oh, The Joyful Sound.
Sandy o'er the Lea.
Sandy & Jenny.
Santry's, Miss, Waltz.
Sareon Volage, finale.
Savage Dance.
Savourneen Deilich
Saw You, My Father, and Saw You . . .
Saxe Coburg Waltz.
Scotch Reel.
Scots Wha Hae.
See the Conquering Hero Comes.
Selina, La.
Seymour, Miss.
Shawl Dance.
Shepherds, I Have Lost My Love.
Shirland.
Shows Waltz.
Si fino all'ora—Norma.
Sicilian Dance.
Sicilian Hymn.
Sicilian Mariners.
Silver Street.
Sitwell, Master.
Sitwell, Mrs.
Slave Come Home.
Slavonian Waltz.
Sleeping Beauty.
Sleeping Maggie. Reel.
Slingsby's Allemande.
Smith, Dr. Sydney: Reel.
Social Powers.
Softly Sleep, My Little Boy.
Soldiers' Chorus from Faust.
Soldier's Joy.
Soldier's Return.
Song of Miriam.
Southbound.
Spacious Firmament.
Spa Dance.
Spanish Chant.
Spanish Dance.
Spanish Patriot's Reel.
Speed the Plough.
Spicer, Major.
Spinning Wheel.
Sprigs of Laurel.
Stapleton La.
Stabilini's Minuet.
Stewart's Col., March.
Stewart, Miss A.
Stir Your Stumps.
Stobell. Miss, Fancy.
Stop Waltz.
Storace.
Stratham.
Straughton.
Strauss Waltz.
Sul Margine.
Sur Carmena.
Sure then I'm doomed.
Sure Sally is the Loveliest.
Sussex Military March.

Sweet Nan of Hemp.
Sweet Spirit.
Sweet with Clover.
Sweethearts' Waltz.
Swiss Allemand.
Swiss Boy.
Swiss Waltz.

Taglioni's Waltz.
Tancredi.
Tanti Palpiti, Di.
Tank, The.
Tars of the Victory.
Tarter Drum.
Tartan Plaidie.
Tekeli, Dance in.
Tell Me the Old Old Story.
Tempête, La.
Temple of Concord.
Thaddie, The.
Thally of the Clyde. cp. Kitty . . .
The Harp that once . . .
The last time I cam' ower the muir.
The Lord's Supper.
Theodore's Jig.
Theodora, La.
There grows a bonnie briar bush.
There's Nae Luck.
They're A' Noddin'.
Thorn, The.
Those Soft Flowing . . .
Tho' dark are our sorrows.
Tho' Love is Warm Awhile.
Thou Art Gone Away.
Thou Art As Near.
Thro' the last glimpse.
Tippers Waltz.
Triumph, The.
Ticonderoga.
Tink a Tink.
Timour the Tartar.
Tit for Tat.
Tom Thumb.
Top Sails Shiver in the Wind. Song.
Torryburn. Reel.
Tracie, Le.
Through the Wood (. . she ran/of Fyvie).
Troubadour. Arie.
True Courage.
Trumpet Tune.
Tulloch Gorum.
Tunbridge.
Turkish March.
Turnpike Gate/Galop.
Turnpike Lad.
Tweeddale Club.
Tweedside.
Tyrolese, La, Waltz.
Tyrolese Song of Liberty.

Up Jenkin.

Variation to Gavot by Dubourg.
Vaudeville.
Vauxhall New March.
Verona.
Vesper.
Victory, The.

Village Ball, The.
Virginella, La.
Voici le Sabre-Grand Duchess.
Voice of Her I Love.
Voluntary by Handel
Von Erith. Hornpipe.
Voulez vous avez.
Voulez vous danser.
Vulcan's Cave.

Waliot's, Mrs. Minuet.
Wars Alarms.
Weber, Carl Von.
Waltz by Mozart.
Waltz by Musard.
Waltz by Spindler.
Waltz from Lucrezia Borgia.
Warwick.
Waterbrook
Waterloo Dance (Waltz).
Waterman, The (Jig).
Waters of Elle.
Weber's Favourite.
Wedderburn, Miss.
Weel may The Keel Row.
We have no abiding City here.
Wellington's Victory.
Welsh Jig.
We may roam thro'.
Westminster Chaunt (Jones).
Weymouth Waltz.
What a Beau My Granny Was.
What is life! 'Tis but a vapour.
When I was a Young One.

When Late I Wandered.
When Love is Warm.
When Pensive I Thought.
When the Rosebud in Summer.
When thro' Life am blest.
When William at Eve Meets Me.
White Cockade.
Whither My Love.
Why those fears, behold 'tis Jesus.
Wife of Bath.
Wilkinson, Miss: Minuet.
Will You Come to the Bower.
William Tell overture.
Willie Brewed a Peck o' Maut.
Willow Song (J. Hook).
Wiltshire March.
Windle.
Wisky Barrel.
Witch of the Glen.
Witches.
With Verdure Clad.
Within a Mile of Edinburgh Town.
Wolds of Sussex.
Wood Robin.
Woodland Maid.
Wybrow, Miss.
Wybrow, Mrs. Waltz.

Ye Banks and Braes.
Yellow Haired Laddie.
Young May Moon.
Young Man's Dream.
Young Rubin Was a Shepherd Boy.

Zodiac.

The author will welcome any additions or corrections to the foregoing list.

MISCELLANEA

From a small book—"The Opinions of Sarah Duchess Dowager of Marlborough, published from original MSS", dated 1/88. There is no author's name. Page 63 is headed "Chamber-Organ", and reads as follows:

1737. I am now in pursuit of getting the finest piece of music that ever was heard; it is a thing that will play eight tunes. Handel and all the great musicians say that it is beyond any thing they can do; and this may be performed by the most ignorant person; and when you are weary of those eight tunes, you may have them changed for any other that you like. This I think much better than going to an Italian opera, or an assembly. This performance has lately been put into a lottery, and all the Royal Family chose to have a great many tickets, rather than to buy it, the price being I think L.1,000, infinitely a less sum than some Bishopricks have been sold for. And a gentleman won it who I am in hopes will sell it, and if he will, I will buy it, for I cannot live to have another made, and I will carry it into the country with me.

By a strange coincidence, the following was noted in *Musical Opinion*, December 1940, page 130:

"Horace Walpole (1717-1797) tried in 1737 to purchase a barrel organ which had been the prize in a popular lottery."

Both quotations refer to the same instrument and indicate the popular interest in barrel organs early in the 18th century.

From "THE TIMES" of 20th December 1810.

"Capital Barrel Organ.

To be sold for 50 guineas a most elegant new one near 7 ft. high, 3 ft. wide, with 17 gilt pipes, of great power and fine soft tone, fine Gothic front and would be a great ornament to any Gentleman's Hall as it may be played by a servant during Dinner. May be seen any day from 2-4 at Mr Purcell's, 11 Queen Street, (London)."

Unfortunately, the name of the maker of this Chamber Barrel Organ is not stated.

PLATE 13

Photo by courtesy of the owner, Mrs. A. E. Greef, Thornham, King's Lynn.

Barrel-organ by Wm. Hubert van Kamp, Lee Street, Red Lion Sq., Holborn. 4 stops plus
drum and triangle. c. 1770. 4 barrels x 11 secular tunes.

CHAPTER V

BUILDERS OF BARREL-ORGANS FOR CHURCH AND CHAMBER USE

No attempt has hitherto been made to compile a list of those organ-builders who made barrel-organs. The present list covers a working period of over a century, but the majority were active between 1775 and 1850. Some were primarily finger-organ builders but others almost exclusively barrel-organ builders, while others built both types and, towards the end of the period, combined finger and barrel-organs.

After each builder's name is a list of churches for which the builder supplied a barrel-organ. The fate of the instrument will be learned from the County lists of churches and the code-letter referring to the organ.

In addition, the names are listed of private owners or Museums having an organ by the particular maker.

For the sake of completeness a few builders' or inventors' names are included though no surviving specimen of their work is known.

Adams, George: Author of *Adams' Micrographia Illustrated* (1747), appended to which is a catalogue. No. 334 therein is a particularly new and curious Machine, containing a Movement which plays either an organ or Harpsichord (or both if desired) in a masterly manner.

Allen, William: 11 Sutton Street, Soho, London ..1794-1835.. William Allen was one of some ten organ-builders in the Soho district of London in the late 18th century. At 11 Sutton Street he was next door to Thomas Elliot (*Vide* Elliot & Hill). He registered pianoforte patents in 1820 and 1831 and was succeeded by a son, Charles, at the same address, until 1838. The ultimate fate of the firm has not been ascertained.
Stanstead, Herts., finger and barrel, 4 barrels, 6 stops, 2 octaves of pedals.
Stagsden, Beds. (from Bedford St. Mary): converted to manual.

Argent: Colchester. c. 1774. In 1930 a "G" organ, converted barrel-organ, 7 stops, black naturals and white sharps, from Buxhall Church, Suffolk, stood in the chancel of Shelland Church, Suffolk, but nothing is known of its later history. *Vide Musical Times,* 1 May, 1930, pp. 460-461, article on Shelland Barrel-Organ. Also *The Organ* No. 163.

Astor, George: 79 Cornhill, London. Traded as G. Astor & Co. (1798-1815). *Vide* article on George Astor, in *Musical Opinion,* Dec. 1934, pp. 283-284.
Birmingham City Museum: Large barrel-organ (ex Rev. L. Mitchell Collection).
Hertford Museum: Chamber B-O. 4 barrels. *Vide Notes & Queries* 172 (1937), 444.
Guy Oldham, London: Miniature Barrel or bird organ, 12½" high. *Vide Music Libraries & Instruments* Paper No. 32, Plates 57 and 58.
Mrs. Brocklebank, Suffolk: Chamber B-O. Five stops. 3 barrels of ten tunes each.
J. P. Hall, Kendal: Chamber B-O. Five barrels. Two drums and triangle.
The late Canon Noel Boston, Lamas Manor, Norwich: Chamber B-O. 4 stops, drum and triangle. 4 barrels.
M. C. Miller, Cape, South Africa: Barrel-organ. 3 stops. 3 barrels x 10 sacred tunes.
Alan Lusty, C.P., South Africa: Chamber barrel-organ. 3 stops. 2 barrels x 10 tunes. In perfect condition.
Independence National Historic Park, Philadelphia, Penn., U.S.A.

Astor & Horwood: 79 Cornhill, London (1815-1831).
Pitt-Rivers Museum, Oxford: Chamber B-O. "Patent 1820." (No such patent can be traced). 4 stops. 3 barrels of 10 secular tunes each. The case bears: " Sold by J. & H. Banks, Musical Inst. Depository, Church Street, Liverpool."

Astor & Lucas: 62 Sun Street, London. Bruce Moss Collection: chamber barrel-organ: 3 stops, plus drum and triangle: 3 barrels, but no tune-list.

Ayton, W.: London 1764-1842. Chamber B-O. Said to be from Oakwood Hill Church, Dorking, Surrey. 22 keys. 6 stops including drum and triangle. 3 barrels of secular tunes. F. G. Turner & Son, Horsham, Sussex.

Balfe, William, (Royal Arms). Chamber barrel-organ: 3 barrels x 10 tunes: A. Campbell, Co. Donegal.

Bates, Theodore Charles: London. Established c. 1812 at St. John Street, Smithfield. Bates was at various addresses on his own account: 7 Jerusalem Passage, St. John Square, Smithfield, c. 1813. 20 St. John's Square, c. 1814-1824.

Additional premises:—18 Holywell Street, Strand, c. 1820-1822, and 490 Oxford Street, c. 1822-1824.

Then followed a period in partnership with G. Longman as Longman & Bates, 6 Ludgate Hill, c. 1824-c. 1833 where they were joined by Samuel Chappell from 1829 to c. 1833. On Chappell's death in 1834 the partnership was dissolved and T. C. Bates continued on his own account at 6 Ludgate Hill till 1847. He was joined then by his son and the business continued as T. C. Bates & Son, 1847-1859 and as Bates & Son, Burdett Road, Stepney, 1859-1863, and at 2 Little Bridge Street, London, until 1864 when the business closed down.

The Daily Telegraph of 23rd January, 1964, republished the last advertisement of Bates & Son (1864) selling off secular organs from £2, 2s. and church organs at £10.

Alvechurch, Worcs. now in Birmingham Science and Industry Museum.

Barkestone, Notts. Rebuilt in 1862 by Forster & Andrews.

Bettws-Cedewen, Montgom. ' Dumb Organist,' 3 barrels of 8 tunes each to fit single-manual Bates 7-stop organ.

Bosbury, Herefs. (now in All Saints Church, Hereford). No. 2578. Foot blown; 3 stops; 19 keys; only 1 of 4 barrels survives. *Vide Country Life*, 31 Mch. 1953, p. 878.

Bradwell-juxta-Mare, Essex, Barrel and finger. Barrels removed.

Bushey Chapel, Dorset.

East Chinnock, Somerset.

Faulkbourne, Essex (from Wickham Bishops).

Cardeston, Salop (Restored 1935). See Plate 27.

Cranford Baptist Chapel, Northants (No. 2888). See Plate 18.

Great Ness, Salop.

Helhoughton, Norfolk: barrel-organ (1852), now manual only; tune-list for four-barrels. (*ex* West Raynham Ch. in 1890).

Hereford Museum (*ex* Bosbury Church and now on loan to All Saints Church, Hereford).

Hertford Museum (*ex* Stocking Pelham in 1937).

Horton, Northants: Finger organ with ' Dumb Organist ' attachment. One of two barrels survives with eight sacred tunes and tune-list for both. 4 stops: clear pleasing tone. (Per F. F. Hill).

Letheringsett, Norfolk (No. 2964). See Plate 8.

Liddington, Wilts. (No. 2189).

London: All Hallows Church, London Wall: (lent by the late Canon Noel Boston): 3 stops: 2 barrels of 11 tunes each.

Lytchett Matravers, Dorset.

Meopham, Kent, 1865. Removed in 1867 to Trottiscliffe, Kent, and now in Rochester City Museum.

Pelton, Durham.

Sarratt Providence Chapel, Herts, Barrel and finger. Barrels removed.

Stocking Pelham, Herts (now in Hertford Museum).

Sutton, Beds. (No. 2917), 5 stops, 3 barrels of 10 ten tunes each. Recently restored. See Plate 29.

Tadlow, Cambs.: Only barrels of a ' Dumb Organist,' but doubtless for the period Bates finger-organ.

Tartaraghan, Co. Armagh: Barrel-organ No. 2031: 5 stops: 2 barrels x 10 tunes.

Toronto: St. John's Anglican Church, York Mills (installed in 1847).

Victoria, B.C.: Christ Church Cathedral (installed in 1859).

Wardley, Rutland (No. 2633). Use revived. *Vide Home-words,* May 1964. See Plate 9.

Welland, Worcs.: Remnants of barrel-organ and case.

West Raynham, Norfolk: barrel-organ presented to the church in 1852: now manual only: transferred to Helhoughton in 1890: 6 stops: 4 barrels including one spiral of 6 voluntaries.

Wickham Bishops (see Faulkbourne above).

Birmingham Midland Institute.

Birmingham Science and Industry Museum: *ex* Alvechurch Church, Worcs.

Birmingham City Museum (*ex* Rev. L. Mitchell Colln. & Liddell Colln).

Birks, C. J., Gerrard's Cross, Bucks. (No. 1741). (*ex* St. Luke's Hospital, Beaconsfield).

Boston, The late Canon Noel, Bury St. Edmunds, Suffolk. (On loan to All Hallows Church, London Wall).

Esquimalt, B.C.: In Dallymore residence. Organ dated 1859.

Geffrye Museum, London.

Hall, J. P., Kendal, Westmorland. (No. 1453) from a Cumberland farm-house.

Hereford Museum: *ex* Bosbury Ch., *vide supra*.

Hertford Museum: *ex* Stocking Pelham Ch., *vide supra.*
Jeans, Lady, Susi, Dorking, Surrey.
Jeffrey, G., Woking, Surrey.
Manx Museum, Douglas, I. of M. (from Old St. Matthew's Church, Douglas).
Ord-Hume, A., London.
Orton Hall, Twycross, Warwicks.
Pole, The late E. R. (formerly Bedwyn, Wilts.).
Robinson, Revd. G. S., Sherborne, Dorset. No. 2728: 3 stops: 3 barrels each of 10 sacred tunes.
Rushworth & Dreaper, Liverpool. (No. 2978), 5 stops, 3 barrels of 10 tunes each.

Bell, Joseph: York. Born 1823. Died 1898. In 1852 he made a barrel and finger-organ for Thirkleby Church, near Thirsk, Yorks., the gift of Lady Frankland Russell. 3 barrels x 10 tunes. (*Vide "Notes on the organists and quires in York Churches since the Reformation,"* and *"York Musicians"* in York City Library). Joseph Bell commenced business in 1847 having been apprenticed to Postill, (*q.v.*)

Beloudy, Joseph: Organ Builder, Lewkin Lane, Drury Lane, London. c. 1784.
Chamber barrel-organ (said to be *ex* Crosthwaite Church, Keswick), but five barrels are each of fifteen secular tunes. Collection of Guy Williams, Birkenhead.

Bevington & Sons: London.
Henry Bevington, an apprentice of Ohrmann & Nutt (successor to Snetzler), commenced business in 1794. His sons, Henry and Martin, continued at 8 Rose Street, Soho Square, London, W., (Ohrmann's premises) where they were in 1883. Other addresses occur on organs:—12 and 48 Greek Street, Soho Square, London ..1827-1855.. Manette Street, London, W.1. ..1907.. Charing Cross Road ..1912-21.. Bird in Bush Lane till c. 1940. Gold Medal awards at Internat. Exhibs., 1855 and 1862. Now incorporated in Wm. Hill & Son & Norman & Beard Ltd. (since 1944).
Bevington is credited with the construction of the Apollonicon organ which took its name from Flight & Robson's famous instrument for the Colosseum in Regent's Park, London.
Barnston, Essex, to be restored to occasional use.
Bressingham, Norfolk, 1851. Restored c. 1959.
Brisley, Norfolk, now manual only.
Croft, Herefs. (only tune list survives). Manual only.
Epping Upland, Essex, barrel organ rebuilt.
Fobbing, Essex.
Kilton, Somerset: 7 stops: 3 barrels.
Llanigon, Herefs.
Nenthead, Cumberland, 1852. Barrel and finger. In bad condition.
Newchurch, Isle of Wight. 'Dumb Organist.' See Plate 1.
Sacomb, Herts. (on loan since 1939 in Hertford Museum).
Shobdon, Herefs.
Tasley, Salop (now in Bishop's Palace, Hereford).
Tonge, Kent, 4 stops, 3 barrels.
Boston, J. L. Bebington, Cheshire. 4 barrels.
Brackenbury Collection, Berwickshire. 3 stops: 3 barrels x 10 tunes.
Dunbeath, Lord, Newtonards, Co. Down. 4 stops: 3 barrels.
Hereford, Bishop's Palace (*ex* Tasley Church), 2 stops, 2 barrels.
Hereford Museum: (*ex* Sacomb Church, Herts.)
Pole, The late E. R., (formerly Great Bedwyn, Wilts).

Binyon (or Bunyon), Robert: Organ maker, Clerkenwell, London.
Recently offered for sale in London: Barrel-organ, 5 stops, stopped diapason, open diapason, principal, twelfth and fifteenth. 3 barrels: marked as above.

Bishop, James C: was an "apprentice to Flight & Robson, Organ Builders to his Royal Highness, The Prince Regent, No. 7, York Buildings, Kent Road, Marylebone." (Trade-card in Banks Collection in British Museum). In 1824 James Chapman Bishop described himself as "Organ Builder and Inventor of the Composition Pedals, 7 York Buildings, New Road, Marylebone." *Vide infra, s.v.* Dungannon.
Founded in 1795 the business was known successively as:—Bishop, Son & Starr. Bishop, Starr & Richardson, c. 1840. Bishop & Starr. Bishop & Son.
In 1827 at New Road, London. At the Great Exhibition, 1851, Bishop showed a cabinet organ (No. 553) describing himself as "Designer & Manufacturer" of 1 Lisson Grove South, London.
In 1883 Bishop & Son were at 250 Marylebone Road, N.W. Today at 16b Finchley Road, N.W. 8, 50 Beethoven Street, W.10., and Bolton Lane, Ipswich, Suffolk.
In 1912 at 20 Upper Gloucester Place, N.W.
Churchill, Oxfords. (Case and barrel only, 1859.)
Fitz, Salop.
Dungannon, No. Ireland: Barrel (weight driven) finger organ: 10 stops: 3 of 6 barrels

survive. Owner, Mr. W. A. N. McGeough Bond, D.L., has the original estimate and specification dated 3rd March, 1824.

East Ham Old Parish Church: In 1880 had in use a barrel-organ by J. C. Bishop (1837): 6 stops: 4 barrels x 11 tunes (Per J. C. Curwen 1888).

Hillmorton, Warwicks., c. 1825. Barrel and finger, but barrel mechanism removed and stored.

Llanfairwaterdine, Salop, (barrel and finger). In order.

London: St. Benet, Paul's Wharf: barrel and finger organ installed 1833. Two barrels had vanished when organ rebuilt in 1897.

Northallerton, Yorks., c. 1820.

North Lopham, Norfolk, (barrel and finger), *ex* Stanhoe Church.

Stanhoe, Norfolk: transferred to North Lopham.

Bremner, Robert: c. 1713-1789, Edinburgh and London.
This Scottish musician and publisher in Edinburgh had a music shop there from 1745 till 1762 when he left for London and was succeeded by John Bryson. On his arrival in London, he issued a '*Compleat Tutor for the Flute*' from "The Harp and Hautboy, opposite Somerset House, Strand." and offered to supply "Barrel organs, all sizes: Bird Organs." *Vide Galpin Society Jl.,* xvii, Feb. 1964, pp. 99-102.
No barrel instrument bearing Bremner's name has, as yet, been noted.

Broderip & Wilkinson: 13 Haymarket, London, (1798-1811).
Apparently this firm supplied almost entirely secular or chamber barrel-organs.

Birmingham City Museum.

Chelsea Antiques Fair, April 1962, (*vide The Music Box* No. 4. Christmas 1963). 4 stops plus drum and triangle.

Culzean Castle, Ayrshire, 8 stops, 4 barrels. Out of order.

Donaldson Collection, R.C.M., London: 3 stops, 3 barrels; under restoration.

Hill, F. F., Godalming, Surrey.

Moss, R., Barton, Beds.

National Maritime Museum, Greenwich, 4 stops and drum and triangle. 4 barrels of 10 popular tunes on each.

Pole, The late E. R. (formerly Gt. Bedwyn, Wilts).

Webb, G., London, W.11.

York Castle Museum, 8 stops, 3 barrels.

Young, Miss, Bushey, Herts. 15 notes: 4 stops plus drum and triangle: 3 barrels x 10 tunes.

Brooking: Organ builder, Exeter, c. 1822-1861. Brooking & Son, Gandy Street, 1822: Upper Paul Street, 1844. In 1847, name becomes H. Brooking and in 1851 the address reverts to Gandy Street. H. Brooking appears in *Exeter Pocket Jl.* 1861 for the last time. (Information by courtesy of the Exeter City Librarian). Table barrel organ: one rank of stopped wooden pipes: 8 tunes, Alec Hodsdon's collection, Lavenham.

Bryceson, Henry: London. Business was founded in 1796, probably at 3 Little Thames Street, St. Catherine's, the address of Henry Bryceson in Holden's Directory 1802 and P.O. Directory 1803 until 1809. In Kent's Directory 1810, Henry Bryceson, organ builder is listed at 22 Market Street, St. James's London. A Chamber barrel-organ bearing this address is in N. P. Mander Collection, London; 5 stops, plus drum and triangle; 22 keys; 6 barrels. This address continued till 1815. Another 5 stop barrel-organ from Pennard Church, Glam., now in Welsh Folk Museum, Cardiff, bears the name: "H. Bryceson, Organ Builder and Piano Forte Manufacturers, No. 38 Long Acre, London. Patentee." No patent by H. Bryceson can be traced but Bryceson remained at 38 Long Acre until 1830 when he appears at 5 Tottenham Court New Road until at least 1855. Other addresses: Euston Road till 1851; Stanhope St., N.W. till 1879; 54 Essex Road, Islington Green, N. till 1893; Church St., Islington Green, in 1898; 155a Marlborough Road, Upper Holloway, in 1912. Brook St., Euston Road, also occurs on a chamber-organ in Langton-by-Spilsby Church, Lincs.

Then, as Bryceson Bros., at Charlton Works, Charlton Place, Islington Green, London. N. in 1893, bought by Kirkland, now Hill & Son & Norman & Beard Ltd. The firm was styled Bryceson Bros. & Morten in 1872 and Bryceson & Ellis, 1880-82.

Burtle, Somerset (now in Mickleburgh Collection).

Colchester Workhouse Chapel (now in Colchester Museum).

Cold Ashby, Leicestershire (now in Leicester City Museum).

Compton Wynyates, Warws. (*ex* Long Compton Church, Glos.). See Plate 31.

Garton-in-Holderness. (now in Castle Museum, York): 4 barrels; 5 stops: 1846. Out of order.

Hampton Gay, Oxon. (c. 1835). See Plate 10.

Hartfield, Sussex. (Remnants scrapped 1939-1945).

Helhoughton, Norfolk. Transferred in 1890 from West Raynham.

Isle Abbots, Somerset.

Luton (now F. F. Hill Collection).
Lilbourne, Warwicks. (Barrel and finger). Remnants only, in Bede House now.
Lyddington, Rutland (barrel and finger).
Milton, Cambs. (1840).
Pennard, Glam. (now in Welsh Folk Museum, Cardiff): 5 stops: 3 barrels. Restored to working order in 1969 by J. Budgen, Ipswich.
Rowde Methodist Chapel, Wilts. (*vide* Scholes *Oxf. Comp.* p. 549).
Shelland, Suffolk. (In regular use. 6 stops, 3 barrels each of 12 tunes). See Plates 11 & 12.
West Raynham: barrel and finger: 1852: transferred in 1890 to Helhoughton: 6 stops and 4 barrels of which one is spiral for voluntaries.
Colchester Museum, Essex. (*ex* Workhouse Chapel).
Ellen, Mr. and Mrs. R. G., Fleet, Hants.: Chamber barrel-organ similar to that of N. P. Mander, *infra*.
Hill, F. F., Godalming, Surrey. (*ex* Luton Church). No longer in collection.
Leicester City Museum (*ex* Cold Ashby, Leics.).
Lubbock, Mr., Midhurst, Sussex.
Mander, N. P. Ltd., London, E.2: 4 stops plus drum and triangle: 1 sacred and 5 secular barrels—1 spiral barrel.
Mickleburgh, E. R., Bristol. (*ex* Burtle Church, Somerset).
Ord-Hume, A., London (Secular organ).
Stuart, Mrs. J. S., Hethersett, Norfolk. (Secular organ).
Welsh Folk Museum, Cardiff. (*ex* Pennard Church, Glam.). Restored 1969.
York Castle Museum. (*ex* Garton-in-Holderness).
The West Sussex Gazette of 25 June 1857 advertised a " Church Organ of 3 barrels, 10 tunes each, by Bryceson Bros. 4 stops, 8 guineas.
Musical Times in 1860 advertised a Bryceson " barrel-organ playing 40 psalm tunes and chants. 4 barrels."—*vide Notes and Queries*, 12th Series, x, 254, 1 April 1922.

Bryson, H: 3 Little Thema Street, East Smithfield, London. " Patent " Barrel-organ, 3 barrels x 10 Scottish Songs etc.; 4 stops plus drum and triangle. Inside is a trade-card " William ... Princes St., Edinburgh, The Turf Coffee House." Owned by R. G, Hopkins, Bishops Stortford.

Buckingham, A: London. c. 1819-1840. " Foreman to the late Mr. Avery and Mr. Elliot," 39 Frederick Place, London. In 1827 he was at 39 Hampstead Road, and he must have been in business before Elliot's death in 1832. A barrel-organ made by him for Brightling Church was sent in 1829 as a gift to Archdeacon Williams, New Zealand and the organ, with its three barrels of ten tunes each, is preserved in Wanganui Museum.

Buckwell, Theodore: 31 Hackney Road, London. c. 1827.
Chamber barrel-organ, 4 stops, tune-list for 4 barrels of which 2 survive. P. M. Campbell-Voullaire, London, S.E.21.

Bunting, John: pre-1815: " Organ builder and Piano Forte Manufacturer,, 22 Swan St., Minories, London," inside the lid of a barrel-organ by Astor & Co, 79 Cornhill.

Butler, James: Born 1780. Died 1863. 4 Hyde Street, Bloomsbury.
This maker may not have made barrel-organs, but is included as " Organ Builder " in Pigot's Directory of 1827—and repeated here in case a barrel-organ bearing his name may come to light.

Button & Purday: 75 St, Paul's Churchyard, London, 1807-08. Secular barrel-organ: 4 stops and drum and triangle: L. Taylor, Wells, Som., and Beazor's shop, Cambridge

Chiappa: 31 Eyre Street, Hill, London, E.C.1.
The last surviving fair-organ builders in Britain. The first of the family served apprenticeship with Gavioli in Paris. In 1864 he set up business near Farringdon Road, London, but soon after went to New York, starting a fair-organ factory there. In 1877 he returned to London and established the present factory at 6 Little Bath Street, Holborn, a street later re-named Eyre Street Hill. The business was continued by a son and is now conducted by a grandson, Victor Chiappa. Street barrel-organs and street barrel-pianos were produced till c. 1910. Clockwork pianos operated by both barrel or perforated strip continued till c. 1923. Large " military band " barrel organs for roller-skating rinks were produced till c. 1910. At one time twenty to forty people were employed and the firm made and pinned barrels for Imhof & Mukle orchestrions made in the Black Forest. Local repairers were named Viazzani and Arigoni. To-day Victor Chiappa has one man and two women employees. (Information by courtesy of Mr. A. Ord-Hume).

Clementi, Muzio: 1752-1832. 26 Cheapside, London and Paris Agency. 1802-1809.
He was successor to Longman & Broderip and was succeeded by (John) Longman, Clementi & Co.
Chamber barrel-organs with secular tunes are in the following public and private collections:—
Angrave, Bruce, London, W.5.
Baines, R., London, W.2.
Birmingham City Museum (*ex* Liddell Colln.)

PLATE 14

Photo by Basil D. King, Markyate, Herts.

Wood Rising Church, Norwich. Barrel-organ by Flight & Robson, London, 1826, in gallery. A particularly pleasing case. The instrument was restored to working order by John Budgen, of Messrs. Bishop & Son, Ipswich, in 1958 as a result of Lord Verulam's agency and rededicated on 1st May 1958. 3 stops: 78 pipes: compass 3 octaves from Bass G but omission of certain notes reduces the number from 37 to 27. Originally 3 barrels of 10 tunes each. One extra barrel was made and fitted by John Budgen to replace one beyond repair.

Burkart, A. J. London.

    R.A.M., London, 4 stops plus drum and triangle, 5 barrels each of 10 secular tunes.

de Vere Green, C., London.

    Yale Collection, U.S.A., N-234 (*ex* Belle Skinner Collection).

Coates, Richard: Oakville, Ontario. A sawmill operator and amateur organ builder who made a barrel-organ for Sharon Temple, now a Museum Owned by York Pioneer and Historical Society of Toronto.

    Chamber barrel-organ owned by Ernest G. Lusty, Rodney, Ontario, a great grandson of R. Coates.

Courcell, John: 26 Judd Street, Brunswick Square, London. Inventor of the " Cylindrichord ": *vide*: Scholes' "Oxford Companion to Music," *s.v.* Mechanical Reproduction, 13, p. 554. Pigot's Directory, 1827. Music Trades Directory 1883 gives J. Courcelle (sic), 12 Sandringham Road, London, E. Organ pipe maker and voicer—presumably a descendant of the earlier inventor. Came from France in 1847, and made pipes for Forster & Andrews (*q.v.*) till they made their own c. 1852. Courcell's successors are Alfred Palmer & Sons (Estab. 1853), Finchingfield, Essex.

Crang, John: "Organ builder . . . Also makes box-organs, etc." c. 1745-1792.

    Great Queen Street, Lincoln's Inn Fields, London, per Mortimer's London Directory, 1763. Crang came from Devon and joined John Hancock, a celebrated reed-voicer, about 1770. Crang specialised in converting old Echo organs into Swell organs. Both Crang and Hancock died in 1792. Per J. A. Gilfillan, Kendal.

Crowshaw: London. c. 1830. A single example with 3 stops plus drum and triangle and piano by this maker came up at Sotheby's Saleroom in July, 1965. No address has been ascertained. *Vide "The Music Box,"* Vol. 2, No.3, p. 123. Now owned by Bruce Moss, Barton, Beds. The instrument has 5 barrels.

Cumming, Alexander (1733-1814). A native of Scotland who became a celebrated Bond Street watchmaker. His advice was sought by John Stuart (1713-1792) Third Earl of Bute who was having a finger and barrel organ installed by John Snetzler and others in Luton Park, the estate purchased in 1762 by the Earl. The organ gave trouble but Cumming's designs for improvement were received too late for incorporation. In 1785, however, Lord Bute invited Cumming to superintend the building of another barrel-organ in the Earl's house, High Cliff, near Christchurch, Hants. Cumming finished the organ in 1787 with various improvements. He wrote a book published in 1812 entitled "A Sketch of the Properties of the Machine Organ, constructed and made by Mr. Cumming, for the Earl of Bute." (A rare copy is in the Patent Office.)

    Unfortunately, the Luton Park organ is presumed to have been destroyed in the fire there in 1843. The High Cliff organ was sold to the Earl of Shaftesbury who in turn sold it back to Cumming, by then resident at Pentonville. The fate of the organ is not known. *Vide "Lord Bute's Barrel Organs" by Michael I. Wilson in Musical Opinion,* Feby. 1966

Davis, James: Chelsea. London. 1762-1827. Assumed to have made a large barrel-organ of which the tune sheet and the windchest bear his name. 5 stops include a Tierce with drum and triangle in addition. A base accommodates 4 of the complement of 10 barrels, each of 10 tunes. Davis established himself in London in the late 18th c. He provided the organ for Wymondham Abbey in 1793. He removed to Preston c. 1800 and was succeeded by Joseph Renn who continued till retiral in 1843. (Renn & Boston, 1827-c. 1831). The business was then acquired by James Kirtland (nephew of Renn) who took into partnership Fredk. W. Jardine, an ex-employee of Bishop. Jardine retired in 1875. *Vide* Obituary notice in *Gentleman's Mag.* xcvii, p. 284, 1827, which states " Mr. Bishop succeeds in all the church business."

Davis, John: 11 Catherine Street, Strand. 1814-1818.

Davis, Joseph: 14 Crescent, Kingsland Road 1805-06, 11 Catherine Street, Strand, 1812-1829, also at 92 Blackfriars Road in 1829 which was his only address, 1830-1843. Finally he was at 20 Southampton Street, Strand, 1844-1848.

    " Organ builder, Military Wind Instrument Maker, Importer and dealer in every article in the musical line. Self-performing Piano-Harp and other musical instruments."

    Organ of two manuals with barrel-organ addition was in Farleigh Castle, then c. 1870 removed to Blount's Court, Potterne, Wilts., and in 1957 to Dauntsey's School, Devizes, Wilts. Weight-driven by worm and pinion. The single barrel, 6 ft. long, turns in a screw, moving laterally—ten turns to complete its repertoire. *Vide Musical Times,* Sept. 1968, pp. 846-848, reprinted in *The Music Box,* Vol. 3, No 8, pp. 534-538.

    Burton-on-Trent Museum; Barrel-organ thought to have been in Repton Ch., then in Bretby Hall: 4 stops, 3 barrels x 10 sacred tunes.

Dawson, Charles: London, c. 1848, took out British Patent No. 12307 of 2 Nov. 1849 being a device for playing pianos or organs using perforated pasteboard instead of barrels.

Dieffenbacher, P. L.: Turbotville, Pa., U.S.A., ..1892-1899...

    Barrel-organs in Hershey Museum, Pa; one of 1892 with 18 notes; another of 1899, 4 stops, 22 notes; 1 barrel x 8 secular tunes. (Per Miss B. Owen, Pigeon Cove, Mass.)

Distin, Henry: Bristol . . . 1847-1854 . . . No entry for H. Distin occurs in Bristol Directories from 1816 to 1853 but he appears in Poll Books of 1847 and 1852 as residing at Church Lane, Temple Parish.

Early piano in the late E. R. Pole's Collection, is marked:—
"Henry Distin (from the late Joseph Hicks). Barrel pianoforte maker, No. 2 Church Lane, Temple Street, Bristol."

Distin appears at this address as Pianoforte tuner in the Bristol Directory for 1871. His patent 1178 of 27 May, 1854 is for drums with barrel-organs. A barrel-piano is in the collection of Roy Mickleburgh, Bristol.

Dixon, Jn.: Conway Street, Fitzroy Square, London "Organ Builder" per Pigot's Directory 1827.

Dobson & Munro: London. Known only by a barrel-organ in collection of Murtogh Guinness, New York. *Vide Music Box,* Vol. 3, No. 8, p. 547.

Dobson, Benjamin: 22 Swan Street, Minories, London ..1799-1827..

Barrel organ dated 1799 on the tracker board. Four stops. 22 keys. 5 barrels with 10 sacred tunes. One barrel is labelled:—Dobson, Organ Builder and Pianoforte Manufacturer, No. 22 Swan Street, Minories, London. Merchants, Captains and the trade supplied. N.B. No communication with No. 21 next door. (This refers to Eveleigh. *q.v.*)

Colln. of T. H. Ashton, Corpus Christi College, Oxford, dated 1799.

Dobson occurs in Pigot's Directory 1827.

Eagle, J. S.: Hackney, London, c. 1846. Barrel-organ installed in 1846 in Enford Church, Pewsey, Wilts. Later converted to manual.

Elliot & Hill: London. (1825-1832). Thomas Elliot was at Wharton's Court, Holborn in 1791. Doane's Directory for 1794 gives "Thomas Elliot, Organ builder, 10 Sutton Street, Soho Square, London." Pigot, in 1827 gives him at 12 Tottenham Court Road, where he was as early as 1819. William Hill (died 1870) was partner of Thomas Elliot from 1825 until 1832 when Elliot died. Hill then continued alone until 1837 when he was joined by F. Davison. *cp.* Hill & Davison.

Barrel-organ dated 1831 in Farnham Church, Yorks. (out of order).

Engman, Erick: London (1773-1784). Orange Court, Leicester Fields, London, for which premises he paid rates during the period stated. Secular barrel-organ. 6 stops. Given by Messrs N. P. Mander Ltd., London, to the Rev. Peter Priest.

Evans, James: London. c. 1762.. Possibly the earliest dated barrel-organ was a chamber instrument marked as above and "A.S.R.M. Dn. Carlos III Ano. MDCCLXII" (To his Royal Majesty Don Carlos III in the year 1762). Delivered to the Spanish Court. *Vide "Musik und Kirche,"* 32 Jhg., 1962, p. 173. Evans substituted Diego for his Christian name, James, in compliment to his customer as his family had a long-established connection with Spain. His address: Royal Exchange, was translated: "Bolsa Real, Londres" on the dial of a musical clock owned by the late Sir W. S. Gilbert. *Vide The Times,* Apl. 12, 1960, reprinted in *The Music Box,* Vol. 2, No. 6, 1966, p. 273: on p. 291 of the same issue reference is made to Higgs & Evans of Royal Exchange, London, c. 1795. The Ilbert Collection in the British Museum contains a pair case alarm watch signed "Robt. & Petr. Higgs & Jas. Evans, London, 440": the date assigned is c. 1870. A bracket clock by "Higgs & Diego Evans" is in Virginia Museum, U.S.A. The firm was at Sweeting's Alley and later Royal Exchange, 1775-1825.

Eveleigh & Co.: 21 Swan Street, Minories, London. "Real Manufacturers of Church Organs, Pianos and Barrel Organs. Successors to Mr. Pistor."

Barrel organ labelled as above and barrels likewise. 4 stops. Horniman Museum, Forest Gate, London.

The maker's label also states: "Instruments exchanged, repaired and tuned, carefully repaired, etc. Also Barrel Organs set to new music with new plans for adding Drum, Triangle, Tabor, Flageolet or Harp on the most reasonable terms for ready money. Wholesale, Retail and for export."

Eveleigh, Joseph: also occurs at same address on a small chamber barrel-organ in possession of the late Dr. W. Greenhouse Allt, London.

Eveleigh, Joshua: 21 Swan Street, Minories, London, in 1827 per Pigot's Directory.

Fentum, J.: London. Jonathan Fentum c. 1763 - c. 1784. John Fentum c. 1784 - c. 1835. Barrel Organ dated 1815 in Colt Collection. *Vide* "Country Life," 17 March, 1950, with two photographs.

A Barrel "No. 2," in E. R. Pole Collection, was labelled "Bought of J. Fentum, 78 Strand, near the Adelphi."

Fincham, John: 110 Euston Road, London, N.W. (Estab. 1837).

Barrel organ in South Weston Church, Oxon. 2 barrels, 5 stops. Independent blowing.

A successor, Henry Fincham, 148 and 150 Euston Road, N.W. appears in the *Music Trades Directory,* 1883, as organ pipe maker.

Flight: This name occurs for over a century in connection with organ building, including barrel organs. The Guildhall Librarian very kindly supplied the following:—
Benjamin & William Flight, Exeter Exchange, 1784-1787. Flight & Kelly, Exeter Exchange,

1788-1800. Benjamin Flight, Senr. Exeter Exchange, 1801-1802; Old Lisle Street, Leicester Square, 1803-1805. Flight & Robson, Old Lisle Street, Leicester Square. 1806; 101 St. Martin's Lane, later known as " The Apollonicon Rooms," 1807-1833. Flight & Sons (i.e. John), 16 King William Street, West Strand, 1834-38. Flight (Benjamin & Co., 16 King William Street, West Strand, 1839-1848, 36 St. Martin's Lane, 1849-1887. The founder, Benjamin Flight, Senior, appears to have had a brother associated with him for a time at Exeter Exchange, and possibly at an earlier address as Scholes' *Oxford Companion to Music s.v.* Mechanical Reproduction, states that Flight advertised barrel-organs as early as 1772. B. Flight and a new partner, John Kelly, continued at the same address from 1788-1800. The firm is included in Doane's Directory of 1794; after which Benj. Flight, Son & Kelly occurs on labels. Thereafter Flight, on his own account issued c. 1802, a trade card (in the Banks Colln. B. D2. 2605 British Museum) as follows:— " Benjamin Flight, Organ Builder, Exeter Change, Strand, London. Makes and repairs in the best manner all sorts of Barrel, Finger and Machine Organs. New barrels made and old ones set to modern music. Likewise tun'd and repair'd in any part of England on the most reasonable terms."
He continued alone from 1801-1805. Benjamin Flight, Junior, (born 1767, died 1847), learned under his father, and probably on his father's death he assumed as partner c. 1806 Joseph Robson, removing in the following year to 101 St. Martin's Lane, where the firm, " Makers to His Majesty the Prince Regent," remained for quarter of a century. When the partnership was dissolved in 1832, Gray & Davison (*q.v.*) bought Robson's share while B. Flight, Junior and his son John Flight as Flight & Son, later Flight & Co., continued until 1887 at various addresses shown above.
T. J. F. Robson of 101 St. Martin's Lane, noted as inventor *inter alia* of the Apollonicon, exhibited an organ at the Great Exhibition of 1851.
Abbots Leigh, Somerset.
Burghley House Chapel, Northants.
Bletchley, Bucks. *Vide " Gentleman's Magazine "* 1849. Converted to manual.
Boldre, Hants.
Burley-on-the-Hill, Rutland. c. 1795.
Calke, Derbyshire (incl. 2 of 5 barrels).
Diss Unitarian Chapel (now with Messrs. Boggis, *infra*).
Fryerning, Essex.
Great Glemham, Suffolk : Now manual only.
Hatfield House Chapel, Herts. 1807. Replaced in 1876.
Heacham, Norfolk. (Transferred to Thornham *q.v.*).
Hersham, Surrey (1845). In use till 1867.
Knutsford Unitarian Chapel, Cheshire. (Removed in 1915).
Milton Abbot, Devon. (4 barrels).
South Elkington, Lincs. (Removed in 1849 and advertised for sale by Forster & Andrews, Hull).
Stratfieldsaye, Hants. The gift of Field Marshal The Duke of Wellington, labelled " B. Flight & Son, Organ Builders & Musical Instrument Makers, 36 St. Martin's Lane, Charing Cross, W.C." (*Vide " Daily News," 21st July, 1924*).
Thornham, Norfolk. (From Heacham and later sent to South Africa).
Waltham Abbey, Essex, (1819). Converted in 1850 by J. W. Walker. *Vide The Organ,* No. 149, Vol. xxxviii, July 1958.
Wood Rising, Norfolk. (1826). Restored to complete working order by J. Budgen, of Messrs. Bishop & Son, Ipswich, and re-dedicated 1st May, 1958. *Vide " Wood Rising Church "* by F. W. Steer, F.S.A. (1959)). See Plate 14.
Boggis, W. & A., Organ Builders, Diss (*ex Diss Unitarian Chapel*).
Cook, Geo., Surrey. Chamber B-O.
Greene, F., London and Oxford.
Guinness, Hon. Desmond, Co. Kildare.
Leigh Court Hospital, Abbots Leigh, Bristol: finger and barrel-organ, 12 stops.
Ord-Hume, A., London.
Osborn, the late Sir G., (1838). *Vide Lincoln, Rutland & Stamford Mercury* of 11 May 1838, quoted in *The Organ,* Vol. 149, xxxviii, July 1958, p. 15.
Perrot, M. Paris. (incomplete).
Peterborough Museum. 3 barrels of 10 tunes each.
Victoria and Albert Museum.
Wootton, The late C., Hove: Serinette Organ, 2 stops and triangle. 2 barrels of 10 tunes each.
Thomas, W. R., Fife. 4 stops: Tune list for 4 barrels, only 2 surviving. By Benj. Flight, Son & Kelly.
Vide article on " Holdich & the Flight & Robsons " *s.v.* Holdich, *infra*
Forman: London. Known only by a small table barrel-organ in the Science and Industry Museum, Birmingham. 3 stops. Drum and triangle missing. 1 barrel of 10 tunes. Tune-list missing.

PLATE 15

Chamber Barrel-organ by Godfrey, London. The late Canon Boston's Collection.

PLATE 16

The late Canon Noel Boston at the Mattishall Burgh Church barrel-organ.

Forster & Andrews: 29 Charlotte Street, Hull. (Founded 1843). Mr. Laurence Elvin has published privately a history of this firm's business in " Foster & Andrews, Organ-builders. 1843-1956 ". (Lincoln, 1968). The book contains 37 illustrations and the annexed list of 7 barrel-organs and 20 barrel and finger organs built by the firm between 1846 and 1862. In 1846 Forster & Andrews, former employees of Bishop in London, advertised " Improved Church Barrel Organs with 3, 4 or 5 barrels in a frame." In 1849 they offered " barrel organs with 12 tunes £15 upwards . . . three or four barrels on an axis to avoid shifting the barrels, playing 36 or 48 tunes, £35 and upwards . . . Barrel and finger organs united, of great use where the services of an organist can be only occasionally procured, from 60 guineas upwards."
In 1849 the firm offered the following second-hand barrel-organs:
1. By Robson & Son, London, barrel and finger organ of 1843. 5 stops, 4 barrels each of 10 psalms etc. Recently removed from Lydlinch Church, Dorset.
2. By Flight & Robson, London. Six stops, 5 barrels each of 10 psalms etc. Recently removed from South Elkington Church, Lincs.
3. By Forster & Andrews, Hull. Three barrels in a frame, 36 tunes, and the most recent improvements in the machinery.
In 1880 they had a London address, 17 Temple St., E.C. The firm was wound up in 1956 and the business taken over by Hill & Son, Norman & Beard.

Barrel-Organs

Adlingfleet Church, Yorks. 1857. 1 barrel. Barkby Church, Leics. 1849. 3 barrels. Atwick Church, Yorks. 1856. 3 barrels. Barrowby Church, Lincs. 1849. 3 barrels. Great Ponton Church, Lincs. 1848. 3 barrels. Huttoft Church, Lincs. 1851. 3 barrels. Staunton Church, Notts. 1852. 3 barrels.

Barrel and Finger Organs combined

Adlingfleet Church, Yorks. 1857. 1 barrel. Barkby Church, Leics. 1849. 3 barrels. Brandsburton Church, Yorks. 1857. 1 barrel. Broughton Church, Lincs. 1847. 1 barrel Colsterworth Church, Lincs 1853. 1 barrel. Dent Church, Yorks. 1854. 2 barrels. Edwinstowe Church, Notts. 1862. 1 barrel. Gamston Church, Notts. 1856. 1 barrel. Grantham, Lincs. Mr. Short. 1851. 3 barrels. Great Chart Church, Kent. 1854 3 barrels. Harlaxton Church, Lincs. 1856. 2 barrels. Hatfield Church, Yorks. 1849. 2 barrels. Hunmanby Church, Yorks. 1846. 3 barrels. Lastingham Church, Yorks. 1857. 1 barrel. Longnor Church, Staffs. 1852. 1 barrel. Louth, Lincs. Holy Trinity Church. 1846. 1 barrel. Owersby Church, Lincs. 1849. 1 barrel.
W. Dawber of Thurgarton, Notts., in 1858 was supplied with nearly the last barrel-organ made by the firm:
Barrel and finger organ. 3 barrels each of 10 tunes. 7 stops. 286 pipes. No pedals. Cost £80 nett or £55 and the old organ. Extra barrels could be supplied at £5 each if ordered before the instrument left Hull. In the same year a 2-barrel-organ was supplied to Sir Peter Coats, Paisley.

Fuzelli, Joseph: 379 Great Ormond Street, London.
Barrel-organ. 4 barrels. 4 stops. Rev. Dr. P. C. Moore's Collection, Pershore, Worcs.

Gavioli & Cie., Paris: ..1872-1889.. Makers of street organs mainly but a reed organ with 3 barrels is in the collection of Mr. R. Baines, London. Another barrel-organ (incomplete) in collection of Mr. John Bentley, Waltham Abbey, Essex.

Gerock, Christopher: London. c. 1804-1821 at 74 Bishopsgate Street Within; c. 1815-21 also at 1 Gracechurch Street.
R. T. Boston, Bebington, Cheshire.
The late E. R. Pole, Gt. Bedwyn, Wilts.
Snowshill Manor (Natl. Trust), Glos.

Godfrey, George: London. c. 1789. Organ Builder, No. 12 in the Strand near Temple Bar. " Makes all sorts of Finger, Barrel and Clock Machine Organs. N.B. Harpsichords and spinets made and tuned."
The late Canon Noel Boston, Lamas Manor, Norwich. See Plate 15.
G. Webb, London. (Incomplete).
A. Ord-Hume, London, with the address: " No. 8 Tufton Street, Westminster, near College Street, Westminster." (c. 1802).
Patent No. 1712 of 8th December 1789 was granted to George Godfry (sic) for additions to barrel-organs, "Tamborine, Tabor or Drum and Pipe."
The Guildhall Library checked 1789-1811 and found only one reference (in the Directory for 1802): " George Godfrey, Organ builder, 8 Tufton Street, Westminster."

Gray, William: London. (Died 1820). New Road, Fitzroy Square. With his brother, formed the firm of R. & W. Gray. On the death of Robert, William continued alone for a time.
Church Barrel and Finger Organ, South Kilworth, Leics. (1846).
Presented on 6th September, 1846 by the Rev. Dr. W. Pearson, a finger organ by Wm. Gray with two barrels for Psalmody. 6 stops. The two barrels have disappeared.

Gray, John: London. (Died 1849). New Road, Fitzroy Square. Succeeded William Gray of R. & W. Gray. In 1837 the business was John Gray & Son. In 1838, John Gray assumed Frederic Davison as a partner in Gray & Davison. The firm is said to have bought Robson's share in Flight & Robson in 1832. (Groves's Dict., 5th Edition, *s.v.* Gray), but as stated above Gray & Davison was formed in 1838, though their trade advertisements state " Founded 1750."

In 1839 Robert Gray of John Gray & Son wrote to *The Musical World* describing his " Improved Church Barrel Organ " with a diagram of 3 barrels on a frame and separate blowing pedal. The ' projector ' is stated to be Robert Gray of 9 New Road, Fitzroy Square.

Wissington Church, Suffolk, by John Gray No. 32. (1840) 4 stops, 3 barrels of 10 sacred tunes each. See Plate 4.

Raithby Church, Louth, Lincs. (restored by John Budgen of Messrs. Bishop & Son, Ipswich). See Plate 17.

Gray, Robert & William: London. The firm is said to have been founded by Robert Gray in 1774. He had an organ factory at Leigh Street, Red Lion Square in 1774 and the firm's trade card of 1793 gives their address as 72 Queen Ann Street East, London. *Vide:* Philip, James, *Early Keyboard Instruments,* London, 1930; and Doane's Directory for 1794 records:

Gray, William & Robert (*sic*) Organ Builders, No. 4 New Road, Portland Road, London. In 1827 they were at 9 Quickset Row, New Road.

The label on a 21-keyed barrel-organ reads:

" Robert & William Gray, Organ, harpsichord and piano makers. No. 4, New Road, near the end of Portland Road."

Chamber barrel organ: 5 stops. 3 barrels, one of which moves laterally as it turns and plays a chorus from "Messiah." J. W. Walker Collection, Ruislip, Middlesex.

Gray & Davison: London. Formed by John Gray and Frederic Davison in 1838, at 9 New Road, Fitzroy Square. In 1851 at the Great Exhib. the firm, as " Designers and Manufacturers " at the same address, showed a " Church organ of the first class." By 1883, as a Limited Company, they were at 370 Euston Road, N.W. and 18 Colquett Street, Liverpool. Today the company is at 3 Cumming Street, London, N.1., and advertises that it incorporates Holdich: Eustace Ingram and G. H. Foskett & Co. The date of foundation—1750—must refer to an assumed date of foundation by Robert Gray of R. & W. Gray, but evidence is lacking prior to 1774.

Muchelney, Somerset, c. 1838. 4 stops. 3 barrels each of 8 tunes, separate blowing pedal. Replaced by a harmonium in 1872 and by a pipe organ c. 1907. The barrel organ remains in a recess in the South wall. One of the tunes, " Wells " was composed by Thomas Shoel, (pronounced locally " Shayell "), the son of a Montacute village blacksmith. He used to walk all over the county and hawk his chants and hymn tunes at 6d. each. See Plate 30.

Grey, Daniel: Organ builder, No. 6 Ely Place, St. George's Road, Southwark, London. M. Perrot, Paris, owns a large chamber barrel-organ: 3 barrels: independent pedal-blown bellows. Incomplete.

Haines, Wm: 1 London Terrace, Hackney Road, London. (Per Pigot's Directory, 1827). No instrument recorded.

Haxby, Thomas: York. Born c. 1737. Died c. 1796. Son of Robert Haxby, a joiner, Thomas Haxby in 1756 opened a shop "The Organ " in York and advertised in the *York Courant:* 'Musical Instruments at T. Haxby's warehouse, Blake Street, are made and sold. Pianos etc." One of his pianos, date 1789, is in the Castle Museum, York. In 1767 he repaired the organ at Leeds Parish Church and in 1760 and 1778 at York Minster.

Harpsichords of Haxby dated from 1764 and square pianos from 1772 to 1790 are recorded by D. Boalch, *Makers of the Harpsichord* (1956) p. 48. On 28th December, 1770, he took out a Patent (No. 977) for a new single Harpsichord. In 1782 a residentiary Canon of York Minster wrote to his Curate:—

" Mr. Haxby, a famous Harpsichord maker, has finished the organ greatly to my mind and it has been tried and still used in the Church of St. Michael-le-Belfry here in the Minster Yard and has as good effect as any played with the hand. It consists of two cylinders and executes 24 tunes."

After Haxby's death, his business in Blake Street was taken over by Samuel Knapton, a music seller and publisher, and from 1795 to c. 1840 by Thomas Tomlinson. No surviving barrel-organ by Haxby is known.

Vide MS " Notes on the Organs, Organists and Quires in York Churches since the Reformation " by John W. Knowles (in York City Library).

Heath, R. J. & Sons: Cardiff. Estab. 1874. Name appears on small barrel-organ in Welsh Folk Museum. 2 barrels each of 10 secular tunes. One barrel marked " Manufactured by Willis & Co., Royal Musical Repository, St. James's Street, London."

Hicks, George: Brooklyn, New York: 1848-64. Barrel-organ: 35 notes: Smithsonian Institution, U.S.Natl. Museum No. 299855.

Hicks, John: London. At Coburg Street, Clerkenwell, London. ..1854-1871.. *Vide* J. E. T. Clark,

"*Musical Boxes*," p. 172, gives Hicks, Chapel Street, Edgware Road, London, as a barrel-organ maker " who made the first street organ in 1810 " (*sic*). Hicks made many cylinder pianos in the first half of the 19th century. London Directories show John Hicks at addresses:—24 Coburg Street, Clerkenwell, 1854-57; 2 St. John Street, Clerkenwell, 1858-60; 6 Chapel Street, Clerkenwell, 1861-65. No entries till 31 Clerkenwell Green, 1870-71. A very small barrel-organ is in the Stranger's Hall Museum, Norwich.

Hicks, Joseph: Bristol. ..1816-1851.. An early pianoforte in E. R. Pole Collection was by:— " Henry Distin (from the late Joseph Hicks), Barrel Pianoforte maker, No. 2. Church Lane, Temple Street, Bristol."

Joseph Hicks, Musical Instrument Maker, was admitted a Freeman of Bristol on 12th October, 1812 in that he was a son of Peter Hicks, cabinet-maker (deceased).

Bristol Directories give Joseph Hicks as " Mus. Inst. Mkr., and Organ Builder " as follows:—1816-1829, 11 Griffin Lane and Trenchard Street. 1830, Trenchard Street. 1831, 3 St. Augustine's Place. 1832-41, 16 Lower Park Row. 1842-44, 17 Lower Maudlin Street. 1845-47, 17 Montague Street (final). By courtesy of Bristol Public Library.

Leicester Museum. The instrument is marked " Hicks, Maker, Bristol, No. 699."

Joseph Hicks removed to London and was at 31 Penton Street, 1849-50 and at 21 Kirby Street, Hatton Garden in 1851. A large barrel piano bears a label on the spruce sound-board, as follows:—Joseph Hicks, Manufacturer of Barrel Organs and Cylinder Pianos, 31 Penton Street, Pentonville, London.

The serial number is 420 and the barrel paper is watermarked 1846, suggesting that Joseph Hicks removed to London in that year. There are 41 keys comprising 38 trichords and 3 bichords. Two large barrels each play 10 tunes—mainly dances. Collection of R. Baines, London. W.2.

Hicks, J. & Son: Bristol. This name occurs on the barrel of a barrel-organ in Bethnal Green Museum. In the windchest of showman's organ by White & Langshaw is written " Repaired by J. Hicks of Bristol, June 2nd, 1821." Ord-Hume Collection.

Hill & Davison: London. 1837-38. William Hill (died 1870) of Elliot & Hill (*vide supra*) was joined by Frederic Davison in 1837. A year later Davison left to join John Gray. The business then became W. Hill & Son. In 1916 it was amalgamated with Norman & Beard Ltd. Addresses: In 1855 at 12 Tottenham Court New Road: In 1883, York Road Works, Camden Road, N.W. From 1912-1921 at York Road, Islington.

Hagley Church, Worcs: 2 barrels of 11 tunes in use 1838-1852.

Wennington Church, Essex. A barrel organ made by Hill & Davison was formerly used. 4 stops, 18 keys and 65 pipes. 2 barrels each of ten psalms and hymns. The instrument has vanished.

Hinton, William: 4 Coalyard, Drury Lane, London. (Per *Pigot's Directory* 1827). No instrument is recorded.

Holdich, George Maydwell: London. Maydwell was the Northants village of his birth. He was established at New Road by 1827. Then by 1837 at 12 Greek Street, Soho (the same premises as Bevington). By 1851 he was at 4 Judd Place East, King's Cross, from which address he showed a " small choir organ " with " diaocton " stop at the Great Exhibition. The Judd Place premises were renumbered 42 Euston Road and he remained there till the 1860's when the site was acquired by the Railway. His new address, 24 Park Place West, Liverpool Road, Islington became almost at once 361 Liverpool Road. Holdich sold out to Eustace Ingram in 1894 and for a time, the firm was Holdich & Ingram, but very soon Gray & Davison took over, leaving the management to Ingram for a time.

An excellent account of " G. M. Holdich and the Flight & Robsons " by the Rev. B. B. Edmonds is in *The Organ Club Handbook*, No. 6, pp. 42-57.

Easton-on-the-Hill, Northants: ' Dumb organist,' presumably by Holdich, as it fits the Holdich finger organ of 1850. *Vide Galpin Socy. Jl.*, xiv, Mar. 1961, pp. 37-40 and Plate.

Edgecott Church, Northants. A barrel and finger organ, dated 1855. 6 stops, 3 combination pedals. 2 barrels each of 6 hymns and psalms.

Piddington, Northants: barrel and finger organ.

N. Vince, East Dereham: secular barrel-organ converted to manual. Bears plate stating rebuilt by G. M. Holdich, Soho Square, in 1847.

Holland, Henry: London. ..1783-1827..

The label in a barrel organ seen in Norfolk in 1959 bears:—

" Henry Holland, (Royal Arms), Organ Builder & Patent Grand & Square Pianoforte maker, Corner of St. James's Street, from Bedford Row, nephew and successor to the late Mr. Pyke, organ builder to His Majesty. Sells all sorts of Music and Musical Instruments, music books, music paper, ruling pens for do., Harpsichord wire, Guittar (*sic*) do; the best Roman Strings, with every other branch in Music on the most reasonable terms. Instruments let out on hire. Tun'd and repair'd by the month, quarter or year. N.B. Any lady or Gentleman having a pianoforte and wishing to have an organ under it may have it made on reasonable terms at the above warehouse."

Holland is stated to have learned his trade with the elder England. He built the organ in St. George's, Bloomsbury in 1788. He appears in Doane's Directory of 1794 as " Organ

PLATE 17

PLATE 18

Photo: F. Huntly Woodcock, Grimsby.

Photo: Nothamptonshire Newspapers Ltd.

St. Peter's Church, Raithby, Nr. Louth, Lincs. Barrel-organ by Gray & Son (1839). 3 stops: 3 barrels, each of 10 tunes. After 90 years disuse, restored in 1963 by John Budgen, of Messrs. Bishop, Ipswich.

Mr. H. W. Geary, of Kettering, with his T. C. Bates & Son Barrel-organ at Cranford Chapel, Kettering. Possibly *ex* Bulwick Parish Church.

Builder, Little Chelsea." Barrel-organ in collection of P. Brennan, Abbeyleix, Eire, dated 1784.

In 1827, Pigot's Directory gives his address as Bedford Row and St. James's Street. A small barrel-organ with "Organ Maker to His Majesty" and these last two addresses is in the N.P. Mander Collection.

Holland: Sutton-on-Trent, near Newark, Notts.

A fair organ with 16 barrels in excellent condition and marked as above is in the C. F. Colt Collection, Kent. This is almost certainly the name of Holland, a Notts., travelling showman.

Hubbard, Edward: 33 Gibson Street, Lambeth, London. "Musical and Dutch Clock Maker." His trade-card on an old clock of c. 1850 advertised repairs etc. "to every description of mechanical and barrel'd instrument." (Per J. Budgen, Ipswich).

Imhof & Mukle: London. Founded 1845, the firm was at 46 Oxford Street, London, in 1870. In 1883 the Music Trades Directory records them as "Piano Makers" and makers of "Mechanical Pianos & Organs" at 110 New Oxford Street, London, W.C. From a factory in the Black Forest they imported Orchestrions and other forms of weight-driven barrel organs. Mr. S. H. Mukle, now retired, recalls that practically no two were alike so that the barrels were not interchangeable. Some instruments had reeds and brass trumpets: others only wood pipes of beautiful workmanship and delicate tone. Bought by the well-to-do and the aristocracy, these weight-driven clockwork organs were operated by a man-servant who wound up the weight and changed the barrels. Some owners had so many barrels that a small room nearby was shelved to accommodate them. The firm exhibited at the 1862 and 1865 London Exhibitions and later occupied premises 547 Oxford Street. Daniel Imhof took out Patent No. 2516 of 29th September, 1866, for "improvements in the machinery of chimes . . . and the striking of drums and other instruments of percussion by self-acting organs." The last member of the Imhof family died in 1962 but the business continues as A. Imhofs Ltd., 112-116 New Oxford Street.

British Piano Museum, Brentford: Orchestrion.
Bruce Angrave, London. (No. 2296).
J. G. Barrack, Aberdeen: Orchestrion No. 2413. 18 barrels of operatic and light music.
Burghley House, Northants, barrel-piano: 4 barrels x 10 tunes.
A. T. Greeve, London.
Colchester Castle Museum, (*ex* Layer de la Haye Church, Essex).
Birmingham Museum: (from Blackpool Tower).
Vide Music Libraries and Instruments (1961) Paper No. 32 (& Plate 56) by Canon Noel Boston, also *Musical Boxes* (3rd Edition) (1961) by J. Clark, p. 220: also *The Music Box, passim.*

Jardine, George: London. (1800-1882). A workman with Flight & Robson, who in 1834 went to America and, with his four sons and two grandsons, built many organs there between 1850 and 1899. He intended to make barrel-organs but finding no demand there, he and his family turned their attention to finger-organs. The firm was dissolved in 1900. Zion Episcopal Ch., Pierrepont Manor, New York, U.S.A., contains the only true church barrel organ and the only known 'finger and barrel' organ in U.S.A.: 3 stops: 53 notes: 2 barrels each of 11 tunes. In excellent order. *Vide The Hymn*, Vol. 11, No. 3, July 1960, art. by Barbara Owen. *Vide The Organ* No. 149, Vol. xxxviii, (July 1958) p. 12.

Johnson, John: 3 Avery Farm Row, Pentonville, London. (per Pigot's Directory 1827). No specimen of his work recorded.

van Kamp, William Hubert: London. ...1767-1772...

An advertisement in "The Liverpool General Advertiser" No. 155 of 9th December, 1768, reads:—

"William Hubert van Kamp, Organ Builder, at the Dial in Lee Street, the second door from Red Lion Square, Holborn, London, makes and repairs all sorts of Barrel-organs . . ." A spinet in the Geffrye Museum, London, is marked:—"Hubert van Kamp Londini fecit, 1762." The Rate Books record:—Hubert van Kamp 1754-1764 . . . William van Kamp 1767-1772 . . .

Vide Galpin Society Journal VII April, 1954, pp. 56-57.

Peter Ward, Grantchester, Cambridge, has a barrel-organ bearing the Lee St. address: 3 stops: 3 original barrels. An almost identical instrument, but without a maker's name, is in the Ord-Hume collection.

Mrs. Anna Greef, King's Lynn: 4 stops plus drum and triangle: 2 of 4 barrels survive and tune-list for four barrels. See Plate 13.

Keith, Prowse & Co. : London. Founded by R. W. Keith who died in 1846. The Company first appeared at 131 Cheapside 1829-32 and at 48 Cheapside 1832-46. Wm. Prowse was on his own account 1846-c. 1865. Then H. Bryan Jones joined Prowse and the title reverted to Keith, Prowse & Co. cp. Prowse, Wm.

Chamber barrel-organs: Tristan Jones, St. Nicholas-at-Wade; T. T. Mayers, Ipswich.

Kelly, John: London. An Irish organ-builder who came over from Ireland in 1785 to seek his fortune. He joined Benj. Flight, Senior in partnership c. 1790, and "Flight & Kelly,

Exeter Change " appears in *The Musical Directory* of 1794. Presumably on the death or retiral of Flight Senior, Kelly continued alone, in the Strand c. 1805, and later at 20 Marylebone Street, Golden Square where he described his business " Late Flight & Kelly." ' Organ Builder, No. 20 Marylebone Street, Golden Square, London, (Late Flight & Kelly)," occurs on the label on a barrel of the organ by Longman & Broderip in Bowes Castle Museum. 4 stops; 3 barrels.

Additions to the organ at Whitchurch, Salop, were carried out in 1805 by " Kelly of the Strand." *Vide The Organ Club Handbook,* No. 6, p. 49.

King, John: Collier Street, London. ..1827.. (Per Pigot's Directory, 1827). No specimen of his work has been recorded.

Kirtland & Jardine: Manchester, Estab. 1843. *Vide* James Davis *supra.*

Advertised their barrel-organs in the 1855 Edition of Hopkins & Rimbault " *The Organ.*" They were then at Dickinson Street, St. Peter's Square. Frederick W. Jardine was an ex-employee of Bishop. He retired in 1875 and the business continues today as Jardine & Co. Ltd. *Vide The Organ,* July 1958, article by L. Elvin.

Kleyser, John & Co. : 66 High Street, Borough, London, Watchmakers and Clockmakers: John Kleyser, High Holborn, 1790-1811; J. Kleyser & Co. Oxford Street, 1820; John Kleyser & Son, High Holborn, 1800-20. J. Kleyser, Boro' High Street, No. 66, 1829-70; J. Kleyser, Boro' High Street, No. 69, 1871-1907.

Barrel-organ playing National Anthem and dances, etc. in collection of Karl Mangold, Zollikon, Zurich. *Vide Glareana,* 13 Jhg., No. 3/4, 31 December 1964.

Lamy, J. Thibouville: Paris. Estab. 1867. Street barrel-organ: 3 stops: 1 barrel x 10 tunes. Birmingham Museum of Science and Industry.

Langshaw, John: Born 1718. Died 1798. London and Lancaster. Organist and barrel-organ builder who was employed about 1761, under the direction of Handel's amanuensis John Christopher Smith, in setting music on the barrels of a very large organ built by Snetzler and others for Luton Park, for the Earl of Bute. This organ was later destroyed by a fire at the mansion. John Langshaw became organist of St. Mary's Parish Church, Lancaster, in 1772 and died in 1798 when his son John (born in London 1763) succeeded him and may have been a partner of White & Langshaw (*q.v.*). John Langshaw, Organist, appears in the Lancaster Poll Book of 1818. He probably sold his interest in White & Langshaw, London, to John Puncher about whom nothing is known.

Vide Mendel's Lexikon, s.v. Langshaw. Scholes' *Oxford Companion to Music*: *s.v.* Mechanical Reproduction. Grove's *Dictionary of Music* (1910): *s.v.* Langshaw. *Musical Opinion,* February 1966: " The Earl of Bute's Barrel Organs." History of Lancaster, (Fleury) p. 523.

J. P. Hall, Kendal: 3 barrels x 10 secular tunes.

R. M. Heintz, California: 3 barrels x10—one sacred and 2 secular.

Lark, George: May's Buildings, London. ...1763...

" Organ Builder: also makes Musical Boxes for Minuet and Country Dances & Concerts and Bird Organs." (Per Mortimer's Directory, 1763). No surviving specimen is recorded.

Last, William: Bury St. Edmunds. Said to have built a number of barrel-organs in East Anglia in the early 19th c. (Per his grandson, G. C. Bedwell, Cambridge organ bldr.)

Leathers, Edward, Jnr.: 3 Dean Street, Soho, London. ...1827... (per Pigot's Directory 1827).

Lincoln, Henry Cephas: 196 High Holborn, London. (Born 1789. Died 1864). Trade Card in Banks' Colln. Brit. Mus.: " Lincoln, organ builder for Church, Chamber, Finger or Barrel. No. 196 High Holborn." This may refer to J. Lincoln of London who built the organ in Bakewell Church, Derbyshire, in 1810, and was probably the father of Henry C. Lincoln. Two barrels of the barrel-organ in Calke Church, Derbyshire, are labelled " Lincoln, Great Bowden, Nr. Harborough " (*i.e.* Market Harborough, Leics.) No other reference to this Lincoln has been noted but a local Directory for 1855 records ' Charles Lincoln, Piano-tuner.'

Baines, R. London: 4 stops, 4 barrels x 10 tunes—one sacred, three secular.

Isaac Balkin, Bettwsycoed: 3 stops, plus drum and triangle.

Bolling Hall Museum, Bradford. (formerly in Newburgh Priory). 4 stops. 4 (now 3) barrels. See Plate 19.

Lord Newborough's Collection, Pwllheli. 4 stops plus drum and triangle.

Fritz Spiegl, Liverpool (*ex* Bernard Miles).

Stoke Dry, Rutland, 1810, converted to manual.

Chiddingstone Castle (D. E. Bower). 4 stops plus drum and triangle. 4 (now 3) barrels.

Longman, John: 131 Cheapside, London. (1801-1816): Giles Longman & James Herron were successors from 1816 to 1822.

Scott Polar Research Institute, Cambridge. 7 stop Church and Secular barrel-organ. 4 barrels. Taken on Scott's Expedition, 1875. Restored in 1955 by the late Canon Wintle and J. D. Budgen. See Plates 20 and 21. No longer playable as a result of neglect.

Chiddingstone Castle. 4 stops and drum and triangle. A label reads: " No. 230. When a new barrel is wanted, please send the above number." Patent Tune Indicator. 1 barrel (3 missing).

Ovington House, nr. Winchester. 4 stops and drum and triangle. 3 barrels. " By His Majesty's Royal Letters Patent, No. 232."

C. L. R. Morley, Lewisham. 4 barrels of 10 tunes each (sacred).

Peter Ward, Grantchester, Cambridge: small chamber organ: 2 stops: 1 barrel x 10 secular tunes.

In 1801 John Longman of Penton Street, Pentonville, Clerkenwell, Organ Builder, took out Patent No. 2468 for Improvements in Barrel Organs.

Longman & Broderip: 26 Cheapside, and from 1783 also at 13 Haymarket, London. 1776-1798.

Victoria and Albert Museum, London: Small chamber barrel-organ. 2 stops. Tune-list for four barrels of 10 tunes each but only two barrels remain.

Bowes Castle, Co. Durham:—Chamber barrel-organ, 4 stops, 3 barrels.

J. Walker, Reigate, Surrey. Chamber barrel-organ. 1794 watermark on paper of barrel No. 1. 4 stops. 18 keys. 3 barrels of 10 tunes each. Bought at Sotheby's 27th July, 1962.

First Universalist Ch. of Gloucester, Mass., U.S.A., had a barrel-organ " made and sold at Longman & Co., Music Shop, No. 26 Cheapside, London," in use 1780-1802: 4 stops: 18 notes: 2 of original 3 barrels survive. (Per Miss B. Owen, U.S.A.)

Dickinson College, Carlyle, Penn. Barrel-organ dated 1784 originally owned by Joseph Priestly.

Mackilwain, Richard: —post 1795.

Victoria and Albert Museum, London. 2 barrels of a barrel organ by John Pistor (q.v) bear the following:—

" Richard Mackilwain, Real manufacturer of Church, Chamber and Barrel Organs, Harpsichords, Grand and Square Piano Fortes. Successor to Mr. Pistor, 21 Swan Street, Minories."

Bethnal Green Museum. One of two barrels of another barrel organ by John Pistor in Bethnal Green Museum bear the label of Richard Mackilwain and the same narration as above.

E. & J. Pistor were at 116 Leadenhall Street in 1794, (per Doane's Directory), but a trade-card in the Ambrose Heal Collection in the British Museum gives John Pistor's address as 21 Swan Street, Minories, the address at which R. Mackilwain continued in business.

Maher, Matthew: London. ...1794-1825... " Organ-builder, Lower Lambeth Marsh," (per Doane's Directory 1794). Charlotte Street, Lambeth Marsh (per Wakefield's Directory 1794). At 1 Westminster Bridge Road, Surrey, c. 1806-1820. 6 Hatfield Place, Westminster Road in 1822, (per Wakefield's Directory).

Birmingham Science and Industry Museum: Large chamber barrel-organ. (ex Rev. L. Mitchell's Colln.). 4 stops and drum and triangle. 4 barrels. Now (1966) dismantled.

Martin: Nottingham and Stamford. c. 1821.

Rampton Church, Notts. 5 stops, 4 barrels, sacred tunes.

Installed in 1821 per *Lincoln, Rutland & Stamford Mercury* of 23rd November, 1821. *Vide The Organ*, No. 149, Vol. xxxviii, July, 1958, p. 12.

Maule, John: Edinburgh. Chamber barrel-organ: 3 stops: 3 barrels—2 of reels and 1 of songs. Mrs. John L. Campbell, Isle of Canna.

Mayor, Thos.: Exeter. Pentonville, London, c. 1827, (per Pigot's Directory).

Meyer, O. & Co.: No. 2 Frith Street, Soho Square, London. c. 1800-1802.

Chelmsford and Essex Museum, (ex Thaxted Church): Barrel organ dated 1800. 4 stops and drum and triangle. It is strange to find percussion effects on a former church instrument. 4 barrels. Repaired 1967.

The Guildhall Library has kindly supplied the following:

1802, John Meyer, 25 Angel Street, St. Martin-le-Grand. 1803, Meyer & Co., 61 Soho Square. 1804, Meyer & Co., 14 Frith Street, Soho Square. 1805, Henry Meyer, 14 Frith Street, Soho Square. 1806-1807, Meyer & Co., 14 Frith Street, Soho Square. 1808, Henry Meyer, 14 Frith Street, Soho Square.

It is not known how O. Meyer & Co., 2 Frith Street, Soho Square, were connected with the foregoing.

Morgan: Old Square, London. Barrel-organ marked thus, converted to manual, was purchased for £5 for a church hall at Cirencester, (per R. Matthews, Organist, Cirencester, Glos.).

Muir, Wood & Co.: Edinburgh. Founded 1796; became Wood, Small & Co. 1818-1830 (q.v.).

E. R. Mickleburgh Colln., Bristol: 5 barrels.

Mrs. C. E. Hill, Wymondham, Melton Mowbray. 10 barrels each of 10 tunes, 6 barrels stored in a separate case. *Vide* Farmer " *History of Music in Scotland* " pp. 400-402.

Nicholls, W. A. A.: London: post 1816.

" Son-in-law and successor to the late Mr. G. P. England, No. 9 Stephen Street, Tottenham Court Road."

The foregoing is found pencilled on the front board of the fine barrel organ in Brightling Church—See Plate 5. The instrument, now restored and in occasional use, was pre-

PLATE 19

Photo: P. Harrison, A.R.P.S., Bradford

Barrel-organ by H. C. Lincoln, 188 High Holborn, London (c. 1800-c. 1825). Height 5′ 8″; width 3′ 1″; depth 1′ 9″. Formerly in Newburgh Priory and now in Bolling Hall Museum, Bradford. Overhauled by Bishop & Son in 1962. 4 stops; 24 notes; 96 pipes. Spiral barrels—4 (now 3) of secular tunes.

sented to the church by John Fuller, M.P., who died in 1834. Geo. P. England, *i.e.* England Junior, died c. 1816.

Parker, Mr: Organ Builder, " at the lower end of Gray's Inn Road, Houlborne " recommended by John Arnold in his *Compleate Psalmodist* (1761), as being " very eminent in his profession ". Box organs of a very small structure . . . likewise of the machinery kind, at ten to fourteen guineas. " Tunes of your own chusing " (*sic*). No surviving specimen known.

Parsons: London. c. 1825- c. 1868. The Guildhall Library reported:
(1) Parsons, G., 25 Duke Street, Bloomsbury: 1825-1838. (2) Parsons, Stephen, 2 Little Russell Street, Bloomsbury: 1839-1845. (3) Parsons, Samuel, 2 Little Russell Street, Bloomsbury: 1846-1868.
Gt. Gaddesden Church, Herts., by Parsons (2 or 3) above. 1 barrel of 7 tunes.
Trelystan Church, Montgom., by Parsons (1) above, as it is dated 1827. The initial G. was misread as T. in an article in *Musical Opinion*, Feb. 1965, p. 295, " A Welsh Barrel Organ " by Eric Dawes. 3 stops, of which only the stopped Diapason pipes remain. *Vide* also " The Four Parsons " by A. Freeman in " *The Organ* " No. 96.

Pemberton, Robert: c. 1856. Hildenborough, Tonbridge, Kent.
Took out Patent No. 1199 of 21st May 1856 for Improvements in Barrel-Organs. He sought to make them fully chromatic with all necessary pipes and double-acting bellows.

Phillips, William: London. c. 1799-1828...
Holden's Directory of 1799 gives " Phillips, William, mus. inst. maker, 3 Manor Row, East Smithfield."
Kent's Directory of 1802 first gives " Little Tower Hill, Corner of Manor Row (facing the bottom of the Minories in Little Tower Hill)." (Note: Manor Row led from southeast of Little Tower Hill to Upper East Smithfield).
Critchett's Directory of 1806 gives him as " grand pianoforte manufacturer " but soon reverts to " Mus., inst., maker," till Critchett & Wood's Directory of 1827.
Kent's Directory of 1826 gives the address as No. 9 Little Tower Hill. From 1828 onwards the address is 78 Minories.
Gt. Leighs Church, Essex. 6 stops. Tune-list for 4 barrels of ten tunes each, 20 sacred and 20 secular. Only 3 barrels survive. The organ was transferred to the church in 1914 by Mr. J. H. Tritton of Lyons Hall. The " voluntaries " were called by the country folk " The Dog-Tunes." *Vide Essex Review*, Vol. 42, 1933, pp. 165-168: article by E. Spurgeon Knights.
J. V. Willins, West Runton, Norfolk: barrel-organ case; mechanism removed. Originally 4 stops and drum and triangle.
Norwich: Strangers' Hall Museum: Small chamber barrel-organ with the 1802 address as above. Tune list for 3 barrels each of 10 tunes but only 1 barrel remains. Restored to working order.

Pilcher, Wm.: London. Stockbridge Terrace, Pimlico. c. 1827. Organ Builder and piano maker. (Per Pigot's Directory). 33 Upper Belgrave Place, Pimlico. c. 1860.
Advertised — Table or Desk Organs, 4 models from £21, £28, £36-£40 depending on the number of stops.
" William Pilcher begs also to inform the clergy that he has a very excellent assortment of fine-toned Revolving Barrel-Organs of great power which contain 30 Psalm Tunes and Chants." from £45-£80: also Finger and Barrel Organs of the best quality from £70-£100.
Wm. Pilcher, Senior, was a Canterbury man with at least two sons. One, William Junior, settled in Pimlico as organ builder and put a barrel into Stanmer Church, Sussex. Another son, Henry, learned organ building from his elder brother and then went to America. (Per Rev. B. B. Edmonds). A builder named Pilcher was working at Chichester Cathedral organ in 1829. (Per Rev. J. A. Gilfillan).

Pistor, John: London. 21 Swan Street, Minories. Sir Ambrose Heal Collection of Trade-Cards in the British Museum includes one of John Pistor, " manufacturer of Church, Chamber and Barrel-organs, Harpsichords, Pianofortes, etc..." c. 1794.
Bethnal Green Museum. 4 stops. 4 barrels playing in all 33 tunes. One barrel bears label of R. MacKilwain (*Vide supra*).
Gunthorpe Hall, Norfolk. 4 stops and drum and triangle. 7 barrels of 10 tunes each. See Plate 22.
Horniman Museum, London. 6 stops. 3 barrels. Out of order.
Barrel-organ bought c. 1767 by Sir George Houston who later gave it to A. D. Woodruff of Savannah, Georgia, ancestor of Joseph F. Mayer from whose estate it was for sale in 1962 at Trenton, New Jersey, U.S.A.
Victoria and Albert Museum, London: Barrel-organ: 4 stops: 4 barrels: 33 tunes.

Pistor, E. & J.: London ..1782-1798.
Edward Pistor, Clock & Organ Maker, occurs at 116 Leadenhall Street, in the Directories for 1763 and 1777. By 1782 Edward and John Pistor, Watchmakers, were at the same address. In Doane's Directory for 1794, " E. & J. Pister (sic) 116 Leadenhall Street "

occurs. Britten's " *Clocks and Watchmakers* " lists Pistor as " musical clock and barrel-organ makers."

Harrogate, Pump Room Museum: (*ex* Fleet Church, Lincs.), restored by F. F. Hill, Godalming.

J. P. Hall, Kendal: Barrel-organ: 3 barrels x 8 tunes and one spiral barrel of 3 tunes. The label reads: Edwd. & Jn. Pistor, Musical clock, Watch, Finger and Barrel Organ Makers at " The Turk's Head and Organ," No. 116 Leadenhall Street, London. Harpsichords tuned and old Organs set to new music."

Postill, Robert: Monkgate, York. (Born 1810. Died 1882.) R. Postill, Senior, c. 1835, took premises in Marygate as organ builder, and was made a Freeman in 1831. He had three sons: Robert, Junior (Born 1838. Died 1918): George and Edward. Premises moved to 3 Monkgate. The firm advertised till c. 1888 frequently in " *The Yorkshire Gazette.*" They made organs for St. Austell, Barton-upon-Humber, Market Weighton, Osmotherly, Yarm, etc. No mention of barrel-organs nor of Blacktoft, Yorkshire (*q.v.*). (Per York City Librarian).

Presbury, Philip: Chester. c. 1767.
Cabinet-maker who advertised: —
" Chamber Organ, consisting of several stops, to be played on either by hand or turning a Wynch, having seven favourite tunes put on the barrel." *Vide Galpin Journal* VII, Apl. 1954, p. 56.

Preston, John: London. 97 Strand, c. 1799-1834.
Guildhall Library reports: —1799 Preston, John, 97 Strand. 1800 Preston & Son, 97 Strand. 1800-1802 Preston T., 97 Strand. Mus. Inst. Mkrs. 1822 Preston T., 97 Strand. Wholesale Mus. Sellers. 1824-34 Preston T., Wholesale Mus. Inst. Maker, 71 Dean Street, Soho.
Cambridge: University Music School. 4 stops plus drum and triangle: 5 barrels (originally): Nos. 1 and 5 now missing: Nos. 2 and 3 secular: No. 4 sacred. In working order.
Church (?) barrel-organ by John Preston, 97 Strand, London. Inside wind chest is pencilled: " Repaired by John Smith, Bristol, June 1820," 3 barrels—34 tunes. One for church use with 12 hymns and chants. One for musical evenings with songs. One with dance tunes for the church hall. Collection of the late E. R. Pole (dispersed). Clark, J. *Musical Boxes* misspells the name as ' Greston.'

Prosser, Henry J.: Rode, Somerset. Founded 1868.
In Music Trades Directory 1883 as " instrument dealer." Canon Boston's Collection, (*ex* Aldridge Church, Staffs.). Cabinet type church barrel organ. 3 stops. 1 barrel with seven psalms etc. *Vide Music Libraries and Instruments,* Article No. 32. Plate 55.

Prowse, Wm.: London. 1846-65. Late Keith Prowse & Co., Manufacturer, 48 Cheapside. Barrel-organ in Winwick Church, Northants: 7 barrels x 10 sacred tunes. (Not by Bryceson as stated by Canon Boston in A. M. Socy. Transactions). Restored in 1969 by K. G. Parrott & E. W. Timmins, both of Rugby. See Plate 32.

Pyke, George: London: pre 1794. " Facing Bedford Row."
Barrel-organ with label: —
" All sorts of machines and other organs made and sold by Geo. Pyke, Maker to His Majesty. Facing Bedford Row."
In possession of the late Mrs D. Winrow-Foster, Sandiacre, Notts. whose father told her the organ used to be in Morley Church but inquiry does not confirm this. It is in good playing order and has two barrels; all secular tunes except for four hymns. On Mrs Foster's death, the organ was sold by auction (1969). *Vide* Chap. VII s.v. Haley. Geo. Pyke was succeeded by H. Holland (*vide supra*) and Holland learned his trade with the elder England. As England's son was named George Pike (sic) England, the family may well have been descended from George Pyke.

Robson, Joseph & Son: 101 St. Martin's Lane, London, " The Apollonicon Rooms."
Mickleburgh Collection: Bristol. Small domestic organ with 5 barrels.
Lydlinch Church, Dorset: Barrel and finger organ, installed in 1843. Removed in 1849 and offered for sale by Forster & Andrews of Hull.
Ossington Church, Newark, Notts. 3 stops, 3 barrels.
The business of J. Robson & Son was acquired in 1876 by Gray & Davison. (q.v.).

Robson, T. J. F.: (known as Joseph),, (died 1876), described himself as Manufacturer, 101 St. Martin's Lane, London, in the catalogue of the Great Exhibition of 1851, where under No. 559 he gave details of his enharmonic organ.
Vide article on " Holdich and the Flights & Robsons." *s.v.* Holdich, *supra*.
Rudham East Church, Norfolk. Robson " Psalmodic Barrel-Organ " costing £105 was installed 22 December 1837. Replaced by a finger-organ in 1880.
Churchill Church, Oxon. Only a barrel with nine tunes survives.
Kings Langley, Herts. Removed.
c.p. Flight & Robson (*supra*).

62

Robson, Thomas: pre-1858. Barrel and finger organ in St. Patrick's Church, Kilrea, County Londonderry. 8 stops on Great Organ, 4 on the Swell, 1 and 2 couplers on the Pedal Organ. Two barrels of 10 hymns and psalms. Independently operated bellows.
The organ installed in Boldre Church, Hants., bears a plate: "Apollonicon Rooms, 101 St. Martin's Lane, Thomas Robson, Organbuilder to Her Majesty." The organ was presented on the restoration of the church in 1855.

Rolfe, William: 112 Cheapside, London. ..1796-1890.
William Rolfe was music-seller and publisher and musical instrument maker at 112 Cheapside in 1796. In conjunction with Samuel Davis, Rolfe took out Patent No. 2160 of 31 Jany. 1797 for improvements on the harpsichord and grand and square pianos. The business became William Rolfe and Sons in 1806. Additional premises were at 28 London Wall in 1813. In 1850 they removed from 112 to 61 Cheapside and from 28 to 31-32 London Wall. After three subsequent addresses the firm disappears after 1890. *Vide Grove's Dictionary* 5th Edit. *s.v.* Rolfe. With Samuel Davis, Rolfe patented pianoforte improvements: No. 2029 of 31st January, 1797. A square piano by William Rolfe is known.
Castle Museum, York: Barrel-organ, 15 keys, 4 ranks of pipes, 4 stops: Stopped Diapason, Principal, Twelfth and Fifteenth. 3 barrels each of 10 secular tunes. H. 4'5": W. 2'1": D. 1'5".

Rostrand, E.: London. c. 1764. Orange Court, Leicester Fields.
"Makes all sorts of Chamber Organs to play with fingers or barrels."
Pitt-Rivers Museum, Oxford. *Ex* Stanton Harcourt Parsonage, Oxon.
Small chamber barrel-organ dated 1764 and labelled as above: 2 barrels each of 8 tunes, all secular except Easter Hymn. 4 stops. In working order.

Rust, John Rayment: Chelmsford. Maker of new barrel No. 4 for Bevington barrel-organ of 1865 in Barnston Church, Essex. A barrel-organ by him was built in 1856 for Croft Church and enlarged in 1858. *Vide* letter to "*The Organ*," No. 49. Rust established his business between 1845 and 1848. He appears in the Essex Directory until 1914. (Information by courtesy of Chelmsford Borough Librarian).

Small, Bruce & Co.: Edinburgh. 54 Princes Street, c. 1830-1833. 101 George Street, c. 1833-1837, and as Small & Co. until 1839.
The senior partner, George Small, previously a partner in Wood, Small & Co., was joined by James Bruce, a skilled organ-builder. The firm became "Musical Instrument Makers to His Majesty," *Vide* H. G. Farmer, *History of Music in Scotland*, p. 402.
F. F. Hill Collection, Godalming, Surrey. 4 stops. 5 barrels with 10 tunes each.
Vide Music Box Journal, Christmas 1963, (No. 4), pp. 18-19, Illustration.

Southwell & White: Liverpool and London.
Liverpool Directories from 1803 to 1832 record:—
Southwell H. J. & F. (later Southwell, Nicholas) of Duke Street, Liverpool, variously described as "Mus. Inst. manufacturers," "pianoforte makers," and "music sellers." It is not known if the Southwell of Southwell & White was before or after the foregoing.
Mr. S. D. Dyer-Gough, Ruthin, Denbighshire. 4 stops plus drum and triangle. 3 barrels, 1 sacred and 2 secular of 10 tunes each.

Tax, John: c. 1753: "At the Bird Organ, in May's Buildings, St. Mary's Lane, London, makes all sorts of Musical Boxes for Birds, for Country Dances, Minuets and to play whole Concertos, all in the neatest manner."
R. M. Heintz: Los Altos, Calif., U.S.A. Pipe Bird-Organ labelled as above.

Taylor, Samuel: Bristol. 1854-56.
Mr. F. F. Hill's Collection, Shackleford, Godalming, Surrey.
Cylinder-piano, labelled: "Samuel Taylor, Musical Instrument Maker, No. 26 Host Street: Next to Colston's School, St. Augustine's Place, Bristol. Manufacturers of Barrel Organs and Cylinder Pianofortes. N.B. Country Orders punctually attended to." In Mathew's Directory 1854 and 1855 as "Organ & pianoforte maker" at 27 St. Augustine's Place, Bristol. In the Rate Books, Samuel Taylor is listed under Host Street for 1855-56. (By courtesy of Bristol City Archivist).

Taylor, Thomas: Sheffield. Cylinder piano, branded as above and "Maker, No. 79." Mahogany case. Trichord stringing. Pleated with silk and brass Royal Arms. Collection of F. G. Turner & Son, Horsham.

Taylor, W. F.: Bristol. c. 1848-56.
Mr. F. F. Hill Collection, Surrey. Cylinder piano dated 1848, labelled:
"W. F. Taylor, Musical Instrument Maker. No. 57 Broad Quay, Bristol."

Taylor, William: Bristol. Born 1808. Died 1847. Mus. Inst. Mkr. at 69 Stokes Croft from 1835 to 1839, after which year he is described as "Mus. Inst. Maker & Nautical Stationer" from 1840 to 1847 at 57 Broad Quay where he died in December 1847 aged 39. A W. F. Taylor (perhaps a son) continued at 57 Broad Quay, as a barrel-piano dated 1848 bearing his name and at that address, is in the F. F. Hill Collection. *Vide* Taylor, W. F. *supra*.

PLATE 20

Scott Polar Research Institute, Cambridge. Chamber
Barrel-organ by John Longman, Patentee, London,
including his "new invented Patent Barrel-organ, with
Drum, Bells and Triangle." 4 stops. 4 barrels—one
sacred (defective) and 3 secular. Taken by Admiral Sir
Edward Parry to the Arctic in 1819-20, etc. No
longer in playing order.

Barrel-organ: 3 ranks of wood pipes and tall case, resembling a street piano, was seen by Mr. Ord-Hume, London, in 1966.

Cylinder piano by William Taylor in almost mint condition was restrung by Mr. Ord-Hume in Sept. 1969.

Telford, William: Dublin. Established 1830. Died 1885.

E. R. Mickleburgh Collection, Bristol: Barrel-organ from a church in the Macroom district of County Cork, labelled on one of three barrels:—

"William Telford, Organ builder to the Cathedrals, Colleges, Chapel Royal etc., 109 Stephens Green, Dublin." 3 barrels are mounted between two large wheels, which when rotated, bring any one of the three barrels into playing position. All pipes are unfortunately missing. *Vide* Grove's *Dict. of Music, s.v.* Telford. *Galpin Society Journal XVII*, Feb. 1964, p. 108.

Thomson, W. P. & Harris M. were granted Patent No. 5646 of 24 Dec. 1881 for a mechanical pipe-organ. No other trace.

Tomasso, Angelo: Clerkenwell, London. Born in Rome 1865. Died in London 1953. The last of the barrel-piano makers in Britain. In the 1920's he was making 50 to 60 barrel-pianos weekly in his Clerkenwell factory. Hundreds were let out on hire to street players; hundreds more were played by electricity in public houses etc. Radio brought an end to the business. Angelo's son, Antonio, makes no more barrel-pianos. He makes watches.

Townsend, Wm.: ..c. 1824-1875. Organ builder etc., 9 and 10 Greenside Place, Edinburgh.

Barrel-organ from East Lothian now in Museum of Childhood, Edinburgh. Thomson commenced in 1824 as a harp maker at 3 Canongate: from 1827 at 92 Princes Street, and from 1829 at 3 So. St. Andrew St., as harp and pianoforte maker. He removed to Greenside Place in 1835. The business finally became Townsend & Thomson, music sellers, 79 George Street, and wound up in 1939.

Vanquish, Peter: London. c. 1800.

This name is found on the barrel access door of an ornate chamber organ of 19 keys and only two ranks of pipes: stopped diapason (4 foot wood) and principal (2 foot metal). Only No. 4 barrel survives, pinned with nine tunes, apparently hymns. The instrument is much damaged—ten metal pipes and the drum are missing. (Information kindly supplied by the owner, A. Ord-Hume, London).

Violet, A.: Coldbath Square, Clerkenwell, London.

Birmingham City Museum: Table barrel-organ. 14 stopped wood pipes. 2 barrels of 9 tunes each, sacred and secular.

Walker, Jos. W. & Sons: London. Founded 1825.

Joseph William Walker was a "parlour apprentice" to George Pike England from c. 1818. He set up his business in 1825. 5 Bentinck St. Soho, London, 1827: Museum Street, 1828: 166 High Holborn, London, 1831: 27 Francis Street, Bedford Square, London, W.C. 1838-1883 . . .

J. W. Walker died in 1870, aged 68, leaving four sons and a daughter, Sarah, who marked the barrels prior to pinning. All sons were apprenticed to their father but three died young and James John Walker continued until his death soon after the incorporation of the firm on 14th June, 1920, leaving E.F., J.H.F., F.P. and R. H. Walker, directors. Braintree Road, Ruislip, Middlesex. *Vide* W. L. Sumner, *The Organ* (1962) p. 240.

Dumb Organists

J. Walker & Sons, Ruislip, in use at Gt. Bookham. c. 1856, complete with barrel of 6 tunes. *Vide* Account & illustration Plate III in "*The Singing Church in Essex*" (1933) p. 14.

Pembury, Kent (1823), 1 barrel of 6 tunes; No. 27.

Barrel-organs

Meldreth Church, Cambs., (From Bassingbourn Church in 1866), converted to finger.
Stondon Massey Church, Essex.
Watford Church, Herts. (1842).
Brightwell Baldwin, Oxon. (1843). See Plate 23.
Parham Church Vestry, Sussex: now in Parham Park House.
Balsham Church, Cambs: Barrel and organ now at Roseworth, Stockton-on-Tees.
Borden Church, Kent, converted to a finger-organ and removed about 1910.
Tolleshunt D'Arcy, Essex, (finger & barrel-organ), 1856.
Fawsley, Northants., (finger & barrel-organ), 1839.
Sutton, Northants., (finger & barrel-organ) c. 1850, (*ex* Great Waldingfield, Suffolk.)
Mattishall Burgh, Norfolk, 1852. See Plates 16 & 24.
Hoxne Church, Suffolk, 1836, converted to finger.
Bathealton, Somerset, 1854. Scrapped in 1901.
Southill, Beds.
Paul Corin Colln. Liskeard, 1855.

Helions Bumpstead, Essex, converted to finger.
Rougemont Anglican Church, Quebec (1844).
Steeple, Dorset (1858). Remnants only.
Horniman Museum, London. Small chamber barrel-organ (3 barrels), labelled " J. W. Walker, 21 Francis Street, Tottenham Court Road, London. W.C."
Norman Vince, East Dereham: barrel-organ dated May 1832 by Joseph Walker, High Holborn: 32 keys: 4 stops: 3 barrels x 10 secular tunes.

Walmslay, F. G.: c. 1800.
Name pencilled on pallet-spring rail of an anonymous chamber barrel-organ; 4 stops plus drum and triangle. 3 barrels of mainly secular tunes. A. Ord-Hume Collection.

Watlen, John: Edinburgh pre-1788-1829: thereafter in London. Organ builder, 5 Leicester Place, Leicester Square.
Church barrel-organ " No. 26 " in Aldro School, Shackleford. Restored by F. F. Hill and re-dedicated for use in the Chapel, June 1969. 21 notes: 5 stops: 5 barrels x 10 tunes. See Plate 6.

Webber, R.: London, post 1821.
Name on label of small barrel-organ, A. Ord-Hume Collection, London. 1 barrel of nine secular tunes: 1 rank of stopped wood pipes: 12 keys: marked " R. Webber, Organ Builder, London."

Wedlake, Henry Thos. : 8 Berkeley Road, London, N.W. (Founded 1858). In *Music Trades Directory*, 1883, as Organ-builder, as Medlake. Fellow apprentice of Henry Willis in Gray & Davison's factory.
Small 12-key barrel-organ, 8 secular tunes. A. Ord-Hume Colln., London.
Ampthill Church, Beds., in 1867 had a 2-manual organ " built by Mr. Wedlake of Hampstead Road, London. " Henry Thomas Wedlake and Francis James Kitsell took out provisional patent No. 2493 of 10 Oct. 1864 for improvements in metal for organ pipes. H. T. Wedlake also patented improvements in harmoniums, No. 1068 of 27 April 1861 and No. 1144 of 23 April 1866. *Vide* Dr. C. W. Pearce's " *Old London City Churches, their organs etc.*" (London, 1908), p. 76.

Weekes, Thos.: Tichbourne Street, London.
Clockwork barrel organ, 19 keys. 4 stops. 76 small scale pipes. Barrel set with 12 tunes; each tune played twice and changed automatically. Engraved on key frame: " Weekes's Museum, Tichbourne Street, Haymarket." W. Vaux Collection, Ilchester.

Wheatstone, C. & W.: London.
Established separately at first—Charles, *ante* 1791 till 1826 and William, his brother, flute teacher and maker from c. 1813 till 1826—the brothers appear to have amalgamated c. 1826 at 20 Conduit Street, Regent Street, where the concern continued for eighty years. A trade-card in the Banks' Collection in the British Museum (D2.2628) c. 1809 records Charles' business: "Wheatstone's Musical Instrument and Music Warehouse, No. 436 Strand, London. Patent Barrel Organs and Military Instruments." At the 1851 Exhibition, William Wheatstone & Co., 20 Conduit Street, Regent Street, designed themselves " Patentees & Manufacturers." Today C. Wheatstone & Co. Ltd., continue as Mus. Inst. Mfrs. at Edgware, Middx.
St. Peter Hungate Church Museum, Norwich, (ex Hoveton St. John, Norfolk). 4 stops: by Wheatstone, Strand, London (*i.e.* c. 1805-c. 1826). 2 barrels—one in very poor condition.
Vide Archeol. Jl. XCIX (1943) p. 65, and Plate iii, fig. D. *Ancient Monuments Society* Transactions, May 1960, fig. 3. Grove's *Dict. of Music, s.v.* Wheatstone.

White & Langshaw: London, pre 1821. Organ Builders, No. 57 Old Street Square, John Puncher, proprietor.
Showman's organ with shoulder strap hooks. Brass plate lettered as above. A. Ord-Hume Colln., London. *cp.* Langshaw, *supra.*

Wilkinson, C. & Co.: London, 1808.
On the dissolution of Longman & Broderip in 1798, Clementi and 3 others joined John Longman at 26 Cheapside. Francis Broderip founded a new company with C. Wilkinson as Broderip & Wilkinson at 13 Haymarket, 1798-1808, when the concern became Wilkinson & Co. No barrel organ by the latter has been recorded as yet.

Willis, Isaac & Co.: Dublin and later in London, c. 1816-1862.
Music publishers, not mus, inst. makers, but dealers.
Dublin, 7 Westmorland Street, c. 1816-c. 1836. London, 56 St. James's Street c. 1824-1835. 75 Lower Grosvenor Street 1835-1848. 119 New Bond Street 1849-1862.
Church or Chamber barrel-organ. Rev. Gordon Paget's Colln., The Provost's House, Bury St. Edmunds. 4 stops: 6 barrels. Sacred and secular tunes. In excellent order. Period 1824-1835. *Vide* Grove's *Dict. of Music, s.v.* Willis, I.

Woffington, Robert: 9 William Street, Dublin. fl. c. 1780-1819, the year of his death.
Chamber barrel-organ: 6 stops: 3 barrels: in National Museum of Ireland, Dublin, 2.

Wolf, R. & Co.: ..1837-45.. Barrel-organ in Yale Collection No. 154. At 79 Cornhill (Gerock's shop) 1837-40: 45 Moorgate Street, 1840-43: 20 St. Martin's Le Grand, 1843-45.

Wood, Small & Co.: Edinburgh. pre-1828. (cp. Small, Bruce & Co.).
Barrel-organ: 4 stops: 1 barrel survives. Not in playing order. Owned by J. A. Mackenzie, Organ builder, Clarkston, Glasgow.
Church barrel-organ bought in 1828 for Ryton-on-Tyne Church, Co. Durham, by public subscription from Wood, Small & Co., later converted to manual. Pedals were added in 1853 and swell and five stops added in 1856. Sold for £5 in 1866 to Greenside Church, Ryton, and probably scrapped in 1905 when a new organ installed by Binns of Leeds. (Information kindly supplied by W. A. Cocks, F.S.A. (Scot.), Ryton-on-Tyne).

Wornum, Robert London. Born 1742-Died 1815. Founded 1772. "Violin & Violoncello Maker, 42 Wigmore St." per Doane's Directory, 1794. At Glasshouse St., London, c. 1772-1777. At 42 Wigmore St., Cavendish Sq. c. 1777-1815. After his death c. 1815, his son, Robert, Junior (born 1780 - died 1852) continued the business as a piano-maker. It seems doubtful if Wornum made any barrel organs but apparently he dealt in them.
Birmingham City Museum. Small barrel-organ (*ex* Rev. Lancelot Mitchell Colln.).
Vide Grove's *Dict. of Music, s.v.* Wornum, Robert (i) and (ii).

Wrenshall, Wm.: Liverpool. 1800-1853. Listed only once in the Liverpool Directory for 1800 as organ-builder and organist at St. Matthew's Church, 60 Paradise Street. Thereafter he appears at various addresses as musician and professor of music up to 1853. His son, Wm. Wrenshall, Jr., first appears in the directory for 1825.
Manx Museum, Douglas, I.O.M. (*ex* Santan Church, I.O.M.).

Wright, J.: Organ builder, 30 Commercial Road, (no town). This appears on the empty case of a barrel-organ with no stops but 5 tune-lists in collection of Ralph Moss, Barton-le-Clay, Beds.

Wright, Thomas, Junior: Stockton-on-Tees, 1763-1829.
An inventive organist who devised a pocket metronome, an organ attachment to a square pianoforte and, in 1789, built for himself a chamber-organ and incorporated two orreries for illustrating and calculating eclipses. It is assumed that this was the Wright who was great-grandfather of Robson (*q.v.*) and credited however dubiously, with having made a barrel-organ for Fulham Church, London. *Vide* Scholes's *Oxford Companion to Music, s.v.* Mechanical reproduction. Grove's *Dict. of Music, s.v.* Barrel-organ and Wright, Thomas.

PLATE 21

Scott Polar Research Institute, Cambridge. Chamber Barrel-organ by
John Longman, London. Interior view.

CHAPTER VI

PARISH CHURCHES AND CHAPELS WHICH HAD OR HAVE STILL A BARREL-ORGAN OR THE REMAINS OF ONE

C—Converted or reduced to finger use only.
D—Dumb Organist
F—Appears on Flight's List but there is no indication that a barrel-organ is referred to (c. 1820).
O—Out of order

W—In working order
R—Remnants only
T—Transferred elsewhere
N—Non-existent
M—MacDermott's Book reports a barrel-organ, past or present.

A mark of interrogation denotes lack of information or uncertainty. The author invites notification of any additions or corrections.

BEDFORDSHIRE

N   **AMPTHILL**—A "singing-engine" was purchased by the Church-wardens c. 1770. *Vide The Story of Music in Ampthill Church* by Andrew Underwood, (Ampthill, 1959).

T   **BEDFORD ST. MARY'S**—Barrel-organ by Wm. Allen, c. 1804. Removed to Stagsden Church. *Vide Etude Music Magazine* (Feb. 1941).

N   **BLUNHAM**—Barrel-organ introduced by The Rev. Porter Breachcroft, Rector of Blunham. *Vide Bedfordshire Magazine,* Winter 1951/52, Vol. 3, No. 19, p. 102.

N   **CLOPHILL**—Barrel-organ perhaps that now at Wymington, Northants., as an organ was sold by Ampthill for £20 in 1870 but this may refer to a finger organ installed at Ampthill in 1833 and the barrel-organ it replaced may not be the organ referred to in 1870.

N   **COCKAYNE HATLEY**—No trace.

N   **CUMNOR**—Barrel and finger organ by Elliot with toe-pedals was transferred here from Eynsham, Oxon., but since c. 1924 has disappeared.

N   **EATON SOCON**—a barrel-organ, "The Playing Engine" was bought by subscription in 1819. No trace. *Vide Beds. Mag.,* 1951-52, Vol. 3, No. 19, p. 100.

N   **EVERTON**—Barrel-organ purchased by subscription and Mr. Peck, 'the organ grinder' was paid a salary of £1 a year. The accounts record "£1 for sale of old organ in April, 1881". Harmonium used till c. 1951 when present two-manual organ bought for £400. *Vide Beds. Mag.,* 1951/52. Vol. 3, No. 19, p. 103. The barrel-organ was transferred in 1852 to Burstwick, Yorks. (*q.v.*).

N   **FLITTON** "Improved barrel-organ" supplied in 1843 by Gray & Davison, but in 1856 a finger-organ was installed. The church now has a Casson Positive.

N   **HIGHAM GOBION**—A barrel-organ was presented by a Rector, the Rev. J. R. Wardale, who died in 1857. *Beds. Mag.* Vol. 10, No. 79, Winter 1966-67.

MR   **LUTON**—Two barrels are still preserved in the parvise museum. *Vide Beds. Mag.* 1951/52. Vol. 3, No. 19, pp. 102-103.

C   **MEPPERSHALL**—Barrel-organ converted to manual many years ago. Two barrels survive in an outhouse.

N   **OLD WARDEN**—Barrel-organ by Gray, 1842, to the order of Lord Ongley. Replaced by a two-manual organ.

N   **PAVENHAM**—Barrel-organ presented in 1841 by Thomas Green, the squire, at a cost of £50. In 1860 it was replaced by a harmonium. *Vide Beds. Mag.,* Vol. 4, p. 61, and in preface to " Old Oak " by Rev. J. E. Linnell (1932).

DN   **RENHOLD**—"Dumb organist" given away some years ago. *Vide Beds. Magazine,* Vol. 6, No. 43, Winter 1957/58, p. 121.

N   **SHILLINGTON**—Barrel-organ purchased by church-wardens but now no trace nor local recollection. *Vide Beds. Mag.* 1951/52, Vol. 3, No. 19, p. 102.

C   **SOUTHILL**—Barrel-organ added to and serviced from 1843 onwards by Messrs. J. W. Walker. (By courtesy of S. C. Whitbread, Esq., of Southill Park).

C   **STAGSDEN**—Barrel-organ by Wm. Allen, London, c. 1805, converted to manual. Formerly in Bedford St. Mary's Church. *Vide Mus. Opinion,* June, 1965, art. by the late Rev. Bonavia Hunt.

N   **STUDHAM**—Barrel-organ by Gray & Davison. 1842, installed by Rev. T. W. Mead.

W   **SUTTON**—Barrel-organ by T. C. Bates & Sons, No. 2917. Restored to use by John Budgen of Messrs. Bishop, Ipswich, after many years in disuse and rededicated 14 January 1967. 3 barrels of 10 tunes each. 5 stops. Foot blown. See Plate 29.

F	WOODBURN—An organ was supplied to a Bedfordshire Parish of this name by **B. Flight**, London. Woburn may be the parish referred to.
C	WYMINGTON—Independent Wesleyan Chapel—Barrel-organ now converted to manual is regarded locally as having come from Clophill, Beds.

BERKSHIRE

F	ABINGDON—
F	ALDERMASTON—
N	ASHBURY—Small barrel-organ reported in *N. & Q.* Vol. 147, p. 363, 15 Nov. 1924. Now no trace.
MN	BARKHAM—No trace.
W	BOXFORD—Barrel-organ by Flight & Robson? 26 notes: 5 stops: 5 barrels x 10: 1 secular and 4 sacred. The name plate is illegible apart from "London" but one of the barrels is labelled.
N	BUCKHOLD—*Vide Ancient Monuments Society Transactions,* May, 1960, p. 109.
C	COXWELL—Barrel-organ converted to manual. *Vide N. & Q.,* 12th Ser. X, p. 437, 3 June, 1922.
C	HAMSTEAD MARSHALL—Barrel-organ till c. 1890 when advertisement in local paper stated "Organist required, knowledge of music essential".
F	PEASEMORE—
F	READING—
F	SHENLEY—
FN	SUNNING HILL—Barrel-organ in church until 1861, when it was removed.
F	WARFIELD—
F	WINDSOR—OLD—

BRECONSHIRE

F	CRICKHOWELL—
N	LLANIGON—Barrel-organ in use till 1911.

BUCKINGHAMSHIRE

C	BLETCHLEY—Barrel-organ by B. Flight & Son, and in use in 1849. *Vide* Description of the Church in *Gentlemen's Magazine* 1849, converted to manual by Messrs. Kirkland under direction of Sir Geo. Martin, organist of St. Paul's who was consulted by the then incumbent, the late Rev. F. W. Bennett Wyndcote.
?	COSGROVE—Barrel-organ included in list by John Watlen (*q.v.*) pasted in his barrel-organ at Aldro School Chapel, Shackleford, Surrey.
W	LATIMER—Barrel and finger organ by Gray & Davison, 1841. (Information by courtesy of Rev. B. B. Edmonds).
F	MARLOW. GREAT—
F	OLNEY—
N	RAVENSTONE—Barrel-organ by Wm. Hill. Supplied and sent in August 1840 by canal from Pickford's Wharf to Newport Pagnell addressed to "Rev. Wm. Godfrey, Vicarage, Ravenstone, Oulney, Nr. Newport Pagnell, Bucks." Present organ may be conversion or replacement but bears no maker's name.
F	TAPLOW—
C?	THORNBOROUGH—Barrel-organ converted, it is thought, but no evidence of this in present organ by Robert & William Gray, London, 1787. 4 stops.
F	WRAYSBURY—

CAMBRIDGESHIRE

T	BALSHAM—Barrel and finger organ by J. W. Walker, 1839, transferred to Roseworth, Stockton-on-Tees. Barrels are lost. *Vide Mus. Opinion,* Jany., 1941: *Ancient Monuments Socy., Trans.* May 1960, p. 109.
T	BASSINGBOURN—Barrel and finger organ by J. W. Walker, (2 barrels), sold to Meldreth Ch. in 1866 for £100.
R	BRINKLEY—A. Claypole, organ bldr., Peterborough, states the original barrel-organ has been so altered over so many years that very little of the barrel-organ remains.
TC	BURWELL—St. Mary's Ch.—barrel-organ converted and brought from St. Andrew's Ch.
N	CAMBRIDGE—St. Edward's Ch. Barrel-organ by Gray & Davison in 1838.
N	GAMLINGAY—Barrel-organ by Gray & Davison 1847, costing £65.
C	COTTENHAM—Originally barrel and finger organ by Hill, 1847. Barrel mechanism removed, and organ restored, improved and dedicated by Bishop of Huntingdon, March, 1966. Tune list of 10 includes one "Cottenham".

N	GRANTCHESTER—Present manual organ includes remains of a barrel-organ, according to a local history of the organs by a previous organist.
C	GREAT WILBRAHAM—Barrel-organ converted to manual prior to 1930 when tune-list survived.
N	HARSTON—Barrel-organ sold to Gray & Davison in 1847 for £12.
C?	HAUXTON—The present single manual organ is thought to be a converted barrel-organ.
N	HISTON—Barrel-organ according to Bryceson's List of Churches (1864). (Per J. Budgen).
T	LANDBEACH—Barrel-organ—anonymous—removed and after 23 years in a shed at Cottenham, restored and brought to Cambridge Folk Museum to illustrate a lecture by Canon Galpin in 1931. Later stood in an attic and allowed to become derelict, till destroyed in 1961.
N	LITTLE ABINGTON—A lady recalls that her father attended Little Abington Church as a boy and there was a barrel-organ with 6 barrels—c. 1853-63. No trace.
N	LITTLEPORT—Barrel-organ by Hill in 1830.
C	MELDRETH—Barrel and finger organ by J. W. Walker. 3 barrels x 12. Bought from Bassingbourn Church in 1866 for £100. *Vide The Antiquary*, Vol. xliii, (1907), p. 248. Converted, rebuilt and enlarged about a century ago.
R	MILTON—Barrel-organ, remnants, by H. Bryceson, London, 1840. One barrel "No. 2" survives with 11 tunes. In 1957, the other two barrels existed: No. 1—12 tunes and No. 3—11 tunes.
N	SAWSTON—Barrel-organ converted to manual by J. W. Walker in 1854. Replaced by present organ by Bishop in 1894.
D	TADLOW—"Dumb organist" for a period finger-organ by Bates. Three barrels x 8; not in playing order.

CARMARTHENSHIRE

F	LLANDILO—
F	LLANDOVERY—

CAERNARVONSHIRE

T	TREMADOC—Barrel and finger-organ by Flight removed c. 1850 to Ynyschanhiaiarn but the barrels were left behind and may have disappeared from Tremadoc Church since c. 1945.
C	YNYSCHANHIAIARN Finger organ by Flight, formerly barrel and finger, transferred from Tremadoc c. 1850. In poor repair and barrel mechanism gone. (Per J. Budgen).

CHESHIRE

F	ASTBURY—
F	BUDWORTHY—
FN	CHOLMONDLEY CASTLE CHAPEL—If Flight installed a barrel-organ, it must have been replaced in 1868 by the present organ by Farr, Manchester, rebuilt 1924 and 1964.
FN	DODDINGTON—Present organ by Wadsworth & Bros. Manchester, evidently a memorial dated 1914.
FN	HIGH LEGH—Present organ a one-manual pipe organ by Abbot & Smith, Leeds, 1894.
T	HURDSFIELD—Barrel-organ now owned by Mr. Eric Robinson, London.
F	KNUTSFORD—Unitarian Chapel—One account states that the organ by Hill, 1893, was rebuilt by Willis in 1963. *Vide Old Cheshire Churches* by R. Richards (1947) where it is stated: "The present organ installed in 1915, took the place of an old barrel instrument". (Per David E. Owen). The Parish Church organ was first installed in 1793 but no indication of builder or barrel and/or finger organ.
N	TUSHINGHAM—A barrel-organ was purchased by voluntary subscription c. 1841. No details. *Vide Old Cheshire Churches* by R. Richards (1947).
F	VALE ROYAL—Private Chapel.
F	WALLASEY—
N	WEAVERHAM—
R	WOODCHURCH—The remains of the church barrel-organ were in 1934 seen in a garden shed at the Vicarage. (Per Rev. G. S. Robinson).

CORNWALL

MN	CAMBORNE—Barrel-organ had drum and triangle. Now no trace.
MN	PROBUS—Anecdote in *"The Old Church Gallery Minstrels,"* Canon K. H. MacDermott (1948), p. 42. Now no trace.

PLATE 22

Photo by A. E. Coe & Sons Ltd., Norwich.

Chamber barrel-organ by Pistor, London, c. 1780. Very handsome case with heart-shaped panel, flanked by two slender towers and surmounted by three gilt urns. 7 barrels with 10 secular tunes on each. 4 stops and drum and triangle. Restored by John Budgen, of Messrs. Bishop & Son, Ipswich, in 1965 for the owner, Mrs. Sparke, Gunthorpe Hall, Melton Constable, Norfolk.

TW	ST. IVES—Barrel-organ transferred to St. Ives Museum. Bought in 1831 for £150. Recently restored by Mr. Dixon Nance, Cumberland. Tune-list for 1 sacred and 2 secular barrels. Only 1 secular barrel survives. 4 stops plus drum and triangle.

CUMBERLAND

T	ALSTON—Barrel-organ transferred to Nenthead (*q.v.*).
F	GOSFORTH—
T	KESWICK—Crosthwaite Ch. had a barrel-organ by Joseph Beloudy, London, 1784. 5 barrels x 15 but all are secular which casts doubt on the origin of the organ— now owned by Mr. Guy Williams, Birkenhead.
O	NENTHEAD—Barrel and finger organ by Bevington & Sons, 1852, rebuilt by a refugee during 1914-18 War. Original tune-list survives. In poor state. Transferred from St. Augustine's Ch., Alston.
F	WHITEHAVEN—

DENBIGHSHIRE

N	BANGOR ISYCOED—Large barrel-organ in the Church c. 1905. Vanished.
F	DENBIGH—
N	LLANGOLLEN—The former barrel-organ in use c. 1840 was scrapped, but a barrel survived until c. 1962 in the church porch. *Vide Musical Opinion*, August, 1958.
R	MARCHWIEL—Barrel-organ removed in 1964 from the gallery as an eyesore and riddled with woodworm. Remains now stand in an outbuilding. American organ used c. 1900 and new pipe organ installed early in the century.
?	RUABON—Barrel-organ in St. Martin's Ch., 3 barrels in a box c. 1907. *Vide N. & Q.* (10) viii, p. 66, 27 July, 1907.
F	RUTHIN—

DERBYSHIRE

W	CALKE—*Vide A. M. Socy. Trans.* May 1960, p. 110. 3 stops: 5 barrels (two by Flight & Robson, two by Lincoln (*q.v.*)) The organ is often used for Voluntaries.
FN	MATLOCK—No trace.
T	MORLEY—Barrel-organ by Geo. Pyke, Bedford Row, London, thought to have come from Morley Ch., was owned by a lady in Sandiacre, Notts., but see Stanton-by-Dale (*infra*)
R	PEAK FOREST—Barrel-organ in Church of Charles the Martyr is said to have been installed in 1700 but no evidence is available. It was still in use in 1870.
T	REPTON—Barrel-organ said to be the first to be installed in Repton Ch. was later removed to Bretby Hall whence it later reached Burton-on-Trent Museum. 4 stops. 3 barrels x 10 tunes.
R	STANTON IN THE PEAK—Church of Holy Trinity contains the case and part mechanism of a barrel-organ and one barrel—in a balcony over the west door.
T	STANTON-BY-DALE—Barrel-organ from Dale Church owned by the late Miss D. Winrow, Sandiacre, Notts. Sold for £680 per "Daily Mail" of 6 June 1969. See Chap. VII *s.v.* Haley.
N	TRUSLEY—Barrel-organ in use c. 1890-1900 according to letter in "Sunday Times", 30 April, 1950. Later removed by a subsequent vicar.

DEVONSHIRE

F	BICTON—
MR	CHIVELSTONE—Two barrels and bellows are all that remained in 1960 of the barrel-organ.
M	CLAWTON—
?	DREWSTEIGNTON—Per Rev. B. B. Edmonds.
F	EXETER—Catholic Chapel.
F	EXETER—Trinity Church.
F	EXMINSTER—
?	GULLIFORD—Barrel-organ (in 1905) in gallery of the Presbyterian Meeting House. It had several barrels and was 'played' by a blacksmith-organist. *Vide Trans.* of the Unitarian Historical Socy., Vol. VI, No. 4 (1938), p. 386. Article by G. E. Evans. (Kindly communicated by Rev. G. L. Clarke, Toxteth Chapel, Liverpool).
R	HARTLAND—Barrel and action—46 keys—survive. Brought from Stoke, near Hartland c. 1846, when it was placed on the rood-screen. In 1849 it was removed to a chamber over the vestry—then open to the church. In 1870 it was removed to the floor of the North aisle and in 1910 to the Chapel-of-Ease at

Harton when the present organ was bought second-hand from Ventnor. Remnants of the barrel-organ are preserved in a chamber over the North porch. *Vide Devon Notes & Queries,* Vol. 14, 1926-27, p. 172.

N   KINGSKERSWELL—Barrel-organ long since disappeared without even reference in churchwardens' accounts. (Per Rev. A. F. C. Rowe, Vicar).

F   LYNMOUTH—

F   LYNTON—

C   MILTON ABBOT—Barrel-organ by Flight & Robson, London: 4 barrels each with 10, 11, 10 and 12 hymns and psalms. *Vide A. M. Socy. Trans.,* May 1960, p. 110. Since 1890's partly incorporated in organ now serviced by Hele, Plymouth.

F   OTTERY ST. MARY'S—

F   PLYMOUTH—Compton Chapel.

M   SPREYTON—

T   STOKE, near Hartland—Barrel-organ transferred c. 1846 to Hartland.

F   TORQUAY—

F   TOTNES—

DORSET

T   BERE REGIS—In 1852, Puddletown Ch. sold the mechanism of their barrel-organ to Bere Regis Churchwardens. *Vide The Choir,* July 1934, p. 150, art. by Canon Galpin. Barrel-organ transferred to Dorset County Museum. 3 barrels. No maker's name visible. 2 of 5 barrels survive. (Per Rev. G. S. Robinson, Sherborne).

MN   BOTHENHAMPTON—The old church is derelict and the nave and west gallery demolished. An old lady in the village remembered " sitting with her uncle who was the organist and the organ worked with a handle which was turned." (From a local Guide-book of 1947).

?   BRIDPORT—No information.

C   BUCKLAND NEWTON—Barrel-organ converted to manual in 1859 at a cost of £60 defrayed by the daughter of the vicar, the Ven. Archdeacon Gunning. The converted organ was superseded by a modern organ in 1937. The tune-list survives.

R   BUSHEY CHAPEL—Barrel-organ by T. C. Bates & Son, No. 3302. 3 barrels each of 12 tunes. Regularly used in 1922 but now derelict. *Vide N. & Q.* (12) X, p. 254, 1 April, 1922.

O   CLOSWORTH—Barrel-organ: 2 ranks of pipes: 20 notes: 2 barrels: no maker's name nor references in church records. Restoration under consideration.

N   LYDLINCH—Barrel and finger organ by Robson & Son, London, 1843; 5 stops: 4 barrels x 10 psalms etc. Removed in 1849 and advertised for sale by Forster & Andrews, Hull. *Vide The Organ,* No. 149, July, 1958, p. 13. In 1850, installed by Forster & Andrews in Rudston Church, Yorks.

F   LYME REGIS—

MO   LYTCHETT MATRAVERS—Barrel-organ by T. C. Bates & Son. Not in working order in 1956.

R   PORTLAND—St. George's Ch. disused, built in 1760, contains remains of a barrel-organ. A barrel from it is preserved in Portland Museum, two miles distant.

MT   PUDDLETOWN—Barrel-organ introduced in c. 1845, sold in 1852 to Bere Regis (q.v.)

?   REFORNE—

N   SHERBORNE ABBEY—Barrel-organ in 1856. (Per Rev. B. B. Edmonds).

FN   SPETTISBURY—No trace.

R   STEEPLE—Remains of barrel-organ made by J. W. Walker, bought in Oct., 1858 by Rev. Nathaniel Bond (*c.p.* Wareham *infra*), now in Vestry of St. Michael's Church. Originally 6 stops: 3 barrels each of 12 tunes. *Vide N. & Q.,* 12, X, p. 254, 1st April, 1922.

C   TARRANT KEYNSTON—Barrel-organ converted to manual. Present organ by Gray & Davison. Traces of barrel mechanism: list of 10 tunes inside the organ case.

F   TYNEHAM—Barrel-organ thought to have been transferred to Steeple in 1939 when Tyneham taken over by the War Dept., but Steeple organ is by Walker and was installed in 1858. There must have been an earlier organ by Flight.

N   WAREHAM—The Grange Chapel—The Rev. Nathaniel Bond bought on 4 Jany., 1850, for his chapel, from J. W. Walker, London, a Psalmodic barrel-organ, 6 stops, 3 barrels in one frame, 10 tunes each, in oak case for £105 plus £1, 10s., for brass rods and side curtains. (Information by courtesy of Messrs. J. W. Walker & Sons Ltd.)

N   WIMBORNE ST. GILES—Barrel-organ destroyed in church fire c. 1908.

FN   WINTERBOURNE WHITCHURCH—No trace since fire in 1870.

?	WOOTTON ST. LAWRENCE—Barrel-organ presented to church c. 1872.
	Note: *Vide Musical Opinion,* November 1969, article "Barrel-organs in Dorset", by A. L. Flay.

CO. DURHAM

F	DARLINGTON—
F	DURHAM—
?	PELTON—Barrel-organ by T. C. Bates & Son, c. 1850. 7 stops. *Vide A. M. Socy. Trans.* May 1960, p. 111.
TN	RYTON ON TYNE—Barrel-organ by Wood & Small, Edinburgh, 1828, bought by public subscription. Later altered to manual and in 1853 pedals were added. In 1856 swell and 5 stops added. Each barrel had 12 tunes. Organ was sold to Greenside Ch., Ryton, for £5 and came into use in June, 1888. In 1886 a 2-manual organ by Lewis & Co. was installed in Ryton Ch. Subsequently a third manual and electric blower were added.
	In 1905 the old organ at Greenside Ch. was replaced by one by Binns of Leeds. (Per W. A. Cocks, Ryton).
?	STOCKTON ON TEES—Barrel-organ by J. Walker 1839, transferred in 1956 from Balsham Parish Ch., Cambs. to Roseworth Parish Ch. (Stockton-on-Tees was included in the list of Messrs. Flight c. 1820).
?	WEST PELTON—
N	WHITBURN—Barrel-organ in use till end of 19th cent. *Vide N. & Q.* 12, X, p. 477, 17 June, 1922.

ESSEX

C	ASHDON—Barrel-organ converted to manual. (Per Johnson & Son, organ builders, Cambridge and the Rev. B. B. Edmonds).
O	BARNSTON—Barrel-organ by Bevington & Sons (1865): 6 stops: 5 barrels x 12 tunes including 2 "new barrels" made by John Rayment Rust of Chelmsford in 1875. In use till 1960 when bellows gave out.
R	BELCHAMP WALTER—A rectangular drum 20″ x 30″ from a barrel-organ is in Colchester Museum.
?	BLACK NOTLEY—
?	BOBBINGWORTH—Barrel-organ, 3′ wide, was standing in the church in 1918 but out of use for many years. *Vide Essex Review,* Vol. 27 (1918), art. by A. V. Phillips.
R	BRADWELL juxta MARE—Barrel and finger organ by T. C. Bates, but barrels removed. (Per Rev. Gordon Paget 13/7/65).
N	CLAVERING—Barrel and finger organ installed by Gray & Davison in 1845: 3 barrels: 5 stops. The present finger organ, however, bears Bishop's plate.
?	CORRINGHAM—Barrel-organ in church in 1930 according to a correspondent in New Malden.
OD	ELMSTEAD—Dumb organist, 1 barrel x 6 tunes; Anonymous. Not applicable to present large organ.
C	EPPING UPLAND—Barrel-organ by Bevington, rebuilt. (Per Rev. B. B. Edmonds).
WD	FAULKBOURNE—Dumb organist by T. C. Bates & Sons: 44 keys: 4 barrels x 8 tunes. Each fits the manual of the existing Bates organ. 7 stops. Bought from Wickham Bishop Ch. by Canon Galpin for £6 and first played at Harvest Festival Thanksgiving in Faulkbourne Church, 25 Sept., 1932. Restored in Nov., 1966 by F. F. Hill.
?	FELSTED—Barrel-organ (per Rev. B. B. Edmonds).
O	FOBBING—Barrel-organ by Bevington & Sons: 3 barrels x 12 tunes: 4 stops. Tune list in *A. M. Socy. Trans.,* May 1960, p. 111 *Vide Essex Review,* Vol. 27 (1918), art. by A. V. Phillips: and *ibid.,* Vol. 42 (1933), art. by E. Spurgeon Knights.
O	FORD END—Black Chapel contains barrel-organ: 2 barrels: 4 stops: 28 keys. In very poor state in West Gallery (1965).
N	FRYERNING—Barrel-organ by B. Flight & Son is known to have been in use *Vide The Singing Church in Essex* (1955), p. 14.
O	GREAT LEIGHS—Small chamber barrel-organ. Tune-list for 4 barrels x 10 tunes each including secular pieces, quadrilles etc. as well as 20 hymns and psalms on two of the barrels: 6 stops. This organ was transferred to the church in 1914 by Mr. J. H. Tritton of Lyons Hall who considered it to date from c. 1838. The maker's label reads "Wm. Phillips, Manufacturers, Little Tower Hill, London." In poor condition in 1960. *Vide Essex Review,* Vol. 42 (1933), art. by E. Spurgeon Knights. Also *Daily Telegraph,* 3 March 1965, letter from the late Alex. Puck and illustration.

PLATE 23

Brightwell Baldwin Church, Oxford. Barrel-
organ by Joseph Walker, 1843. 5 stops:
3 barrels each of 10 tunes. Tune-list now
illegible. Restored in 1960 by R. H. Walker
& Son Ltd., Chesham, Bucks.

N	HADSTOCK—Barrel-organ, maker unknown, existed in the Church of St. Botolph till 1884 when it was removed. Said to have "played 8 tunes all by Tate & Brady."
C	HELIONS BUMPSTEAD—Barrel and finger organ by J. W. Walker, 1851, converted to finger organ and barrel mechanism removed and destroyed. 5 stops.
N	INGATESTONE—Barrel-organ known to have been used. Now no trace. *Vide The Singing Church in Essex* (1955), p. 14.
T	LAYER - DE - LA - HAYE—Barrel-organ long disused was presented to Colchester Museum prior to 1918. *Vide Essex Review*, Vol. 27 (1918), art. by A. V. Phillips. In 1965 the organ was stated to have been repaired.
RF	LEYTONSTONE—St. John's Church, built in 1832, had a barrel-organ in its early days. Displaced by a finger organ c. 1865. Some of the barrels were in the belfry in 1950. *Vide The Organ*, No. 117, July 1950.
R	LITTLE ILFORD—A barrel lay for many years on top of a cupboard in the Church of St. Mary the Virgin. Nothing is known of the barrel-organ formerly in use there.
N	MORETON—Barrel-organ in use till 1905 when it was disposed of owing to removal of the gallery. *Vide Essex Review* Vol. 27 (1918).
F	ORSETT—
T	RAMSEY—Barrel-organ transferred in 1852 to Rimswell Church, Yorks., and put in order by Forster & Andrews, Hull.
N	ROYDON—Barrel-organ was in use until 1866.
R	STANSTED—Barrel-organ by B. Flight & Son c. 1820. Keyframe and barrel still in the church but removed from the manual organ when an electric blower was fitted. (1966).
N	STOCK—In former gallery a barrel-organ with 3 barrels x 12 tunes each. *Vide "Rectors in Two Essex Parishes"*. (Stock & Ramsden Bellhouse in plurality), by the late Rev. F. W. Austen, p. 380.
?	STONDON MASSEY—Barrel-organ by Walker in 1850. *Vide The Singing Church in Essex*, p. 14 and *The West Gallery Minstrels*, p. 41.
T	THAXTED—Barrel-organ by O. Meyer & Co. now in Chelmsford and Essex Museum: 5 barrels, one sacred, remainder secular: 6 stops: 24 keys.
?	THORPE-LE-SOKEN—Barrel-organ by Flight & Robson c. 1839, bought from St. Barnabas Church, Islington c. 1835. *Vide Country Life* of 30 Sept. 1965.
N	TOLLESHUNT D'ARCY—Barrel-organ—no trace now. In 1957 there was a single manual barrel and finger organ by J. W. Walker 1856, but only the slotted bar and the list of 10 tunes remained: 5 stops: 1½ octaves of pedals pulling down the keys of the manual. Two "combination pedals."
?	UPMINSTER—Barrel-organ known to have been in use. *Vide The Singing Church Essex* (1955), p. 14.
C	WALTHAM ABBEY—Barrel-organ by Flight & Robson installed in 1819. J. W. Walker made additions in 1850. The barrel-organ had 8 tunes. In 1860 its pipes were incorporated in a new 2-manual organ by Walker. For full account, *Vide The Organ*, No. 57, July 1935 and No. 149, July 1958, pp. 26-33.
R	WENNINGTON—Barrel-organ by Hill & Davison c. 1838: 4 stops: 2 barrels x 10. Tune-list survives.
T	WICKHAM BISHOPS—Small barrel and finger organ by T. C. Bates: also Dumb Organist bought in 1932 by Canon Galpin for Faulkbourne Ch. (*q.v.*).

FLINTSHIRE

R	WORTHENBURY—Barrel-organ was recalled by a writer in *N. & Q.* (12) x 363 (15 Nov. 1924). Today only two barrels remain.

GLAMORGANSHIRE

N	COWBRIDGE (ST. HILARY)—Barrel-organ c. 1850 in regular use during incumbency of the Rev. Geo. W. Traherne, but had vanished by 1913 according to Rev. L. S. Crockett, Vicar, 1913-1962.
C	LLANDAFF—Barrel-organ by T. C. Bates in the Cathedral. Converted to manual. *Vide* Cathedral Brochure.
T	PENNARD (GOWER)—Barrel-organ by H. Bryceson stood in gallery till c. 1935 when it was transferred to the Welsh Folk Museum, St. Fagan's, Cardiff. 5 stops. No tune-list. Restored in 1969 by J. Budgen of Bishop & Son, Ipswich.
F	WENVOE—

GLOUCESTERSHIRE

F	AVENING—
F	BADMINTON—

F	BISLEY—
N	BRIMPSFIELD— Barrel-organ stood in a gallery erected in 1833 and taken down in 1885. It provided six tunes according to a leaflet in the church. *Vide* Church leaflet.
C	CHIPPING CAMDEN—Baptist Church has a converted barrel-organ with a long history. Originally the property of Albert, Prince Consort, was installed in Buckingham Palace. Thence it passed to the Baptist Church, Chipping Norton, Oxon., when a manual was fitted. After fifty years it was transferred to Chipping Camden when more pipes and pedals and an electric blower were added. Has a "flute" stop said to be unique. A recording was made during the ministry of the Rev. S. G. Dudley, 1946-1955.
C	CIRENCESTER—A converted barrel-organ was bought for £5 and installed in the Church Hall. (Per R. Matthews, organist, aged 78), in a letter of 8 Apr. 1965.
T	DAGLINGWORTH—Barrel-organ was shipped to Malta but sunk by mine during 1939-45 War. 5 stops: Foot pedal for bellows: 3 barrels each of 8 hymns and 2 chants.
T	LONG COMPTON—Barrel-organ by H. Bryceson was stored in a room under the church tower in 1903. By 1910 the organ had been removed to Compton Wyngates, Warws., (*q.v.*) through the agency of the Marquis of Northampton, land owner in both parishes. (Information by courtesy of C. M. Taylor & L. Morgan, Morecambe).
C	NORTH CERNEY—Barrel-organ recalled by writer in *N. & Q.* (12), x 363 (1924). As present organ is by J. W. Walker c. 1850 or earlier, it was presumably a former barrel and finger organ.
F	RODMARTON—
FN	STOW IN THE WOLD—Barrel-organ by Flight repaired in 1842 by Gray & Davison.
R	STROUD, Congregational Chapel—Present organ includes remains of a barrel-organ. The Chapel is to be closed. (Per Evan Rigby).
N	WORMINGTON—Barrel-organ was in use. By 1820 a two-manual organ had been installed. *Vide* E.A. B. Barnard's "Old Days," No. 510, 11 July, 1931 in *Evesham Journal*: also article by A. Freeman in *The Organ*, Vol. 19 p. 110.

HAMPSHIRE

W	AVINGTON—Barrel-organ, maker uncertain, presented by Mrs. Shelley in 1849: 3 stops: 2 barrels each of 11 hymns and psalms. Restored by John Budgen, of Messrs. Bishop, Ipswich, in 1960. See Plate 26 *Vide Country Life*, 6 Apl. 1961.
F	BASINGSTOKE—
F	BISHOPSTOKE—
N.F.	BOLDRE—Formerly (prior to 1855) there was a gallery over the Western door . . . in it was installed a Barrel Organ which played three tunes . . . *Vide Boldre* by W. F. Perkins, 4th Edit. (Sept. 1935), p. 17. This statement must be accepted with reserve. More precise details are lacking except that Boldre is included in the list of B. Flight & Son's organs.
F	CHICHESTER—No record of a barrel-organ locally. (Per F. W. Steer).
N	CRONDALL—A barrel-organ replaced the church band in 1842: 3 barrels: maker unknown. Chanting was introduced in 1847, unaccompanied until 1859 when a harmonium was introduced. Pipe organ was installed in 1861 and again in 1871. (Per Rev. J. Hunt and Mr. C. Howkins).
F	GODSWORTH—
F	HIGHFIELD—
F	RAMSDEN—
CW	STRATFIELDSAYE—Barrel-organ by Flight & Sons presented by the first Duke of Wellington. Later converted to manual but barrel mechanism retained. 3 stops: 2 barrels: 27 keys: foot-blown. A very interesting tune-book of 16 psalms and hymns was found in the foot of the organ case. The tunes are included in the Chapter on tunes.
F	SWARRATON—
F	WARBLINGTON—
?	WEST TYTHERLEY—Small barrel-organ dated 1834 has 3 barrels of 10 tunes each. Maker: H. Bryceson and presented by the Hon. H. Bouverie. 4 stops: 24 keys.
?	YATELEY—Barrel-organ purchased in 1836 by subscription replaced a band of three clarinets and a bassoon in the gallery erected in 1755. *Vide* letter in *The Times* of 10 June 1939. A piccolo, 3 clarinets and a bassoon are preserved in the church.

HEREFORDSHIRE

R ASHPERTON—The case of a barrel-organ survives in a small west gallery. The mechanism was removed by a previous vicar.

T BOSBURY—Barrel-organ by T. C. Bates & Son in All Saints Church, Hereford, on loan from Hereford Museum. Originally 4 barrels each of 10 tunes. Only one survives. *Vide Country Life* 31 Mch. 1953, p. 878 and *A. M. S. Trans.*, 1960, p 112.

N BYTON—Barrel-organ recalled in use in 1870's.

C CROFT—The present finger organ by Bevington formerly had barrel mechanism but only the tune-list remains and includes a tune "Nayland", nr. Colchester, a 'local' tune probably added by Rust of Chelmsford (q.v.).

N DINEDOR—Barrel-organ said to have been in the church c. 1905 according to Miss R. M. Clarke, (aged 92), former organist for 70 years .

R EARDISLAND—Barrel-organ installed in 1834 was converted to finger in 1864. One barrel survives in the church and the organ in a house nearby. (Per Rev. B. B. Edmonds).

O LLANIGON—Barrel-organ by Bevington, disused since c. 1856, but still in the church. Three barrels: in very poor condition. (Per Rev. K. V. Evans, Vicar).

N MADLEY—In 1844 Gray & Davison installed an " Improved Barrel-Organ."

? SHOBDON—Barrel-organ by Bevington, presented c. 1842 by the family of Lady Bateman. Played 20 tunes.

N WESTON under PENYARD—Recorded that in 1840 John Robbins, a string bass player and bootmaker, made a new barrel for the church barrel-organ.

HERTFORDSHIRE

MR ALDENHAM—A barrel-organ by Gray was first installed during incumbency of Vicar Lomax (1806-25). This was replaced by a larger barrel and finger organ of Gray & Davison in 1853-54 and a 2-manual pipe-organ of Gray & Davison in 1866. *Vide The Parish Registers of Aldenham, Herts.* (Published privately in 1902), p. 204. In 1887 the Vicar opened an old oak chest and found the remains of an old barrel-organ with its list of 12 tunes. The organ front and tune-list were preserved in the Vestry (1902).

R AYOT ST. LAWRENCE—A barrel and finger organ—maker uncertain—of c. 1790. Restored in 1964. Too little of barrel mechanism remained for complete restoration in 1964.

N BARNET—Barrel-organ by Flight & Robson supplied in 1824: 5 stops: 3 barrels x 10 psalms. Replaced in 1850 by Bevington who allowed £45 for it.

NF BARNET, EAST—

? BROUGHTON—Barrel-organ listed by John Watlen on list pasted on his barrel-organ in Aldro School Chapel, Shackleford, Surrey.

? BUSHEY HEATH—Formerly barrel-organ by Holdich, 1845.

CHESHUNT—A small chamber barrel-organ with 5 barrels each of 10 tunes was in use as late as 1929. Maker's name effaced and only Royal Arms remain. 6 stops including drum and triangle. One barrel bears Gavioli & Cie., . . . Paris & London. *Vide* A.M.S. Trans. May 1960, p. 111.

N COTTERED—Barrel-organ in West Gallery in use until 1870. (Per Rev. B. B. Edmonds).

N ELSTREE—Barrel-organ of 1820, vanished.

MD GREAT GADDESDEN—Dumb organist survives. Maker not stated but the sole surviving barrel is by "S. Parsons, 2 Little Russell Street, Bloomsbury". Seven tunes.

M HUNSDON—

T KINGS LANGLEY—Barrel-organ by Robson, in church till 1935 when removed to Flitton, Beds. but no longer at Flitton.

N MUCH HADHAM—Barrel-organ by Gray & Davison in 1844.

N MUCH WYMONDLEY—Barrel-organ recalled. Vanished.

MT SACOMBE—Barrel-organ by Bevington, 3 stops, 1 barrel. Very derelict condition. Since 1939 on loan to Hertford Museum.

O ST. ALBANS—Barrel-organ, 4 stops still (1965) stored in bottom of tower of St. Michael's Church. Not in playing order. 4 stops: 2 barrels x 10 hymns. *Vide* Galpin *Old English Insts. of Music,* (1913), p. 237.

M ST PAUL'S WALDEN—Barrel and finger organ installed in 1850. The barrel was used until 1855 when an organist was appointed. The old organ and gallery were removed in 1900 when a new organ was erected. This was in turn superseded in 1936 by a Hammond 2-manual electric organ. *Vide Mus. Times* August 1937, p. 733.

G

PLATE 24

PLATE 25

Mattishall Burgh Church, Dereham, Norfolk.
Barrel-organ by J. W. Walker, 1852. 3 barrels
each of 10 tunes.

Ex Attleborough Church, Norfolk. Now in
the Collection of the late Canon Noel Boston,
Lamas Manor, Norwich.

R	SARRATT—Providence Chapel had a barrel and finger organ by Theodore Bates, c.1840. 58 notes. 1 octave of pedals. All pipes enclosed in a swell box. No pedal pipes. Pedals pulled down the lowest octave of the manual. Barrel mechanism has been removed and no barrels survive.
F?	STANSTEAD—Barrel and finger organ in St. Margaret's Church. 4 barrels: 6 stops: 2 octaves of pedals. Made by William Allen, London. Presumably Flight supplied a previous organ.
MT	STOCKING PELHAM—Barrel-organ by T. C. Bates & Son in use till 1917. Placed in Hertford Museum in 1937. *Vide* N. & Q., 12th series, IV, June 1918, pp. 164-165.
M	WATFORD—Barrel and finger organ by Walker, 1842, in St. Mary's Parish Church. One barrel played eleven tunes. *Vide The Old Church Gallery Minstrels*, p. 41.
?	WHEATHAMPSTEAD—Barrel-organ recorded as having been repaired by J. W. Walker in January 1863.

HUNTINGDONSHIRE

R	BUCKWORTH—The remnants of a barrel-organ are now used as a vestry cupboard. (Per Rev. B. B. Edmonds).
?	KIMBOLTON—
F	RAMSEY—
F	STILTON—
R	WARESLEY—The pipes of the old barrel-organ have been incorporated in the present organ. *Vide Bedfordshire Magazine* Vol. 3, No. 19 p. 103

IRELAND

B. Flight & Son included the following places in the list of those to which organs or barrel-organs had been supplied by the firm c. 1820.

F	BARONSTOWN—
F	BALLYNAKILL—
F	BALLYMENA—
F	CORK: CATHEDRAL—
F	CORK: COVE CHURCH—
F	CORK: ST. PETER'S—
F	CLOUGH—
F	DUBLIN: ST GEORGE'S—
F	DUBLIN: ST. MARY'S—
F	LIMERICK CATHOLIC CHAPEL—
F	MACROOM—
T	MARINA PASSAGE—
F	SWORDS—
F	THURLES—

ISLE OF MAN

T	DOUGLAS—St. Matthew's Church. Barrel-organ by T. C. Bates now in The Manx Museum, Douglas.
T	SANTAN—Barrel-organ by W. Wrenshall, Liverpool, now in The Manx Museum, Douglas.

ISLE OF WIGHT

N	BEMBRIDGE—Holy Trinity Church had a barrel-organ from c. 1827. In 1857 a barrel and finger organ was acquired for £96 nett, after allowance for the original organ. The Brighton Railway carried the new organ free of charge from London. In 1887 an organ was purchased for £325 from Forster & Andrews, Hull. *Vide The History of Holy Trinity Church, Bembridge 1827-1852*.
F	COWES—
F	GODSHILL—
DW	NEWCHURCH—Dumb organist and organ by Bevington & Sons. One barrel of 6 tunes. Restored by Mickleburgh, Bristol, 1961 as a gift of the Bishop of Malmesbury. 6 stops: 44 keys: fine carved Gothic case and exceptionally fine tone. See Plate 1.
T	VENTNOR—Barrel-organ by Robson, 4 barrels: transferred in 1859 by Forster & Andrews to Spridlington Church, Lincs.

KENT

M	BARHAM—
?	BELGRAVE—
F	BLACKHEATH—

CN	BORDEN—Barrel-organ by J. W. Walker was converted to manual and removed c. 1910. The organ has reappeared in Tunstall, Kent, in private hands.
F	BRASTED—
O	BREDGAR—Barrel-organ, no maker's name, in Church of St. John the Baptist. Only one of 3 barrels survives with 10 hymns and psalms, 4 stops. Organ in poor condition. Used within living memory.
F	BROMLEY—
F	CHIDDINGSTONE—
F	CHISLEHURST—
F	CHEVENING—
F	DEAL—
F	DOVER—
F	EAST SUTTON—
?	GREAT CHART—Barrel and finger organ by Forster & Andrews in 1854; 3 barrels.
R	HARTY, Isle of Sheppey—Only the case of a barrel-organ remains in church.
F	LEE—
F	LEWISHAM—
T	MEOPHAM—Barrel-organ by Bates in 1855 removed to Trottiscliffe in 1865.
F	MERSHAM—
F	NEW ROMNEY—
F	OSPRINGE—
DO	PEMBURY—A barrel by " J. W. Walker No. 27. 1823 " was given in 1823 in memory of Bishop Willcox, at one time Bishop of Rochester. The barrel was used in conjunction with an organ like "an oversized harmonium" until 1860 when a Hill organ was introduced. After long neglect in the belfry, the barrel was cleaned and placed by the West Door in the 1950's. Some parts, including the handle are missing. The barrel has six tunes.
R	SHOREHAM—Barrel-organ used till c. 1860 in the Church of St. Peter and St. Paul in a west gallery taken down in 1863. In 1847 the choir organ from Westminster Abbey, built by Schreider in 1730 and used for the Coronation of George III, was transferred to Shoreham and though remodelled and modernised the original case remains. (By courtesy of the Rev. D. E. Benbow, Vicar).
N	SHORNE—Barrel-organ barrel seen c. 1906 on second floor of Church tower.
CW	SMEETH—Barrel-organ converted to manual in Willesborough in 1857 and sold to Smeeth Church in 1884.
F	SOUTHEND—
F	SUNDRIDGE—
FM	SUTTON VALENCE—
O	TONGE—Barrel-organ by Bevington: 4 stops: 3 barrels each of 10 tunes. *Vide A. M. S. Trans.,* 1960, p. 114.
N	SWALECLIFFE—Barrel-organ by Bevington & Sons, 48 Greek Street, Soho. London: 4 stops: 24 keys: 80 pipes: 2 barrels x 10 tunes. On sale in London, Oct. 1969 for £375.
TW	TROTTISCLIFFE—Barrel-organ by T. C. Bates, in use till 1937. 6 stops: 6 barrels each of 10 tunes. Bought from Meopham Church in 1865. Restored in 1950 by Noel Mander and after being shown at Kent Music Exhibition it was finally placed in Rochester City Museum. Unfortunately, this barrel-organ, one of the largest of its type, is no longer in good order. Barrel No. 5 was recently restored at a cost of £100, but the winding shaft is broken. In *Country Life,* 24 March, 1966, a correspondent stated that the organ can still be used in emergencies.
F	WALMER—
F	WEST WICKHAM—
MTC	WILLESBOROUGH—Barrel-organ bought in 1817 for £42 from William Goldfinch. 33 tunes and 6 stops. In 1849 the West Gallery was removed and the organ placed in the chancel where it was converted to manual between 1849 and 1857. In 1884 a new organ was installed and the converted barrel-organ was sold to Smeeth Church (four miles distant). (Per W. P. Garner, Willesborough).

LANCASHIRE

R	GRESSINGHAM—Remnants of a barrel-organ installed in 1859, stand above a porch inside the South Door.
F	LIVERPOOL—St. George's—
F	LIVERPOOL—Corporation—
F	PADIHAM—
F	WARRINGTON—

LEICESTERSHIRE

N BARKBY—Barrel and finger organ installed by Forster & Andrews in 1857: 1 barrel. Removed in 1899 when present organ was installed.

DN COALVILLE—Barrel and finger organ by Walker, *Vide The Organ*, Vol. 17, p. 168. It appears that a barrel attachment to fit over the manual was still present in 1894.

T COLD ASHBY—Barrel-organ by H. Bryceson now in Leicester City Museum. *Vide* Chap. VII *infra*.

FT COLD OVERTON—It would seem that a later barrel-organ by Bryceson replaced the Flight organ. The Bryceson instrument is now in Leicester City Museum.

T DINGLEY—Barrel-organ by Bates removed pre-1892 to Brigstock Congregational Chapel, Kettering, Northants.

? NORTON juxta TWYCROSS—Barrel-organ with 3 barrels installed in 1840.

T ORTON-ON-THE-HILL—Barrel-organ transferred to Orton Hall.

R SOUTH KILWORTH—Barrel and finger organ by Wm. Gray. A board near the door gives the date 1846. Tune-list mislaid. 6 stops: 2 barrels. (Per Rev. R. F. Seal, North Kilworth).

LINCOLNSHIRE

N ALLINGTON—Barrel-organ by Forster & Andrews. 3 barrels; installed in 1849. Present organ bears no maker's name. No record of its installation. (Per Rev. J. M. Ashley).

? BARROWBY—Barrel-organ by Forster & Andrews in 1849: 3 barrels.

N BELTON—Barrel-organ vanished.

? BISHOP NORTON—Old barrel-organ from (Market) Rasen, Lincs.: 2 barrels: installed in 1854 by Forster & Andrews.

? BROUGHTON—Barrel and finger organ by Forster & Andrews in 1847: 1 barrel.

N BURTON-ON-STATHER—St. Andrew's Church had a barrel-organ in mid 19th century. *Vide N. & Q.* (12), x, p. 353, 6 May 1922. Apparently no record of organ prior to Forster & Andrews organ installed in 1867.

N CARLTON-LE-MOORLAND—Probably one of the last churches to replace the church band by a barrel-organ in 1863. This was replaced by a manual organ in 1885. *Vide The Organ* No. 149, p. 16. July 1958.

? COLSTERWORTH—Barrel and finger organ by Forster & Andrews in 1893: 1 barrel.

N DONINGTON—Church of St. Mary and the Holy Rood had a barrel-organ in a West Gallery till c. 1864 when both were removed.

T FLEET—Barrel-organ: 4 barrels each of 8 tunes: transferred to Royal Pump Room Museum, Harrogate. Made by E. & J. Pistor. Restored by F. F. Hill in 1961. Tuned by J. E. Quarmby, organ tuner of York Minster. *Vide Harrogate Advertiser*, 13 January, 1962.

F GOSBERTON—

? GREAT PONTON—Barrel-organ by Forster & Andrews in 1848: 3 barrels.

F GRIMSBY—

N HARLAXTON—On Dec. 21, 1856 it was announced that Forster & Andrews of Hull had just fitted a very handsome organ . . . played by hand or by barrel. Five stops, an octave and a half of German pedals and could be blown by the hand or foot. 2 barrels. Tunes shifted by a notched plate. Erected by suscription. This organ was replaced in 1948.

O HUTTOFT—Barrel-organ by Forster & Andrews in 1851. 3 stops: 3 barrels each of 12 tunes. Not in working order.

LOUTH—Barrel and finger organ supplied by Forster & Andrews in 1846 to Holy Trinity Church: 1 barrel. This refers to a daughter church, south of the present church built in 1866. Forster & Andrews supplied the 3-manual organ in 1870 for the present church. The earlier organ was re-built as a 1-manual and pedal, 8-stop organ for Stocksbridge Wesleyan Chapel, Yorks., in 1870. *Vide* L. Elvin, *Forster & Andrews, 1843-1956*, (Lincoln, 1968), Illus. No. 19.

? MANTHORPE—Barrel-organ in use till at least 1867 and probably installed when present church was built in 1848. *Vide N. & Q.* (12), x, p. 353, 6 May 1922. The performer is stated to have maintained a uniform pace so, in the *Te Deum*, without any regard to the length of the different verses, the singers were obliged to get in the words as best they could.

N MARKET RASEN—Barrel-organ with 2 barrels removed in 1854 by Forster & Andrews and installed in Bishop Norton, Lincs.

F NOCTON—

? OWERSBY—Barrel and finger organ by Forster & Andrews in 1849: 1 barrel.

PLATE 26

Photo by E. A. Sollars, Winchester.

Barrel-organ, maker unknown, presented by Mrs. Shelley to Avington Church, Hants. in 1849. Restored by John Budgen, Ipswich, in 1961. 3 stops and 2 barrels. The Georgian Royal Arms in front of the gallery are dated 1771.

W	RAITHBY, Nr. Louth—In St. Peter's Church, a fine barrel-organ by Gray & Son, installed when the church was rebuilt in 1839. After 90 years disuse the barrel-organ was restored to good working order by John Budgen, of Messrs. Bishop, Ipswich, in 1963. As the only barrel-organ in working order in Lincolnshire, it has featured on East Anglian Television. See Plate 17.
N	SCREMBY—Barrel-organ said to have existed but present organ is a Snetzler.
N	SOUTH ELKINGTON—Barrel-organ by Flight & Robson. 6 stops: 5 barrels each of 10 tunes. Removed in 1849 by Forster & Andrews and advertised for sale by them. *Vide The Organ*, No. 149, July 1958, p. 13.
N	SPRIDLINGTON—Barrel-organ by Robson, 4 barrels, from Ventnor, I.O.W., installed by Forster & Andrews in 1859.
N	THEDDLETHORPE-ALL-SAINTS—Barrel-organ recalled in N. & Q. (12), x, p. 353, 6 May 1922. Vanished without trace.
?	WEST HALTON—
F	WRANGLE—

LONDON

W?	EAST HAM—Barrel-organ in old parish church by J. C. Bishop, 1837: 4 barrels x 11 tunes. *Vide Studies in Worship Music*, by J. S. Curwen.
F	DUCHY OF LANCASTER—
F	FULHAM PALACE—
F	GUY'S HOSPITAL—
F	HARLEY STREET CHAPEL, BOW—
T	ISLINGTON, ST. BARNABAS—Barrel-organ by Flight & Robson c. 1830, sold c. 1835 to Thorpe le Soken, Essex (*q.v.*).
F	LINCOLN'S INN: SOCIETY'S CHAPEL—
F	MAGDALEN INSTITUTION—
N	PAUL'S WHARF, ST. BENET'S—Barrel and finger organ by J. C. Bishop in use 1833-1897, by which time the two barrels had vanished. *Vide Old London City Churches*, by C. W. Pearce, Mus.D. (London, 1908). pp. 175-177.
F	ROLLS CHAPEL—
F	ST. BARNABAS, ISLINGTON—The barrel-organ bought in 1830 was found to be too small and was resold c. 1835 to Thorpe-le-Soken, Essex. *Vide* Letter in *Country Life* of 30 Sept., 1965.
F	ST. GEORGE'S HOSPITAL—
F	ST. PANCRAS—
N	SOUTHEND CHAPEL, LEWISHAM—This former private chapel had a barrel-organ which was replaced c. 1922. The earlier organ was said to have had a "grinder" by Flight 1854 and later converted to manual.
T	STRATFORD—Barrel-organ in 1840, said to have been transferred to East Ham.
F	YORK STREET—

MERIONETH

N	DOLGELLY—Barrel-organ by Gray & Davison, 1841: 3 barrels x 10 tunes.

MIDDLESEX

R	CRANFORD HAYES—Barrel-organ, incomplete, now (1956) in stable of Cranford House.
N	HANWELL—Barrel and finger organ by Gray & Davison.
FN	HARROW—WEALD—Barrel-organ by Gray & Davison 1843. Presumably replacing an earlier Flight organ.
F	HENDON—
N	KINGSBURY—Barrel-organ by Gray & Davison, 1841.
N	SOUTH MIMMS—Barrel-organ introduced in 1813 but criticised by a local lady. *Vide* S. Baring Gould "*Old Country Life.*"
F	SUNBURY—
N	UXBRIDGE MOOR—Barrel and finger organ by Bryceson, long since replaced.

MONMOUTHSHIRE

R	GROSMONT—Barrel of organ formerly in use in the church is still preserved in church.
F	LLANGATTOCK—
C	NEWPORT—Barrel-organ, 6 stops, converted to manual. (Per R.V. Gill, Cardiff Organ Works).

D   BETTWS CEDEWEN—A one-manual organ by Bates with a 'Dumb-Organist': compass CC to F''' (4½ octaves): 7 stops: pedal pull-down 1½ octaves from CC: 44 Keys: 3 barrels each of 8 tunes are labelled "Bates, 6 Ludgate Hill, London." 6 barrels were present in 1908. Presented by Lord Sudeley in 1872.

?   MACHYNLLETH, CHRIST CHURCH—Barrel-organ by J. W. Walker & Sons, 1855: 3 barrels x 10, originally built for Wellington Hospital, Salop. Sold c. 1859 to Christ Church. On closure of the church pre-1967, the organ was bought back by J. W. Walker & Sons, and restored by them.

W   TRELYSTAN—The sixth century Church of St. Mary in the Wood contains a small barrel-organ by G. Parsons, London 1827. The organ was in use till 1862 (when harmonium was bought) and was out of repair for a century. In 1962 it was restored by D. V. Owen of Manchester and the B.B.C. made a T.V. recording of a short service using the barrel-organ. 3 stops: 14 keys. *Vide* Article by E. Dawes in *Musical Opinion*, Feb. 1965, p. 295.

NORFOLK

T   ATTLEBOROUGH—Barrel-organ from the church in the collection of the late Canon Noel Boston, Bury St. Edmunds. No maker's name. See Plate 25.

R   BARNHAM BROOM—Barrel and finger organ by an unknown maker. Now in use as a finger organ only.

C   BARTON TURF—Barrel-organ given to the church by the Preston family who in the 1870's had it converted to manual.

R   BOUGHTON—Anonymous barrel and finger organ restored by Bishop & Son in 1968. Barrel mechanism either removed or never completed. Very primitive workmanship. Date c. 1850. (Per J. Budgen).

DW   BRADENHAM, WEST—'Dumb organist' discovered in the West Church by the late Canon Noel Boston in 1954 who actually used it. 2 barrels of 7 tunes each: 42 keys. *Vide* Tune-list in *Ancient Monuments Society* Transactions, 11 May, 1960, p. 115.

W   BRESSINGHAM—Barrel-organ (probably by Flight) presented by the Rev. G. H. C. Bidwell in 1859. 6 stops: 2 barrels of 12 tunes each including 6 chants. Footblowing for pointing chants. 3 short octaves—28 notes from G. Restored to working order by John Budgen of Messrs. Bishop, Ipswich. *Vide* tune-list in *A. M. S.* Trans., 11 May 1960, pp. 115-116.

C   BRISLEY—Barrel and finger organ by Bevington, 1832. Used as manual since c. 1870.

F   CARLTON RODE—

F   CASTLE RISING—

F   DISS—The inclusion of Diss in Flight's list, conflicts with extract Vestry Minutes of 1844 which record the purchase of a Bates organ.

N   EAST RUDHAM—A "Psalmodic" barrel-organ by Robson was installed on 22 Dec. 1839 at a cost of 100 guineas. Replaced in 1880 by a finger organ.

N   FELTWELL—Barrel-organ by Hill, 1838: 1 barrel. (Per Rev. B. B. Edmonds).

N   HARDINGHAM—A barrel-organ formerly stood in the West Gallery which has now vanished.

T   HEACHAM—A barrel-organ by Flight & Son stood in the West Gallery in 1850. A coloured drawing appears in the Supplement to Blomefield's "Norfolk". The organ was transferred to Thornham and thence to a mission church in South Africa. *Vide A.M.S. Transactions* 1960, p. 116.

R   HELHOUGHTON—Barrel and finger organ by H. Bryceson presented to E. & W. Raynham in 1852. 6 stops: Tune-list for 4 barrels: (1) 12 hymns. (2) 12 hymns and chants. (3) 12 hymns and chants. (4) spiral, playing 6 voluntaries. Organ brought from E. & W. Raynham in 1890. Now used as manual only.

F   HILGAY—

T   HINDRINGHAM—Barrel-organ by T. C. Bates removed to Letheringsett Church in 1955 after being for years in a private house. *cp.* Letheringsett *infra.*

TF   HOUGHTON—Barrel-organ by B. Flight & Son formerly in church is now stored in the stables of Houghton Hall.

T   HOVETON ST. JOHN—Barrel-organ by Wheatstone in 1820. Now in St. Peter Hungate Church Museum, Norwich. *Vide Archaeol. Jl.* (1943), p. 65 with plate iii fig. D. 6 stops.

W   LETHERINGSETT—Barrel-organ No. 2964 by T. C. Bates, c. 1835. Formerly in Hindringham Church and thereafter in a private house till 1955. Restored in 1956 by C. Hyatt, Trunch, Norfolk. 6 stops: 3 barrels each of 10 tunes of which 26 are hymns and 4 are chants " the latter having to be fitted into a psalm or canticle as best one can." Blowing pedal and separate crank handle for barrel. (Per Rev. Gordon Paget). See Plate 8.

W	MATTISHALL BURGH—Barrel-organ by Walker 1852. 3 barrels of 10 tunes each. *Vide* Tune List in *A. M. Socy.* Trans. 1960 p. 117. In working order. See Plates 16 & 24.
C	NORTH ELMHAM—Barrel-organ converted to manual.
W	NORTH LOPHAM—Barrel and finger organ by J. C. Bishop, transferred from Stanhoe Church: 1 barrel of 10 tunes. Installed in No. Lopham Church in 1953 by W. & A. Boggis, Diss.
F	REYMERSTON—
R	SISLAND—Barrel-organ remnants in church. *Vide* Letter in *"Sunday Times"* of 23 April 1950 from Rev. Gordon Paget.
C	STANFIELD—Formerly barrel-organ or barrel and finger. Two barrel tune-list. Now manual use only. (Per Rev. A. F. Mellows).
T	STANHOE—Barrel and finger organ by J. C. Bishop, and transferred to No. Lopham Church. *Vide supra.*
F	STARSTON—
C	SWAFIELD—Barrel-organ by Flight converted to finger in 1880 by J. Rayson, Ipswich and restored more recently by Martin Williamson, Trunch, Norfolk. Still in use.
T	THORNHAM—Barrel-organ from Heacham Ch. afterwards sent to a mission church in South Africa.
FN	TITCHWELL—Barrel-organ with 2 barrels replaced by manual organ in 1890 by Forster & Andrews.
T	WEST RAYNHAM—Barrel and finger organ by H. Bryceson presented in 1852. Transferred as a finger organ only to Helhoughton in 1890.
R	WEST SOMERTON—The case of an early 19th century barrel-organ is preserved. Abortive attempts at conversion appear to have destroyed most of the mechanism. 3 stops. (Per J. Budgen, Ipswich). *Vide* Letter in *Sunday Times* of 23 April, 1950, and *The Organ*, April 1932.
W	WITTON—A barrel and finger organ formerly in Witton Vicarage was placed in the church by the Rev. Francis Procter, who became Vicar in 1847. 7 stops: 3 barrels of 10 tunes each. *Vide A. M. S.* Trans. 1960, p. 118 for tune-lists: also *Archaeol. Jl.* 1943, pp. 64-65. Now used as manual only.
W	WOOD RISING—An excellent barrel-organ by Flight & Robson, St. Martin's Lane, Westminster, 1826 stands in the West gallery. 3 stops: 78 pipes: compass 3 octaves from Bass G, but omission of certain notes reduces the number of notes from 37 to 27. Originally 4 barrels of 10 tunes each but only two usable. J. Budgen of Messrs. Bishop, Ipswich, who restored the organ in 1958 made and fitted an extra barrel. The repairs resulted from Lord Verulam's agency. The organ was rededicated 1 May 1958. *Vide Woodrising Church* by Francis W. Steer, F.S.A. (1959). See Plate 14.

NORTHAMPTONSHIRE

R	BRIGSTOCK CONGREGATIONAL CHAPEL—Organ rebuilt in 1892 by a local organ-builder, clock-maker etc., a native of Dingley, A. E. Elliot (died 1946), from a Bates barrel-organ. Only part of the case remains—no mechanism. Probably had 5 stops and operated from the back. Two barrels were last seen in 1910. *cp.* Dingley, Leics. *supra.*
F	BRINGTON—
NT?	BULWICK—Barrel-organ with 40 tunes mentioned in Hart's *Nineteenth Century Parson.* Probably the barrel-organ by Bates No. 2888 now in Cranford Baptist Chapel. The Bulwick barrel-organ was replaced in 1874 by a Holdich 2-manual and pedal organ. The Rector of the time, the Rev. J. H. Holdich, brother of the organ-builder, wrote of the barrel-organ: "It has 30 tunes of which we are all tired". See Plate 18.
FN	BYFIELD—A large barrel-organ is shown in a gallery at the East end, over the altar, in plans drawn prior to restoration of the church.
W	CRANFORD BAPTIST CHAPEL—Barrel-organ by Bates, No. 2888, in working order. May have come from Bulwick in 1874, but bought in Kettering by H. W. Geary who placed it in the chapel on permanent loan. 5 stops: 3 barrels each of 10 tunes. See Plate 18.
F	CULWORTH—
R	DRAUGHTON—Present organ-case, which came from elsewhere c. 1877, bears no maker's name but a tune-list for 3 barrels of sacred music. (Per Rev. C. H. Davidson, Maidwell Rectory, Northants).
DW	EASTON-ON-THE-HILL—'Dumb organist', in good order, fits the Holdich organ bought in 1850. *Vide* article by H. B. Sharp in *Galpin Socy. Jl.* XIV March 1961 pp. 37-40 & plate: also *The Organ*, April 1957.

PLATE 27

Barrel-organ by T. C. Bates, London. 2 barrels each
Cardeston St. Michael's Church, Shropshire.
with 10 tunes, c. 1850.

W	EDGECOTT—Barrel and finger organ by G. M. Holdich 1855. 6 stops: 2 barrels each with 6 psalms and hymns: 3 combination pedals: 'Loud', 'Medium', 'Soft'.
W	FAWSLEY—Barrel and finger organ by J. Walker, 1839. Tune-list in *A. M. Socy. Trans.* (1960), pp. 114-115.
N	GREENS NORTON—Now no trace of a "neat" barrel-organ presented in 1826 by John Elliott, Esq., & costing 100 guineas.
DO	HORTON—Small finger organ by Bates with dumb organist: 1 barrel of 8 tunes.
R	LILBOURNE—Barrel-organ said to have been originally at Catthorpe, Leics., but neither barrels nor mechanism remain. Originally by Bryceson, 1855. Faded tune-list and Bryceson's advertisement inside the case. Organ now electrically blown, but pedal lever still usable. Single manual: 4 stops: the duplicate set of pallets for the former barrel action remains. (By courtesy of K. G. Parrott, Rugby).
C	PIDDINGTON—Finger organ by Holdich which originally had a barrel attachment: 4½ octaves: 9 stops.
W	SUTTON, (WANSFORD)—A barrel and finger organ in St. Michael's Church by Walker 1855 came from Great Waldingfield, Suffolk in 1888. Bought by Rev. Wm. Hopkinson, Vicar of Sutton, and presented to his church. Restored in 1961 by J. W. Walker & Son Ltd. 1 barrel of 10 hymns.
?	UPTON—Barrel-organ by Holdich. *Vide The Organ,* Apl. 1957.
N	WANSFORD—Barrel-organ is included by John Watlen c. 1807 in a list pasted in his barrel-organ at Aldro School Chapel, Shackleford, Surrey. The present organ dates from only c. 1900.
W	WINWICK—Barrel-organ by Wm. Prowse, 1864. 7 barrels x 10 tunes in removable shelves; fully restored in 1969 by K. G. Parrott, and E. Timmins of Rugby. See Plate 32.

NORTHUMBERLAND

FN	ALNWICK—Barrel and finger organ by Robson was removed from St. Michael's Church in 1868 by Forster & Andrews and sent to the Bethel Chapel, Demerara. The reference by Flight is probably to another Alnwick church.
F	BENTON—

NOTTINGHAMSHIRE

C	BARKESTONE—Barrel-organ by Bates rebuilt in 1862 by Forster & Andrews. Evidently converted to finger organ.
FN	COLWICK—No trace. The old church has been a roofless ruin for some twenty years. The Rector could find no one who recalled a barrel-organ.
DR	EDWINSTOWE—St. Mary's Parish Church had a barrel and finger organ by Forster & Andrews of 1862. One manual and a 'dumb organist' set to play six tunes. The barrel mechanism, removed many years ago, now rests with the barrel on a window sill in the North Aisle.
N	GAMSTON—Barrel and finger organ by Forster & Andrews 1856. 7 stops: 291 pipes: 1 barrel of 10 tunes: 2 composition pedals: 1½ octaves German pedals. Deal case and gilded front. Cost £105. 7 lower notes of open diapason etc. added at extra cost of £20 on order of the Rev. J. Twells. The tune-list was found in 1961 but a two manual organ was installed in 1964 by T. L. Jubb & Son and the former organ scrapped.
N	HARWORTH—Barrel-organ now vanished, but recalled in *N. & Q.* (12) X 20 May 1922, p. 398. On one occasion the Vicar called to the gallery to ask the reason of the delay in playing the Psalm. The Parish Clerk called back, "T'andle's brok".
W	KINOULTON—St. Luke's Parish Church built in 1793 for the Earl of Gainsborough contains a barrel and finger clockwork organ in a beautiful walnut case. This organ by Flight & Robson was bought in 1946 by Cedric Arnold, Williamson & Hyatt Ltd., at the sale of the contents of Gosfield Hall, Braintree. In 1947 they sold the organ to Kinoulton Parish Church and erected it, leaving the barrel mechanism *in situ*. Tone very small but bright and clear. Barrel mechanism disconnected. 6 barrels in West Gallery are very well made of sheet metal and longer than usual. 8 stops: compass 3 octaves: keyboard is drawn forward for playing.
W	OSSINGTON—Parish Church of the Holy Rood built 1782/83 contains a barrel-organ by Robson c. 1840 in a small recess at the West end. Operated from rear from a platform in the tower wall. Foot blown. 3 stops: compass 27 notes: 3 barrels stored in cases. The barrel-organ after restoration by N. P. Mander, London, at the instance of the Bishop of Sherwood, the Rt. Rev. K. G. Thomson and Dr. W. L. Sumner and was broadcast on radio on 13 May 1968.

N RAMPTON—Barrel-organ by Martin installed in November 1821: 5 stops: 4 barrels: 10 feet high, 5 feet wide. (Per *Lincoln, Rutland & Stamford Mercury*, Nov. 23, 1821.) Replaced by a harmonium in 1871 and on restoration of the church in 1893 by a 1-manual and pedal organ by Abbot & Smith, Leeds.

W STAUNTON IN THE VALE—Parish Church of St. Mary the Virgin contains barrel-organ by Forster & Andrews, erected 14 March 1852. 3 barrels each of 10 tunes in a revolving frame. Foot blown: 3 stops: no tune-list. *Vide The Organ* No. 149, July, 1958, p. 14. The organ has been restored in 1969 by Herbert Friskney, Sutton-on-Trent. An earlier barrel-organ was removed by Forster & Andrews and installed in 1854 in Hook Church, Yorks.

OXFORDSHIRE

C BLADON—Barrel-organ converted to manual. *Vide N. & Q.* (12 X 3 June 1922, p. 437.

W BRIGHTWELL BALDWIN—Barrel-organ, made by Joseph Walker, London, 1843. 5 stops: 22 notes: 3 barrels each of 10 tunes. Still used for voluntaries since restoration in 1960 by R. H. Walker & Son Ltd., Chesham, Bucks. Foot blown. Local tradition maintains that this is the Watlington Organ pre. 1877. *Vide* letter in *Sunday Times*, 13 August, 1939. Also *Ancient Monuments Socy. Trans.* 11 May, 1960, p. 118. See Plate 23.

F CHADLINGTON—

R CHURCHILL—All Saints Church has a barrel and finger organ by Bishop. A barrel discovered in 1961 has 9 tunes including one "Sarsden"—the name of the neighbouring village. This large 58-note barrel was made by J. C. Bishop for Squire Langston of Sarsden in 1859. It was made to the scale of the Churchill organ in its GG compass days, and (in 1958) was exhibited in the tower.

N DUNSDEN—Barrel-organ was in use till c. 1907 but has vanished since then.

? EWELME—A small barrel and finger organ by Wm. Hill, 1840, is in Dr. Hampden's Church." In a letter of 1840 to Dr. J. H. Gauntlett, Hill states: " One barrel supplied and more can come later." It is not known if the barrel mechanism survives. (Per Rev. B. B. Edmonds).

N EYNSHAM—Barrel-organ recalled in *N. & Q.* (12), X, 3 June 1922, p. 437. The barrel and finger organ by Elliot had toe-pedals. It was transferred c. 1924 to Cumnor, Beds., but has disappeared. (Per Rev. B. B. Edmonds).

W HAMPTON GAY—Barrel-organ by Bryceson exists in the small chapel beside a ruined Manor house in a wood in a field remote from any village. The organ has 5 stops, each having 22 pipes, and 3 barrels each of 10 tunes. Tune-list of 2 barrels in *A. M. Socy.* Trans., 11 May 1960, p. 118. Third barrel list is indecipherable. *Vide Old Church Gallery Minstrels* p. 40. A report of 1956 was that it played reasonably well and was used for the occasional services held in the chapel. See Plate 10.

M OXFORD—The Church of St. Giles is stated to have had a barrel-organ.

M SHIRBURN—

W SOUTH WESTON—A barrel-organ by John Fincham probably c. 1860 when the church was rebuilt. 2 barrels: 22 keys: separate blowing. Pine varnished Gothic case.

WARNEFORD ASYLUM Chapel—Barrel and finger organ in use till c. 1900. *Vide N. & Q.* (12), x, 3 June, p. 437.

PEMBROKESHIRE

N MILFORD HAVEN—Chapel of Ease had a barrel-organ in a gallery. *Vide* Richard Fenton's *Historical Tour Through Pembrokeshire* (London 1811) p. 188. John Rees (born 1860) as a lad, turned the handle of the organ, but a centenary account of the church contains no reference to the barrel-organ. (Per J. F. Rees, Cyncoed, Cardiff).

RADNORSHIRE

N KNIGHTON—Barrel-organ installed in 1844 replaced in 1869 by an organ of Gray & Davison, costing £250.

F LLANFIHANGEL RHYD ITHON—

RUTLAND

M BELTON—

N BURLEY-ON-THE-HILL—A barrel-organ by B. Flight & Son was in the church in 1795. *Vide History of Burley-on-the-Hill, Rutland,* by Pearl Finch (London 1901). Vol. I. p. 18.

TR	LYDDINGTON—Barrel and finger organ by Bryceson, c. 1825-30 was removed to Bede House where remnants consist of 4 barrels—3 in good condition—and a section of fascia front.
?	NORTH LUFFENHAM—
C	STOKE DRY—A converted barrel-organ by "Lincoln, London, 1810" is in the church. 7 stops and pedals. No church records refer to the barrel-organ which is said to have come from Tallington, near Stamford, Lincs., in the 1880's.
W	WARDLEY—The church of St. Botolph has a barrel-organ by T. C. Bates & Son, No. 2633: 3 stops: 3 barrels: tune-list, *Vide A. M. Socy.* Trans., 11 May 1960, p. 119. After long disuse, the barrel-organ was revived by the late Rev. Walter Noy, the Rector in 1964. It was described in *"Musical Opinion"*—(August 1928) by J. N. Phillips. The present Rector, the Rev. E. Casson is interested in having the barrel-organ thoroughly restored. See Plate 9.

SHROPSHIRE

T	BISHOPS CASTLE—Barrel-organ sold to Llanfairwaterdine Ch., Salop when a new organ was installed. (Per Rev. J. C. Williams, Withington Rectory, Hereford).
W	CARDESTON—Barrel-organ by Bates, last used c. 1879 till restored in 1935 and preserved in the church. *Vide The Old Church Gallery Minstrels* (1948), p. 42. 2 barrels each of 10 tunes. See Plate 27.
R	CLUN—A barrel from the former barrel-organ was kept in the tower c. 1948. Barrel 5′ 3″ long; 10″ diameter. 49 keys: length of key frame 5′ 9″.
S	CORELEY—Barrel-organ converted completely to a finger-organ and, in spite of considerable alterations, showing evidence of work by Snetzler (fl. 1746-1781). *Vide Country Quest*, Spring 1965, p. 21.
C	EYTON-ON-THE-WEALD-MOORS—Barrel-organ converted to manual. *Vide. Archaeol., Jl.* 1943, p. 65.
O	FITZ—Barrel-organ by Bishop in the West Gallery. Crank operates both barrel and bellows. *Vide Country Quest,* Spring 1965, pp. 20-21: *Church Times,* 25 Nov. 1966.
R	GREAT NESS—Barrel-organ by T. C. Bates, c. 1840. 5 stops: 3 barrels survive but the organ was dismantled on account of woodworm.
N	HENGOED—Barrel-organ in use c. 1880 and recalled by writer in *Musical Times* June 1, 1930, p. 544.
?	KNOCKIN—Barrel-organ existed in c. 1937.
W?	LLANFAIRWATERDINE—Barrel-organ by J. C. Bishop with barel of 10 tunes. From Bishop's Castle, Salop. Still playable in 1957. Vide Art. in *Musical Opinion* Dec. 1957.
?	OSWESTRY, ST. MARTIN'S—Barrel-organ existed in c. 1937.
T	PRESTON-ON-THE-WEALD-MOORS—Barrel-organ by J. W. Walker, 1855, now in Collection of Paul Corin, Liskeard, Cornwall.
T	TASLEY—Barrel-organ from Parish Church now in the Bishop's Palace, Hereford. 2 barrels each of 10 hymns, psalms and chants. 2 stops. Made by H. Bevington & Son. *Vide Country Quest,* Spring 1965, p. 21.
D?	WESTBURY—Barrel and finger organ by Walker 1847. Rebuilt 1927. One barrel of 12 tunes survives. This may have been a 'dumb organist'. There is no tune-list and no mention of the organ in the Parish Records. (Per Rev. P. E. Booth, Vicar of St. Martin's, Oswestry).

SOMERSET

?	ABBOTS LEIGH—Barrel and finger organ by Flight & Co.
?	AISHOLT—Barrel-organ, (recalled by C. Trelease, Sutton, Surrey).
N	ASH PRIORS—Barrel-organ still in the church in 1873. *Vide N. & Q.* Vol. 147, 1 Nov. 1924, p. 326. No information as to disposal.
?	ATHELNEY—
N	BATHEALTON—Barrel-organ "by Mr. Walker of London" installed in 1854 at a cost of £95. 36 hymns and 12 chants. *Vide N. & Q.* (12), X, 22 Apl. 1922, p. 316. Worn out in 1901 and scrapped.
T	BEDMINSTER—Barrel-organ from St. John's Church, presented to Bristol City Museum in 1950 by Mrs. Britton, Long Ashton.
R	BERROW—A barrel survives in St. Mary's Church. *Vide Country Life,* 24 June 1965.
T	BISHOP'S HULL—Barrel-organ by Bevington & Son in the Church was bought for £10 by Rev. Samuel Sheddon (1819-1891) for Kilton Church. (Per Rev. S. H. Sheddon (1856-1952), Vicar of Kilton-cum-Lilstock, son of Rev. S. Sheddon above.

PLATE 28

Photo by Dr. G. F. Wigglesworth, Howden.

Holy Trinity Church, Blacktoft, Goole, Yorkshire. Anonymous barrel-organ installed by Postill of York in 1841. 4 stops: 30 notes. Pedal bellows. One of the two barrels survives. Restored by John Budgen of Messrs. Bishop, Ipswich. The barrel-organ now stands under the organ-gallery (see separate photograph).

F   BROCKLEY—

T   BURTLE—Barrel-organ by H. Bryceson, rescued from destruction in 1950 by E. R. Mickleburgh, Bristol, and now in his collection (q.v.).

N   CHARLTON MUSGROVE—Barrel-organ in use in living memory, converted to keyboard. *Vide N. & Q.* (12), X, 1922 p. 316 and Vol. 147 1 Nov. 1924, p. 326.

MF   CHEW STOKE—

C   CHURCH STANTON—Barrel-organ in use in living memory, converted to keyboard. *Vide N. & Q.* (12), X, 1922, p. 316 and Vol. 147, 1 Nov. 1924, p. 326.

C   CLOSWORTH—Barrel-organ, no name: 20 notes: 2 ranks of pipes: 2 barrels, h. 6' 6", w. 3', d. 1' 10". Restoration under consideration.

?   CORFE—Barrel-organ in list of John Watlen pasted inside one of his organs.

?   EAST CHINNOCK—Barrel-organ by Bates. (Per Rev. B. B. Edmonds).

?   EDINGTON—Barrel and finger organ by H. Bryceson. 4 barrels and tune-list: G compass with mahogany case. (Per Rev. B. B. Edmonds).

F   FROME—

F   GLASTONBURY—

N   HEATHFIELD—Barrel-organ was still in the church in 1873. *Vide N. & Q.* Vol. 147, 1 Nov. 1924, p. 326.

W   ISLE ABBOTS—Barrel-organ by H. Bryceson, 4 stops: 4 barrels each of 10 tunes: 27 notes. *Vide N. & Q.* (12), X, 22 Apl. 1922, p. 316 and Vol. 147, 1 Nov. 1924, p. 326.

O   KILTON—Barrel-organ by Bevington & Son; 7 stops: 3 barrels each of 12 tunes: out of order and very neglected since 1925. Brought from Bishop's Hull, *supra.* Tune-list, *Vide A. M. Socy.* Trans., 11 May 1960, p. 119.

N   KINGS BROMPTON—In 1770 a gallery for the Psalm-singers was erected at the West end of the church. In 1846 the Vicar, Rev. R. Beague presented a barrel-organ and the Rev. Hartwell Horne's *Manual of Psalms & Hymns* was introduced. In 1853, the old gallery was removed during restorations and alterations. In 1870 the barrel-organ was removed and a harmonium took its place. (Extracted from Parish Magazine 1928).

N   MISTERTON—Barrel-organ. *Vide N. & Q.* (12), X, 22 April 1922, p. 316. The organ and the church were destroyed by fire c. 1900.

W   MUCHELNEY—Barrel-organ by Gray & Davison presented 1848. Separate blowing pedal: 4 stops: 3 barrels each of 10 tunes. For list, *Vide A. M. Socy.* Trans., 11 May 1960, p. 120. Replaced by a hired harmonium, July 1872, and later by a pipe organ, but the barrel-organ was used at Harvest Festival in 1954 to accompany singing of the first hymn at Evensong. The instrument stands on a platform in a recess in the south wall. *Vide The Antiquary* xliii (1907) p. 248 and *N. & Q.* (12), X, (1922), p. 316. See Plate 30. According to Gray & Davison's shop-book, the makers were Wedlake & Skeat. Wedlake (q.v.) was an apprentice of the firm.

F   NORTON MALREWARD—

N   PRISTON—Barrel-organ in use till 1879. *Vide N. & Q.* Vol. 147, 1 Nov. 1924, p. 326.

N   STAPLEYMORE—Barrel-organ in use till 1846. *Vide N. & Q.* (12), X, (1922), p. 316 & Vol. 147, 1 Nov. 1924, p. 326.

T   STAWLEY—Barrel-organ dated 1820: maker unknown: 4 stops: 3 barrels in a rotating frame. *Vide N. & Q.* (12), X, 22 Apl. 1922, p. 316. Presented to the Bristol Museum by Rev. W. R. Ford in 1938. No tune-list. An amusing account of a Harvest Festival Service at Evensong in the Autumn of 1908 is given in "*Somerset County Herald*" of 10 Oct. 1908. At Stawley the service was taken by two eccentric brothers, both parsons and both enthusiastic hunting men—Rev. J. P. Hayne (Vicar), assisted by his brother Rev. E. R. Hayne.

R   STOKE ST. GREGORY—Barrel-organ from the church was in the schoolroom in 1920. *Vide N. & Q.* (12), X, (1922), p. 316 and Vol. 147, 1 Nov. 1924, p. 326. Two barrels survive, each in a box, in the vicarage stable-loft. (Per F. L. Balmforth).

N   WEST BRADLEY—Barrel-organ in use till 1866. *Vide N. & Q.* Vol. 147, 1 Nov. 1924, p. 326.

STAFFORDSHIRE

T   ALDRIDGE—Barrel-organ by Henry J. Prosser of Roade, Somerset. (Founded 1868). In use till recently. Now in the collection of the late Canon Noel Boston. *Vide Archaeol. Jl.*, (1943) p. 66 with illustrations, Plate iii, figs. A. and B. Also *Music Libraries and Instruments*, paper No. 32, Plate 55. An earlier barrel-organ by John Watlen is included in a list of his c. 1807, pasted in his organ in Aldro School Chapel, Shackleford, Surrey.

F	ELFORD—
F	LICHFIELD—St. Mary's Church—
R	LONGNOR—Barrel and finger organ by Forster & Andrews, Hull, 27 May, 1852. 8 stops. 1 barrel x 10 tunes. Cost £106. Only a barrel remains in the porch. *Vide The Organ,* No. 149, July 1958, p. 14.
F	NEWCASTLE-under-LYME—

SUFFOLK

N	AMPTON—Barrel-organ in use till c. 1870. The present organ is by John Lewis, 1889.
N	BUXHALL—Barrel-organ converted to manual dismantled and sold in 1944. *Vide* Art. on Shelland Chapel in *Mus. Times,* 1 May 1930, pp. 460-461. Noel Mander removed a purely pipe organ c. 1956 and installed another.
N	DALHAM—Barrel-organ in very poor state. Reduced to manual. No maker's name and no mechanism left. *Vide The Organ,* April 1927.
N	DENHAM—Barrel-organ replaced by a small organ by "F. Norman, Organ Builder, Diss", undated. This Norman later associated with Norman & Beard at Norwich. (Per R. MacKinnon, organist of Hoxne Ch.)
FR	GREAT GLEMHAM—Finger organ by Flight restored by Bishop & Son in 1968 but barrel mechanism absent: 5 stops: whole woodwork of mahogany.
T	GREAT WALDINGFIELD—Barrel and finger organ by J. W. Walker & Sons, 1855, was transferred to Sutton, Northants, as a gift from the Vicar of Sutton in 1888. 1 barrel of 10 tunes.
N	HARTEST—Barrel-organ by Flight & Son. 30 tunes and list. Sold in 1923. Untraced.
R	HENLEY—Barrel-organ in use till 1848-1863. 2 barrels each of 10 tunes: 4 stops: no tune-list. Now only the case remains. *Vide East Anglia Daily Times,* Miscellany Column, items 4949, 4972, 4992, 5002, 5087, 5287.
N	HERSHAM, Holy Trinity—Barrel-organ by Flight & Son 1845, in use till 1867.
CN	HOXNE—Barrel-organ presented by General Sir Edward Kerrison, Bart., K.C.B., in 1836. No maker's name. Converted to single manual in 1867 by J. W. Walker and rebuilt again by them in 1906. The electric blower was the gift of Noel Mander. (Per Roy Mackinnon.)
N	KNODISHALL—Barrel-organ in the church in 1884. *Vide Studies in Worship Music* (2nd Edition 1888), p. 184, by J. S. Curwen, F.R.A.M. Replaced by a Binn's organ of Edwardian period.
?	LITTLE CORNARD—
N	MONKS ELEIGH—Barrel-organ presented in 1852 and replaced by present organ in 1879. *Vide Notes on the History of Monks Eleigh* by the late Rev. —. Northcote, Rector.
N	NEEDHAM MARKET—Barrel-organ in use in church recalled by old inhabitants in 1925. A serpent in use before the organ, is still in private ownership in the town.
C	POSLINGFORD—Barrel-organ converted to manual but without supplying the missing notes! (Per Rev. B. B. Edmonds).
W	SHELLAND—Church of King Charles the Martyr dating from 1767 has the only barrel-organ known to be in regular weekly use in England. By Bryceson Bros., c. 1810. 3 barrels each of 12 tunes. Tune list in *A. M. Socy.* Trans. 11 May 1960, p. 120. Overhauled in 1956 by Noel Mander. 6 stops of 31 notes: Broadcast on BBC Third Programme 28 Dec. 1957. *Vide* art., by the late S. Godman in *East Anglian Magazine* June 1959; also *Musical Times* June 1959, pp. 348-349: also *Romance of Old Village Choirs* by the Rev. C. Morrell, p. 16. Plates 11 & 12. *Vide* Tune-list in Appendix I.
R	SOUTH ELMHAM—St. Margaret. Barrel-organ relics according to Arthur Mee.
W	WISSINGTON (WISTON) — Fine large barrel-organ by John Gray (No. 32). Acquired by subscription in 1839. 4 stops: 27 keys: hand blown: In playing order. 3 barrels each of 10 tunes. Plate 4. *Vide* Tune-list in Appendix I.
N	YOXFORD—"A barrel-organ of good tone, playing both tunes and chants, was in use up to 1868." *Vide Studies in Worship Music* (2nd Edition 1888), p. 184, footnote, by J. S. Curwen: also *Suffolk Archaeol. Socy. Proc.* (Per J .Budgen.)

SURREY

F	ALDBURY—
F	ASHSTEAD—
F	BAGSHOT—
N	BEDINGTON—Barrel-organ included in John Watlen's list pasted inside one of his organs.

N   CHALDON—Use of a barrel-organ recalled by a local inhabitant in 1962. *Vide History of Caterham and District* (1963).

F   ESHER—

TDR   GREAT BOOKHAM—Barrel-organ? Brass barrel with 6 tunes: J. W. Walker Ltd. have a 'dumb organist' said to be from Gt. Bookham.

N   HERSHAM—Barrel-organ by Flight & Son, 1845, in use till 1867 in Holy Trinity Church. 3 barrels x 10 tunes. Cost £60. Church demolished in 1887.

R   MORDEN Remnants of a barrel-organ in a box in the tower.

N   PETERSHAM—St. Peter's Church has a Minstrels' Gallery. Had a barrel-organ 1838-53, with 30 tunes later increased to 40. This church is included in list of church organs supplied by Bryceson (1864).

N   SANDERSTEAD—Wilsdon Church—Barrel-organ is included by John Watlen in a list pasted inside one of his organs.

R   SHERE—Barrel of organ remains.

F   STREATHAM—

SUSSEX

The list for this country is exceptionally complete as the late Canon MacDermott of Selsey and latterly of Buxted, made a special study which he embodied in his two delightful little books, *Sussex Church Music in the Past* (Chichester, 2nd Ed. 1923) and *The Old Church Gallery Minstrels* (London, 1948).

M   ALBOURNE—

M   ANGMERING—Barrel-organ installed in 1852.

M   BERSTED—

M   BERWICK—Clockwork barrel-organ. Apocryphal anecdote *re* same: *Vide Sussex Ch. Music*, p. 52.

O   BEXHILL—St. Peter's Ch. has a small chamber barrel-organ in use before the first manual organ was installed in 1881. 4 stops: 17 keys: 4 barrels each of 8 tunes but only 1 barrel remains. Not in working order. *Vide Sussex County Magazine*, Vol. 29, No. 1, Jan. 1955.

M   BISHOPSTONE

M   BOXGROVE—

MW   BRIGHTLING—Church of St. Thomas à Becket has the distinction of possessing in the West Gallery the only Sussex church barrel-organ in perfect working order. Presented by the eccentric John Fuller, M.P., (1757-1834) it bears in pencil the name of "W. A. A. Nicholls, son-in-law and successor to the late Mr. G. P. England, No. 9 Stephen Street, Tottenham Ct. Rd." It was used to play Voluntaries before and after morning and evening services until the death in 1934 of the old man who had played it for 40 years. Very well restored in 1964 by Harrison & Harrison, it is used occasionally, but always at Harvest Festival when the Rector, the Rev. Eric Knowles gives a short talk and recital. 7 stops: 2 barrels each of 12 tunes; 43 notes. Foot blower. *Vide Country Life*, 15 Aug. 1903, p. 192: *Sussex County Magazine*, Vol. 29. No. 1, Jan. 1955: See Plate 5. *The Organ, April* 1927.

F   BRIGHTON—Faithful's Chapel.

F   St. Mary's.

F   St. Margaret's.

M   BUXTED—

M   CHIDDINGLY—

M   CROWHURST—

M   EASTBOURNE—

M   EASTERGATE—

M   FALMER—

M   FERNHURST—

M   FERRING EAST—Barrel-organ installed c. 1870.

M   FIRLE—

M   FITTLEWORTH—

M   FUNTINGDON—In Bryceson's list of c. 1854.

F   GRINSTEAD EAST—

M   GRINSTEAD, WEST—

M   GUESTLING—

M   HARTFIELD—The remains of a barrel-organ said to be by Bryceson and to have been installed in 1726 were in the belfry, but this must be an error for 1796. Other opinion is that the remains are of the old church clock! In any event, as the metal was sent to a munitions factory in 1939-45, the true facts may never be known. *Vide Sussex Ch. Music*, p. 52. *Sussex County Magazine*, Vol. 29, No. 1, Jan. 1955.

MR   HARTING—Only the case of a spare barrel survives.

M   HENFIELD—

F   HORSHAM—

R   HORSTED KEYNES—Some of the " mellow pipes " of the barrel-organ were incorporated in the new organ in 1904.

M   IFIELD—

M   JEVINGTON—Barrel-organ installed c. 1830. Anecdote recorded in *Sussex Church Music*, p. 53 and *Old Church Gallery Minstrels*, p. 41. Also in *The Choir*, May 1958.

N   LAUGHTON—An inventory of 1873 described the barrel-organ as dilapidated. A new organ was installed in 1883. (Per the late S. Godman).

M   LEWIS, SOUTHOVER—

M   NORTH CHAPEL—

M   OVING—

M   PAGHAM—

M   PARHAM—Chamber barrel-organ by Walker, formerly in the church now stands in the Long Gallery of Parham House. 3 barrels each of 10 secular tunes and 1 barrel of hymns, psalms, etc.: 4 stops: 24 notes. Restored in 1931, but unused and now in very poor condition. *Vide Sussex Church Music*, p. 52 and *Sussex County Magazine*, Vol. 29, No. 1, Jan. 1955. The barrel-organ was in the church till c. 1870 when a harmonium was installed and the organ removed.

MO   PIDDINGHOE—Barrel-organ in bad condition: 3 stops: 2 barrels each of 10 tunes: 28 notes. Restored in 1790, the organ has now no casing and pipes are missing but the barrels remain. *Vide Sussex Church Music*, p. 51 and *Sussex County Magazine*, Vol. 29, No. 1, Jan. 1955 with illustration.

F   PORTSLADE—

M   PULBOROUGH—

NM   ROGATE—George Marshall of Rogate played in the church for sixty-five years— flute, barrel-organ, harmonium and finally a pipe organ and retired when nearly eighty years old. *Vide Sussex Church Music*, p. 13. Some remnants of the barrel-organ said to survive in the village are no longer known.

M   ROTHERFIELD—

NM   RYE—Barrel-organ installed in 1811 but by 1870 had long since vanished.

M   SALEHURST—Barrel-organ installed in 1836.

N   SEDLESCOMBE—Church records include a photograph taken between 1866 and 1868 when the West Gallery was removed. It shows a barrel-organ resembling that at Brightling. (*Vide supra*.) There is no record of what became of it. *Vide Sussex County Magazine*, March 1955, p. 150.

M   SENNICOTTS—

M   SHIPLEY—

M   SINGLETON—Barrel-organ in Bryceson's list of churches (c. 1864). *Vide Sussex Church Music*, pp. 50-51. The organ was converted to manual c. 1870 but was playable only in D.A. and E.

NM   STANMER—Barrel and finger organ now vanished. Anecdote *vide Sussex Church Music*, p. 53. Wm. Pilcher, Junior, is recorded as having put a barrel in the organ (Per Rev. B. B. Edmonds). Two barrels survive in the belfry. (Per A. V. Sheppard).

NM   STEYNING—Barrel and finger organ was converted to manual in 1853 but the barrels were left inside the case till 1894 when the present 3-manual organ replaced it.

M   STOPHAM—

N   STORRINGTON—Barrel-organ is listed by John Watlen c. 1807 in a list pasted in his organ in Aldro School Chapel, Shackleford, Surrey.

M   TANGMERE—

M   THAKEHAM—

N   TWINEHAM—Barrel-organ out of use till 1904 when church was restored. No trace.

O   UDIMORE—Barrel-organ, formerly in the church, was removed in 1897 and later found in an oast-house. The organ case and a barrel were seen in the church in 1951, and thereafter were transferred to Winchelsea Museum. 4 stops: 29 keys: 4 barrels each of 12 tunes. Not in working order. *Vide The Times*, 28 March, 1938: *Sussex County Magazine*, Vol. 29, No. 1, January 1955, with illustration.

M   WADHURST—

M   WANNOCK—Clockwork barrel-organ. Anecdote *Vide Sussex Church Music*, p. 53.

MN	WARBLETON—Barrel-organ in use till c. 1880, then stored in an oast-house at Markly. 4 barrels: 4 stops. *Vide Sussex Church Music*, p. 52. The oast-house and contents were destroyed by a flying bomb during 1939-45. *Vide Sussex County Magazine* Vol. 29, No. 1, Jan. 1955.
M	WILLINGDON—
M	WINCHELSEA—

WARWICKSHIRE

F	ATHERSTONE—
?	BIDFORD-ON-AVON—Wesleyan Chapel had a barrel-organ converted to manual. *Vide Musical Boxes* by the late J. Clark, p. 163.
W	COMPTON WYNYATES—Barrel-organ by H. Bryceson in working order. 4 stops: 2 barrels of 11 tunes: tune-list pasted on organ case: 24 notes: bellows worked by two cranks on the handle shaft. See Plate 31.
?	FELDON—Two derelict barrel-organs are said to survive.
?	FRANKTON—
F	GRENDON—
?	HAMPTON-IN-ARDEN—A barrel-organ was presented in 1839. *Vide Hampton-in-Arden* by J. C. Adams, (1951).
O	HILLMORTON—Barrel and finger organ by J. C. Bishop, c. 1825. 8 stops: 58 notes: 1 barrel of 10 tunes (disconnected). (Per K. G. Parrott).
O	IDLICOTE—Barrel-organ in very dilapidated state. Maker unknown. 1 barrel and no tune-list. Restoration under consideration.
F	KINGS BROMLEY—
T	KINETON—Barrel-organ was removed and parts installed in Kineton Wesleyan Methodist Chapel.
R	LILBOURNE—Barrel and finger organ by H. Bryceson, 1855. Tune-list barely legible. 4 stops. Now finger organ only. Barrel mechanism removed. (Per K. G. Parrott).
R	LONG COMPTON—Remnants of barrel-organ described in *Musical News* of 17 July 1920.
N	OLD BILTON—Barrel-organ till c. 1883 at least, when removed to Wednesbury, locality not known, except for wings of the case which remain at Old Bilton. Designed by Rev. F. H. Sutton, author of "*Church Organs*," member of the Camden Socy., and authority on cases. (Per Rev. B. B. Edmonds).
N	RADFORD SEMELE—Barrel-organ with 12 tunes, recalled in *Quaint Tales of Old Warwickshire* (1923). Reputed to be the organ now in the County Museum, Warwick (by Broderip & Wilkinson).
F	TILDERSLEY—
F	WARWICK—
?	WEETHLEY—Barrel-organ converted to manual according to the late J. Clark, *Musical Boxes*, p. 163.
F	YARDLEY—

WILTSHIRE

C	ENFORD—Barrel-organ by J. S. Eagle of Hackney in 1846. Converted to manual. (Per Rev. N. A. H. Lawrance, M.A., Vicar).
N	GREAT DUNFORD—Barrel-organ stated in 1949 to be stored in church tower for disposal.
W	LIDDINGTON—Barrel-organ by Bates, No. 2189. 2 barrels each of 15 tunes. 10 frontal pipes: 5 stops. Restored by F. F. Hill in 1967.
R	PURTON—Barrel only survives in church.
O	ROWDE METHODIST CHAPEL—Barrel-organ by Bryceson. 3 barrels each of 11 tunes. *Vide Oxford Companion to Music* by P. Scholes, *s.v.* Mechanical Music
F	SEDGEHILL—
F	STEEPLE ASHTON—

WORCESTERSHIRE

T	ALVECHURCH—Church of St. Laurence had a Bates barrel-organ: 1 barrel of 10 tunes: 19 keys: 3 stops. Now in the Birmingham Museum of Science and Industry. (*Ex Liddell Collection*).
?	BOBBINGTON—
F	DROITWICH—
N	HAGLEY—Barrel-organ of Hill & Davison, 1838 with 2 barrels each of 12 tunes, replaced in 1852 by manual organ.

PLATE 29

Photos: B.B.C. copyright.

Sutton (Beds.) barrel-organ recently restored and rededicated on 14th Jan. 1967.
Maker: T. C. Bates & Sons, London. No. 2917. 5 stops. 3 barrels of 10 tunes each.

?	KEMPSEY—Barrel-organ included by John Watlen in list pasted on his barrel-organ in Aldro School Chapel, Shackleford, Surrey.
C	LINDRIDGE—Barrel-organ installed in 1858 was converted to manual in 1874. (Per Rev. B. B. Edmonds).
N	SOUTH LITTLETON—Barrel-organ sold c. 1903. *Vide "Old Days"*, No. 513, 1 Aug. 1931 in *Evesham Journal*.
?	STRENSHAM—John Noake, the Worcestershire historian found in use, about 1848, at Strensham Church, near Pershore "one of the very few good grinding organs."
R	WELLAND—In the church, built in 1877 to replace an older one, the case and a pipe of a T. C. Bates barrel-organ from the old church were seen in 1941. (Per Rev. B. B. Edmonds).

YORKSHIRE

?	ALDBOROUGH—Barrel-organ by Forster & Andrews in 1846: 3 barrels.
?	ARDINGFLEET—Barrel and finger organ by Forster & Andrews in 1857: 1 barrel.
?	ATWICK—Barrel-organ by Forster & Andrews in 1856: 3 barrels.
W	BLACKTOFT—Barrel-organ c. 1850. No maker's name. Installed in gallery of Holy Trinity Church by Postill of York after rebuilding of the church in 1841. 4 stops: 40 notes: pedal bellows: one of two barrels survives with 10 tunes on each. Restored by John Budgen of Messrs. Bishop, Ipswich. See Plate 28.
?	BRANDSBURTON—Barrel and finger organ by Forster & Andrews in 1857: 1 barrel.
N	BURSTWICK—In 1852 a second-hand barrel-organ from Everton, Yorkr.? was installed by Forster & Andrews.
N	CRAYKE—Barrel-organ anecdote by Rev. Dr. Inge *re* incident in the time of his grandfather when Rector. *Vide York Guide*, p. 14.
?	DENT—Barrel and finger organ by Forster & Andrews in 1854: 2 barrels.
O	FARNHAM—Barrel-organ presented by Rev. Thomas Collins, curate, Oct. 1831. Made by Elliott & Hill, London and dated 1831. 3 stops. Quite unplayable through neglect. Pipes in disorder and keys rusted. *Vide N. & Q.* (12), 22 Apl. 1922, p. 316: *"Records of the Parish of Farnham"* by the Rev. A. T. Waterer, p. 80 and *Country Life*, 16 Sept. 1965.
R	FYLINGDALES—Old church contained 2 barrels in a show case. The church has also a 3-tier pulpit and box pews..
T	GARTON-IN-HOLDERNESS—Barrel-organ by Bryceson. 4 barrels of sacred tunes. Now in York Castle Museum.
F	GATESFORTH—
D	HATFIELD—'Dumb Organist' added in 1849 by Forster & Andrews. 2 barrels to suit their finger organ installed in 1849.
R	HOLME-ON-SPALDING-MOOR—Barrel and finger organ: 3 barrels in the vestry. Organ dismantled and a 2-manual organ installed after 1953.
?	HOOK—Barrel-organ, maker unknown, removed from Staunton, Notts., in 1854 and installed, with 1 barrel in addition to the existing 2, by Forster & Andrews.
F	HORNBY—
F	HUDDERSFIELD—Trinity Church.
?	HUNMANBY—Barrel and finger organ by Forster & Andrews in 1846: 3 barrels.
?	LASTINGHAM—Barrel and finger organ by Forster & Andrews in 1857: 1 barrel.
F	LEEDS—
N	MARSKE—Barrel-organ recalled by Canon N. A. Vesey, son of a former Rector of the Parish. His mother 'played' the organ and he as a boy c. 1905 often worked the bellows.
N	NORTHALLERTON—Barrel-organ by Bishop installed 29 Sept. 1819. *Vide Grove's Dictionary of Music* (5th Edit.) *s.v.* Mechanical Appliances.
?	OUSEBRIDGE—St. John's Church. "Between 1847 and 1850 there was a barrel-organ which was limited to 5 or 6 tunes (*sic*) but could be adjusted to long or short metre." *Vide* John Ward Knowles MS. *Notes on the Organs . . . of York Churches since the Reformation.* (In York City Library).
?	RIMSWELL—Barrel-organ from Ramsey (Essex?) "put in order" in Rimswell Chapel in 1852 by Forster & Andrews.
F	ROUNDHAY—
?	RUDSTON—Barrel and finger organ by Robson: 5 barrels: transferred in 1850 by Forster & Andrews from Lydlinch, Dorset, to Rudston.
F	SKIPTON—
C	STOCKSBRIDGE WESLEYAN CHAPEL—Barrel-organ formerly in Trinity Church, Louth, Lincs., was rebuilt as a 8 stop, 1 manual and pedal organ for this chapel in 1870 by Forster & Andrews.

PLATE 30

Photo by courtesy of The Rev. E. W. Plowright.

Muchelney Church, Somerset.   Barrel-organ by Gray & Davison,
London, c. 1838.   3 barrels each of 10 tunes.   4 stops.
Separate blowing pedal.

F   STOKESLEY—

R   SYKEHOUSE—Remains of a barrel-organ exist. (Per Rev. B. B. Edmonds).

?   THIRKLEBY—" In 1852 Joseph Bell made a barrel (and finger) organ for Thirkleby Church, the gift of Lady Frankland Russell. It had 3 barrels and played 10 tunes, (presumably each barrel), and could be used as a finger organ also." *Vide* John Ward Knowles MS. *Notes on the Organs . . . in York churches since the Reformation.* (In York City library).

Note: Joseph Bell commenced business in 1847 having been apprenticed to Postill. He died in 1898, aged 75.

?   THORNE—Barrel-organ anecdote in *York Castle Museum Guide,* p. 14.

?   YORK—St. Michael le Belfrey Church—" In 1782 a barrel-organ was placed in the church by Mr. Haxby, musical instrument maker of Blake Street. It contained 2 cylinders and played 24 tunes. The price was 40 guineas." *Vide MS Notes on the organs . . . in York churches . . . by J. W. Knowles.* (In York City Library).

PLATE 31

Compton Wyngates Church, Warwickshire. Barrel-organ by H. Bryceson, London. 4 stops:
2 barrels each of 11 tunes. In working order.

CHAPTER VII

BARREL-ORGANS IN PUBLIC OR PRIVATE COLLECTIONS

Chamber barrel-organs are those designed for use in the home. They were made in large numbers from the close of the 18th century. Usually equipped with stops for drum and triangle, they had barrels pinned with the secular tunes of the time. The tune-list in chapter IV includes a wide variety of folk-music, songs, dances and almost invariably the National Anthem. Numbers of these chamber barrel-organs have been preserved in country houses, where, in the early part of the 19th century, a servant would change the barrels and play to the company assembled after dinner. Fortunately, some of these chamber barrel-organs have survived the ravages of wood-worm to which barrels seem to have been particularly susceptible. The cases of Gothic design or Sheraton are often very beautiful as will be seen in the illustrations in the present work.

It also happens sometimes that these organs reached public and private collections where they have been preserved though seldom in playing condition. The recent revival of interest in musical automata has given rise to *The Musical Box Society (International)* in U.S.A. with over 400 members and the *Musical Box Society of Great Britain* with over 250 members. These societies include in their membership collectors of a wide variety of automata and where barrel-organs are concerned, the owner's name appears below.

In a few cases, church barrel-organs have been presented to or acquired by Museums. This is noted under the list of churches by counties in chapter VI and again with fuller details under the particular Museum in the following list with a cross-reference under the name of the maker (where known), in chapter V.

The author will welcome information regarding any additions or corrections to the list.

ENGLAND, SCOTLAND & WALES

ALDRO SCHOOL CHAPEL, Shackleford, Surrey: Barrel-organ by J. Walten. See Plate 6.

ALLT, The late Dr. W. Greenhouse: London—small barrel-organ by Joseph Eveleigh, London.

ANGRAVE, Bruce: London, W.5.—Imhof & Mukle German clock-work barrel-organ. 9 barrels. Also chamber barrel-organ by Clementi.

ASHTON, T. H.: Oxford—B. Dobson, dated 1799, 4 stops, 22 keys, 5 barrels each of 10 sacred tunes.

BAINES, R.: London, W.4.—Small collection of reed organs and early cylinder piano bq Joseph Hicks (1846) etc.

BALKIN, Isaac: Bettwys-y-coed. Lincoln, 3 stops plus drum and triangle. Restored by F. F. Hill.

BARCLAY, V.: London, S.W.1—Fentum.

BARNSLEY, Yorks.: At Cannon Hall, barrel-organ, 40 pipes, 6 barrels. The organ bears inscriptions showing that it belonged to Verdi.

BARRACK, J. G.: Aberdeen. Imhof & Mukle Orchestrion No. 2413, weight-driven: 18 secular barrels: 74 keys. From Udny Castle. In excellent condition.

BATEMAN, Col. Hanbury: Barrel-organ, four stops.

BEDSTONE SCHOOL, Salop: Orchestrion.

BENTLEY, J.: Waltham Abbey. Gavioli et Cie., incomplete. Said to have come from Cheshunt Church, Hants., but the 5 barrels each of 10 tunes are all secular.

BETHNAL GREEN MUSEUM: John Pistor, 4 stops, 4 barrels playing 33 listed tunes. One barrel is labelled "Richard Mackilwain ... 21 Swan St., Minories, Successor to Mr. Pistor."

BIRKS, C. J.: Gerrard's Cross. 'Sacred' barrel-organ by Theodore Bates No. 1741 acquired from St. Luke's Hospital, Jordans, Beaconsfield in 1907. 3 barrels.

BIRMINGHAM CITY MUSEUM: An important collection including the former Mitchell and Liddell Collections. Theodore Bates, G. Astor & Co., Broderip & Wilkinson, Wornum (1810), and several small barrel-organs. From Liddell Collection: Bates, (said to have come from Alvechurch, Worcs.): & M. Clementi.

BIRMINGHAM MUSEUM OF SCIENCE AND INDUSTRY: Street barrel-organ by J. Thibouville-Lamy, Paris. 3 stops: 1 barrel of 10 tunes. Table barrel-organs by A. Violet, London & Forman, London.

BIRMINGHAM MIDLAND INSTITUTE: T. C. Bates & Son: 2 stops. In working order.

BOGGIS, W. & A.: Diss. Flight & Son, 3 stops: 4 barrels each of 10 tunes. From the local Unitarian Chapel.

BOLTON: Hall i' the Wood Museum: 'The Manor Organ' out of order. 6 stops with drum and triangle. From Great Brockhill Manor, Northants.

BOSTON, J. L. & R. T.: Bebington, Cheshire. Bevington, 2 sacred and 2 secular barrels. Gerock, 5 barrels, secular except for part of one.

BOSTON, The Late Canon Noel, Lamas Manor, Norwich: T. C. Bates church instrument on loan to All Hallows Church, London Wall. Anonymous *ex* Attleborough Church: 2 stops: 1 barrel of 10 sacred tunes. Plate 25. Chamber instrument by George Astor, 4 stops and drum and triangle. 4 barrels. Miniature instrument by Geo. Godfrey. Plate 15. 8 secular tunes. Church instrument by H. J. Prosser (*ex* Aldridge Church, Staffs.).

BOWES MUSEUM, Barnard Castle: Longman & Broderip, 4 stops: 15 keys: 3 barrels, one labelled " John Kelly . . . late Flight & Kelly."

BRACKENBURY, C. H.: Tweedhill: Bevington. 3 stops: 3 barrels x 10 tunes. Another anonymous. 1 barrel x 8 secular tunes.

BRADFORD, BOLLING HALL MUSEUM: H. C. Lincoln (*ex* Newburgh Priory) 4 stops: 3 (of 4) barrels. Plate 19.

BRISTOL CITY MUSEUM: Anonymous Church Barrel-organ dated 1820 (*ex* Stawley Church, Somerset).
Barrel-organ (*ex* St. John's Church, Bedminster).

BRITISH PIANO MUSEUM: Brentford. Orchestrion (from Imhof's, London).

BROCKLEBANK, Mrs.: Stoke-by-Nayland, Suffolk (postally: Colchester, Essex). Astor & Co.: 5 stops including drum and triangle. 3 barrels each of 10 tunes.

BURKART, A. J.: London. Clementi.

BURGHLEY HOUSE CHAPEL: Lincs. B. Flight & Son: 2 barrels: 3 stops: in good order.

BURNETT, Dr. R.: Birkenhead.

BURTON-ON-TRENT MUSEUM: Barrel-organ from Bretby Hall, thought to have been previously the first organ to be installed in Repton Church. Used at Bretby when Benjamin Disraeli was a frequent visitor to the Hall. 4 stops: 3 barrels each of 10 tunes.

CAMBRIDGE FOLK MUSEUM: Anonymous Barrel-organ (*ex* Landbeach Church) was 23 years in a shed at Cottenham prior to being restored and brought to the Museum to illustrate a lecture by Canon Galpin in 1931. In 1938 stored in a derelict attic and in 1961 so damaged as to be beyond repair.

CAMBRIDGE: SCOTT POLAR RESEARCH INSTITUTE: John Longman, 4 barrels each of 8 tunes—8 sacred and 24 secular. 7 stops. No longer in playing condition. See Plates 20 & 21.

CAMBRIDGE: University Music School: Preston, 4 stops plus drum and triangle: 3 of 4 barrels survive. Also small barrel-organ, anonymous: 1 barrel minus its tune-list. (Presented by the Exors. of the late Dr. J. Bryan, Elsworth).

CAMPBELL, Mrs. J. L.: Isle of Canna. John Maule, Edinburgh: 3 stops: 3 barrels each of 10 reels and songs. In very good condition.

CAMPBELL-VOULLAIRE, P. M.: London, S.E 21. Buckwell, c. 1827: 3 stops plus triangle: tune-list for 4 barrels of which Nos. 2 and 3 survive.

CARISBROOKE CASTLE MUSEUM: Isle of Wight. Anonymous small barrel-organ acquired from Fritz Spiegl. 1 barrel but no tune list. Formerly used in the private chapel of Nunwell Manor, Brading, Isle of Wight. (Per Dr. J. Bruce Williamson).

CHELMSFORD, ESSEX MUSEUM: Meyer & Co., Date c. 1800. (*ex* Thaxted Church): 6 stops: 4 barrels including 1 of sacred tunes. Repaired in 1967 by J. Budgen of Messrs. Bishop, Ipswich.

CHIDDINGSTONE CASTLE, Kent: (D. E. Bower): ' Johannes Lincoln, Londini, fecit.' 4 stops plus drum and triangle: 15 keys: 3 barrels (originally 4). John Longman: 4 stops plus drum and triangle: 16 keys: Patent tune indicator: 1 barrel (3 lost). A label on left door reads: " No. 230. When a new barrel is wanted please send the above number."

CHRISTIE, A.: Great Bardfield, Essex. Clementi: 4 stops plus drum and triangle: 4 barrels each of 10 tunes.

CHRIST'S HOSPITAL, nr. HORSHAM: Flight & Robson in Music School. Only barrel No 3 of original 5 survives. Organ now reduced to manual but barrel mechanism is present. Also small chamber barrel-organ by C. Gerock.

CLAYTON, The Rev. A. E.: London, S.W.17. Clementi & Coy., London, 4 stops plus drum and triangle: Longman, London, 4 stops. Remnants of a dumb organist.

COATES, Sir Peter: Paisley. Barrel and finger organ built by Forster & Andrews in 1858. 2 barrels. Subsequent history unknown.

COE, N.: Felixstowe. Longman & Broderip. 4 stops: 3 barrels each of 10 tunes.

COLCHESTER CASTLE MUSEUM: Bryceson, 5 stops: 3 barrels each of 10 tunes. In bad condition. (*Ex* Colchester Workhouse Chapel). Imhof & Co. 1 barrel, no tune list. Anon.: 2 barrels each of 10 tunes. Tune list for 4 barrels.

COLLINS, D. N., London, W.11. Secular barrel-organ by Flight & Robson: 4 stops plus drum and triangle: 3 barrels.

COLT, C. F.: Bethersden, Kent. Fentum dated 1815: 3 stops and triangle: 3 (of 5) barrels. *Vide Country Life* 17 March 1950. Also a fair-organ marked Holland, Sutton-on-Trent, (A showman): 16 barrels.

COOK, Geoffrey, Godalming: Flight & Robson, 4 stops: 3 barrels each of 9 tunes.

CORBETT, R. C. V.: Winchester. John Longman, No. 232. Purchased at Sotheby's in 1960 for £34. 6 stops, including drum and triangle. 3 barrels.

CORIN, Paul: Liskeard. Barrel and finger organ by J. W. Walker, London 1855. 7 stops: 3 barrels x 10 hymns etc. Built for Preston Hospital, Wellington, Salop, for £150. Restored in 1968 by Hele & Co. Ltd., Plymouth. *Vide* Descriptive brochure of the Corin Collection.

CULZEAN CASTLE, Ayrshire. Broderip & Wilkinson: 8 stops: 4 barrels each of 8 secular tunes, dances, etc. Out of order. Owned by the National Trust.

DAUNTSEY'S SCHOOL, nr. Devizes. J. Davis, London, dated 1813. Barrel and finger organ (2 manuals). Bought at the Great Exhib. 1851 for Farleigh Castle. Removed *c.* 1860 to Blount's Court. In 1957 the then owner, Mr. J. Sword, presented it to the chapel of Dauntsey's School. Repaired by Percy Daniel, Clevedon, Somerset. *Vide Musical Times* Sept. 1968, pp. 846-848.

DAWBER, W.: Thurgarton, Notts. Barrel and finger organ built by Forster & Andrews in 1858: 3 barrels. Subsequent history unknown.

DONALDSON COLLECTION, R.C.M. London. Broderip & Wilkinson: 3 stops: 3 barrels.

DORCHESTER, DORSET COUNTY MUSEUM: Small (chamber?) barrel-organ, (*ex* Bere Regis Church): 4 stops: 5 barrels each of 10 tunes, but only 33 survive.

DYER-GOUGH, Mrs. J. Ruthin, Denbighshire: Southwell & White: 6 stops: 3 barrels each of 10 tunes—1 barrel sacred, 2 secular.

EARLE, Paul: Barrel-organ listed by John Watlen, c. 1807 without other details.

EASTNOR CASTLE, Herefordshire: included in list of places supplied by B. Flight & Son, c. 1820.

EDINBURGH, Royal Scottish Museum: several small anonymous barrel-organs out of order.

ELLEN, Mr. and Mrs. R. G.: Fleet, Hants. H. Bryceson. Barrel-organ.

EUROCLYDON HOTEL, Drybrook, Glos., has an Orchestrion.

FITZROY, General: Towcester. Barrel-organ listed by John Watlen c. 1807 inside one of his organs. No other details.

FONTHILL HOUSE: Wilts.: In this house destroyed by fire in 1755, Richard Pococke, travelling through Wiltshire in 1754, noted "a very fine large organ in the Hall, which plays thirty tunes without a hand and costs about £1500." *Vide Camden Socy.,* 1889, p. 47.

FOOTIT, J. T. H.: Rugby. Chamber barrel-organ bought from the late Canon Wintle of Lawshall. 3 stops plus drum and triangle: 5 barrels but no tune list. Out of order.

FROME COURT, Herefs. included in list of places supplied by B. Flight & Son, c. 1820.

GASCOIGNE, Mrs. E., Evanton, Ross-shire. Small chamber barrel-organ.

GEARY, H. W., Kettering, Northants. T. C. Bates No. 2888: 5 stops: 3 barrels each of 10 sacred tunes. Bought in a Kettering Warehouse and now on indefinite loan to Cranford Baptist Chapel, Northants.

GEFFRYE MUSEUM, London. T. C. Bates, chamber barrel organ: 3 stops.

GLASGOW, City Museum: Chamber barrel-organ in store. No details available.

GREEF, Mrs. Anna: King's Lynn. Chamber barrel-organ from nursery of Melton Constable Hall: 4 stops plus drum and triangle: 2 of 4 barrels survive: tune-list for 4. Made by Wm. Hubert van Kamp, London. (*q.v.*) Plate 13.

GREEN, C. de VERE: London: Clementi.

GREENACRE, F. S.: Gorleston-on-Sea.

GREENE, F.: London. Flight.

GREEVES, T. A.: London, W.4. Weight-driven barrel-organ by Imhof & Mukle.

GRIST, Michael R., Baldock, Herts. Muir & Wood, 4 stops (percussion missing): 1 barrel: restored by the owner.

HALEY, J. T.: Aldridge, Staffs., Barrel-organ by Geo. Pyke, London, c. 1790. Two barrels. *Vide* Chap. V. *s.v.* Pyke & Chap. VI. *s.v.* Stanton-by-Dale, Derbyshire.

HALL, Bryan, Banningham: Flight & Sons. 2 barrels.

HALL, J. P., Kendal: T. C. Bates, No. 1453: 1 barrel of 11 tunes. Astor, 5 barrels of 8 tunes (including 1 sacred barrel), 9 stops including tabor, drum and triangle. Autophone Coy., New York, 1885, cabinet roller organ. *Vide Music Box,* Christmas 1965, p. 184. Anonymous reed barrel-organ: 1 barrel of 6 dances: John Langshaw, 3 barrels x 10.

HARDING, Keith, London, N.1.

HARROGATE, Royal Pump Room: E. & J. Pistor (*ex* Fleet Church, Lincs.): 4 barrels of 8 tunes each. Restored by F. F. Hill in 1961.

HATFIELD HOUSE CHAPEL, Herts. Flight & Robson barrel and finger organ " enclosed in a Venetian swell and a neat mahogany case with one barrel £262, 10/- as supplied to Lord Salisbury in 1812 for his house in Alborough (sic), Suffolk. The fate of this organ is not known, but it is assumed that an organ costing £97 supplied by Flight & Robson in 1807 was removed and disposed of when the present chapel organ was installed by Lewis & Co. in 1876. Another manual organ in Hatfield House was made by Dallam in 1611 (though not so marked) and painted, it is believed, by Rowland Buckett. (Information by courtesy of Lord Salisbury).

HEREFORD, All Saints Church: On loan from City Museum, T. C. Bates, No. 2578, (ex Bosbury Church). Foot blown: 3 stops: 19 keys: originally 4 barrels each of 10 tunes, now only 1 barrel.

HEREFORD, Bishop's Palace: H. Bevington & Son (ex Tasley Church, Salop), 2 stops: 2 barrels each of 10 tunes.

HERTFORD MUSEUM: T. C. Bates & Son, (ex Stocking Pelham Church, where it was in use till 1917 and transferred in 1937): 3 barrels. Astor, 4 barrels each of 10 tunes. Vide N. & Q. 15, 19 June 1937, p. 444. Bevington (lent by Vicar of Sacomb Church in 1939), 1 barrel of 10 tunes. Anonymous English barrel-organ. 1 barrel of 10 tunes.

HILL, Mrs. C. E., Melton Mowbray: Muir, Wood & Co., 5 stops: separate case for 10 barrels each of 10 tunes, mainly secular.

HILL, F. F., Godalming: Clementi & Co., 6 stops including drum and triangle: 4 barrels each of 10 tunes. Small Bruce & Co., 4 stops: 5 barrels each of 10 tunes. Broderip & Wilkinson. Samuel Taylor: cylinder piano.

HODSON, A., Lavenham: Brooking & Son, Organ builders, Exeter, table barrel-organ, 8 tunes.

HOPKINS, R. G., Bishop Stortford: H. Bryson, 6 stops including tabor and triangle, 3 barrels and tune-list of Scottish songs.

HORNIMAN MUSEUM, London: Collection includes barrel-organs by Pistor, Eveleigh & Co., J. W. Walker: a small table organ, an Orchestrion and a street piano by M. Taylor.

JACKSON-BARSTOW, Miss M., Weston-super-Mare: chamber clockwork barrel-organ: 6 barrels—2 of hymns, 2 of Dances, 2 of Marches. Out of order.

JEANS, Susi, Lady: Dorking. Bates: 3 stops: also bird-organ.

JEFFREY, G., Woking: T. C. Bates.

JEFFS, Julian: Newbury. Henry Holland barrel-organ: 3 stops: 1 barrel x 10 secular tunes.

JEPHCOTE, E. W., Birmingham. Anonymous: 15 tunes.

JONES, Tristan, St. Nicholas at Wade, Kent: Keith Prowse & Co., 48 Cheapside, 2 stops: 3 barrels each of 10 sacred tunes. Also street piano marked Keith Prowse.

KILBOURN, W. G. K., Chertsey: Bates barrel-organ, bearing a plate " The Gift of His Royal Highness Prince Albert." 3 barrels sacred and secular. Mechanism now removed.

KIRKCALDY, St. Michael's Mission Chapel. Barrel-organ reduced to manual, with tune-lists on the panels, was sold in 1951 when the chapel was closed.

LEICESTER, City Museum: H. Bryceson (ex Cold Overton Church, Rutland), 4 stops. In playing order. Hicks: barrel-piano No. 699. Small box-organ. Anonymous serinette.

LEIGH COURT HOSPITAL, Bristol: Flight & Co., barrel and finger organ.

LEIGHTON BUZZARD, Beds.: Barrel-organ in Eggington House.

LINDGREN, Rev. D. N., Musselburgh: Barrel-organ by T. C. Bates: 2 stops: 1 barrel x 10. Barrel-organ by Astor, No. 331, 3 stops (percussion removed) 3 barrels x 10 sacred and secular tunes.

LINDSAY, Mr. Croft, Leics.: Barrel and finger organ by Clementi and a smaller one by Longman & Broderip. The two had been combined but are now to be separated (1969).

LUBBOCK, Mr., Midhurst: H. Bryceson: 6 stops: 14 keys. Restored to playing order in 1965.

LYDDINGTON, Rutland: Barrels of a musical box survive in Bede House, adjacent to the church.

MACKENZIE, J. A., Glasgow: barrel-organ by Wood, Small & Co., Edinburgh: 4 stops: 1 barrel.

MANCHESTER, Wilbraham District Library: barrel-organ said to have been used by John Upton, in Newborough Church, near Burton-on-Trent in the 1840's. Maker's name removed: 4 stops bear no names: 4 barrels in damaged state and tune-lists are illegible.

MANDER, N. P., London, E.2: Henry Holland, Bedford Row and St. James's Street, London: small barrel-organ. H. Bryceson. 4 stops plus drum and triangle: 6 barrels—1 spiral, others secular. Serinette: 12 pipes: anonymous.

MANX MUSEUM. Douglas, I. of M.: Wrenshall, Liverpool: (ex Santan Church): 3 barrels each of 12 tunes sacred and secular: 4 stops. Theodore Bates (ex Old St. Matthew's Church, Douglas).

MASSEY-STEWART, J., London, W.2.: Bryceson: 6 stops including drum and triangle: 5 barrels attractively labelled, each of 10 tunes: 16 keys.

MAYERS, T. T., Ipswich: Keith Prowse & Co.: 1 stop: 1 barrel x 10 hymns.

MICKLEBURGH, E. Roy, Bristol: H. Bryceson, (ex Burtle Church, Somerset), 5 stops: 5 barrels each of 11 tunes.

Wm. Telford, Dublin (*ex* a church in Macroom district of County Cork), incomplete: 3 barrels.

J. Robson & Son, 4 stops: 23 keys: 5 barrels including one set to turn in a spiral.

Muir, Wood & Co. 4 stops: 16 keys: 5 barrels.

MILLER, F. H., Dorking, Surrey: Barrel and finger organ, 3 stops. Barrel mechanism removed and only tune-list (10) survives.

MILLER, M. C., Pinelands, Cape, So. Africa: Astor & Co. 3 stops; 3 barrels x 10: in working order.

MOORE, The Revd. Dr. P. C., Pershore: collection of barrel-organs: Longman & Broderip: 4 stops: 4 barrels each of 10 tunes.

 Meyer & Co. : 5 stops including drum: 3 barrels each of 10 tunes.

 Anonymous: 6 stops including drum and triangle: 3 barrels.

 Edward Pistor: 5 stops: 3 barrels.

 Joseph Fuzelli, London: 4 stops: 4 barrels.

 Anonymous: Small 18th c. barrel-organ in shape of a chest of drawers: (*cp*. Rostrand barrel-organ in Pitt Rivers Museum *q.v.*): 4 stops.

 Anonymous: 2 stops and 2 barrels: another with 4 stops and 3 barrels.

 Bates: in pieces.

MORLEY, C. L. R., Lewisham: John Longman, possibly a church barrel-organ as 4 barrels give 40 sacred tunes.

MOSS, BRUCE, Barton-le-Clay, Beds. : Astor & Lucas, 5 stops incl. drum and triangle: 3 barrels but no tune-list. Crowshaw, London: 3 stops plus drum and triangle: piano combined. *Vide Music Box,* Vol. 2, No. 3, p. 123. 5 barrels x 8 tunes.

MOSS. R. A., Barton-le-Clay, Beds. : Weight-driven barrel-organ of orchestrion type. Empty case of barrel-organ labelled " J. Wright—Organ Bldr., 30 Commercial Road." 5 tune-lists: no stops.

 Broderip & Wilkinson: 6 stops incl. drum and triangle: 3 barrels each of 10 secular tunes.

NATIONAL MARITIME MUSEUM, London: Broderip & Wilkinson, 7 stops: 6 barrels each of 10 tunes mainly secular.

NEWBOROUGH, Lord, Pwllheli: H. C. Lincoln, 4 stops plus drum and triangle: 2 barrels each of 10 tunes, one sacred, the other secular. A third barrel of 10 sacred tunes has vanished. The organ is in Bodfean Hall, Pwllheli.

NORWICH, St. Peter Hungate Museum: Wheatstone barrel organ, *ex* Hoveton St. John, Norfolk: 6 stops: *Vide Archaeol Jl.,* xcix (1943) p. 65 and plate iii, fig. D. Tune-list in *A.M. Socy. Trans.,* 11 May 1960, p. 117.

NORWICH, Strangers' Hall Museum. Small chamber barrel-organ. No stops: 1 barrel x 10 tunes. but no tune-list. Restored in 1965. Also barrel-organ by W. Phillips, London. 1 barrel x 10 tunes: tune-list for 3 barrels. Barrel-piano by John Hicks, London.

OLDHAM, GUY, London: Miniature barrel-organ (Serinette or bird-organ): Geo. Astor. *Vide Music Lib. & Insts.,* Paper No 32, Plates 57 and 58.

ORD-HUME, A. W. J. G., Isle of Wight and London. Barrel-organs by White & Langshaw·: James Davis: Bryceson: Webber: T. C. Bates: P. Vanquish: H. Wedlake: W. F. Taylor: Clementi: J. Fentum: Rolfe (empty case): Flight & Robson (empty case): Serinette by Thibouville-Lamy: Street barrel-organs by Chiappa and A. Corvi et Cie. Also two large and two small anonymous barrel-organs; a reproduction 3 stop and percussion barrel-organ by A. Ord Hume; and an Aeolian Orchestrelle.

ORTON HALL, Leics. Barrel-organ *ex* Orton-on-the-Hill Church: T. C. Bates.

OSBORN, The late Sir George: Purchased in 1838 a barrel-organ by Flight & Co. Subsequent history unknown.

PAGET, Rev. Gordon, Bury St. Edmunds. I. Willis & Sons: 4 stops: 6 barrels each of 10 tunes: 2 sacred and 4 secular.

PETERBOROUGH MUSEUM: Flight & Robson, chamber barrel-organ: 3 barrels each of 10 secular tunes.

 Anonymous: chamber barrel-organ: 1 barrel of 10 dances, etc.

 Anonymous: Small barrel-organ: 1 barrel. Not in working order.

PITT RIVERS MUSEUM, Oxford: Astor & Horwood, London. *c.* 1820: 4 stops including triangle: 3 barrels each of 10 tunes. In order.

 E. Rostrand, London, dated 1764: 2 barrels each of 8 tunes. In order.

 Anonymous: Gift of Dr. Scholes: 4 stops: 3 barrels each of 9 sacred tunes. In order.

PLYMOUTH, Longdon Hall: John Watlen listed a barrel-organ for the house c. 1807.

POLE, The late E. R., formerly of Gt. Bedwyn, Wilts. Very large and valuable collection of automata, but now dispersed. It included barrel-organs by T. C. Bates, Bevington, Broderip & Wilkinson, C. Gerock and John Preston.

PORTLAND MUSEUM: Barrel of organ formerly in use in the disused St. George's Church, Portland, is preserved in the Museum: barrel 3 feet long and 10 inches in diameter: played 6 sacred tunes.

PORTMEIRION HOTEL, Merioneth: Large barrel-organ in Gothic case with Hanoverian Royal Arms is said to have come from a church but this seems doubtful as there is a barrel of dances. The instrument, however, is not in playing order.

PRESTON-ON-THE-WEALD-MOORS, Salop. Jas. W. Walker: barrel and finger-organ of 1855: in Hall of the Almshouses. *Vide Country Quest,* Spring 1965, pp. 20-21.

PRIEST, Rev. Peter: Erick Engman: secular barrel-organ: 6 stops.

ROBINSON, Eric, London: Barrel-organ *ex* Hurdsfield Chapel, Cheshire.

ROBINSON, Rev. G. S., Sherborne: Bates barrel-organ No. 2728: 3 stops: 20 notes: 3 barrels each of 10 tunes.

ROCHESTER City Museum: T. C. Bates: *ex* Meopham Church and Trottiscliffe Church: 6 barrels each of 10 tunes. Restored by Noel Mander in 1947.

ROYAL ACADEMY OF MUSIC, London: Clementi & Co.: Patent: 4 stops plus drum and triangle: 15 keys: 5 barrels each of 10 tunes.

ROYAL COLLEGE OF MUSIC, London: Broderip & Wilkinson, 3 stops: 1 barrel of sacred tunes, others secular.

RUSHWORTH & DREAPER, Liverpool: T. C. Bates, No. 2978, 5 stops: 3 barrels each of 10 tunes. Exhibited and played in London in 1928.

ST. IVES Museum, Cornwall: Barrel-organ from Parish Church: maker's name illegible: 1 sacred and 2 secular barrels each of 10 tunes.

SCOTT, A. B., Runton: Barrel-organ. No details.

SHERRIFF, T., Saltford, Somerset: Orchestrion: clockwork barrel-organ by Imhof & Mukle: 85 open wooden pipes and 32 barrels.

SHORT, Mr., Grantham: Barrel and finger organ built by Forster & Andrews in 1851; 3 barrels: subsequent history unknown.

SNOWSHILL MANOR, Glos.: C. Gerock: 3 stops: 1 barrel of 8 tunes.

SPARKE, Mrs., Melton Constable: Pistor, London. c. 1780: 7 barrels x 10 secular tunes: 4 stops plus drum and triangle: restored in 1965 by John Budgen of Bishop & Son, Ipswich. See Plate 22.

SPIEGL, Fritz, Liverpool: H. C. Lincoln: 3 barrels each of 10 tunes: *ex* Bernard Miles who bought it in Scarborough.

STAMFORD, Masonic Temple, Lincs.: J. W. Walker & Sons, barrel and finger organ: 7 stops: 1 barrel of 10 double chants for psalms, but no tune list. Acquired by the Lodge in 1926 after being at Wainfleet, Lincs. and earlier at Monkton Farleigh Rectory, Wilts.

STANTON HARCOURT, Oxon: E. Rostrand dated 1764: 4 stops: 2 barrels each of 8 tunes, all secular except Easter Hymn. Restored by F. F. Hill.

STONELEIGH ABBEY, Warwickshire: Barrel-organ in working order. One barrel.

STUART, Mrs. J. S., Hethersett. Bryceson Bros., chamber barrel-organ. In need of repair.

TAYLOR, Leonard, Wells: Button & Purday, 4 stops plus drum and triangle (drum missing). Tune-list for 6 barrels of which only one survives.

THOMAS, W. R., Burntisland, Fife: B. Flight, Son & Kelly: 4 stops: tune-list for 4 barrels—1, 2 & 3 secular, 4 sacred—but only Nos. 2 & 4 survive.

TOWNER, H. J., Eastbourne: J. Fentum: 3 stops: 4 barrels each of 10 tunes.

TURNER, F. G. & Son, Horsham: W. Ayton, supposed to be *ex* Oakwood Hill Church, Dorking. 4 stops plus drum and triangle: 3 barrels.
Anonymous: 6 stops including drum and triangle: 18 keys: 4 barrels.

VAUX, Wm., Ilchester, Somerset: Thomas Weekes, clockwork barrel-organ: 4 stops: 19 keys: 76 pipes: 1 barrel of 12 tunes. Weekes made this organ for his Museum of Mechanical Instruments, Tichbourne Street, Haymarket, London.
Other barrel-organs by Flight & Robson, D'Almaine & Co., John Longman, Astor, and mechanical barrel-organ in a clock by Geo. Pyke, London, c. 1770.

VICTORIA & ALBERT MUSEUM, London: Longman & Broderip, 2 stops: 15 keys: tune-list for 4 barrels but only 2 barrels remain.
Two anonymous miniature barrel-organs.

VINCE, Norman, East Dereham: Joseph Walker (1832), 3 barrels x 10 tunes: 4 stops. Also a barrel-organ said to be from Belvoir Castle: 5 stops plus flute and drum: 5 barrels: reduced to manual. A plate states re-built in 1847 by G. M. Holdich.

WADMORE, Mrs. J., Tunbridge Wells: Barrel-piano by Canon Wintle, Lawshall, Suffolk: also other various automata.

WALKER, J., Reigate. Longman & Broderip, '1794' watermark on paper of barrel No. 1: 4 stops: 18 keys: 3 barrels each of 10 tunes. Purchased at Sotheby's 27 July 1962.

WALKER, J. W. & Sons Ltd., Ruislip, Middx. J. W. Walker, 'dumb organist': 6 tunes: *ex* Great Bookham, Surrey.
R. & W. Gray, chamber barrel-organ: 5 stops: 3 barrels.

WARD, P. D., Cambridge: J. Longman, 1 barrel of 10 secular tunes.
Kamp, 4 barrels each of 11 secular tunes.

WEBB, G., London. Broderip & Wilkinson: & Geo. Godfrey (latter incomplete).

WELSH NATIONAL FOLK MUSEUM, Cardiff: H. Bryceson (*ex* Pennard Church). 5 stops: 3 barrels badly worm-eaten. No tune-list.

R. J. Heath & Son, small roller organ. 2 stops: 2 rollers each of 10 tunes.

WILLIAMS, Guy, Birkenhead: Joseph Beloudy, dated 1784: (*ex* Crosthwaite Church, Keswick ?): 5 barrels each of 15 tunes but all secular.

WILLIAMSON, Dr. J. Bruce, Ventnor, two table barrel-organs.

WILLINS, J. V., West Runton, Norfolk: Wm. Phillips, 6 stops incl. drum and triangle, but mechanism now removed.

WILLIS, Henry, London. Orchestrion.

WOOTTON, The late C., Hove: Serinette by Flight, 2 barrels x 10 tunes.

YORK, Castle Museum: H. Bryceson, 1846: *ex* Garton-in-Holderness: 5 stops: 28 keys: 4 barrels. Not in playing order.

Wm. Rolfe: 4 stops: 3 barrels each of 10 secular tunes. In playing order but in need of tuning.

Broderip & Wilkinson, Patent: 8 stops including tabor and triangle: 36 keys: 3 barrels.

IRELAND AND NORTHERN IRELAND

The author is indebted to Mr. John Holmes, Monasterevan, Co. Kildare, for much of the following list.

BEATTY, Mrs., Co. Wexford: remnants only of a barrel-organ.

BOND, W. A. N. McGeough, D.L., Dungannon: Weight-driven barrel and finger organ by James Bishop, London, 1824, whose specification and contract is preserved. 10 stops: 3 of original 6 barrels survive. Barrels 75" long and 12" wide. Organ is regularly serviced and in perfect order.

BRENNAN, Patrick, Abbeyleix: small barrel-organ by Henry Holland, dated 1784: 5 stops, 3 barrels made by Flight & Robson.

CAMPBELL, A., Ardara, Co. Donegal: Wm. Balfe & Royal Arms: 3 barrels of 10 tunes each.

COCHRANE, Sir Stanley, Bray: Aeolian organ, 30 stops, 2 manuals: player attachment. Organ removed to West Orchard Church, Coventry, 1912.

CRUMLIN, Co. Antrim: Barrel-organ seen in the Church c. 1937. (Per Rev. G. L. Clarke, Liverpool).

DAMES, Longworth, Athlone: Keys of barrel-organ by Bevington sold at auction 1883.

DOMVILLE, Sir C., Co. Dublin: Keys of barrel-organ sold in 1880 to H. V. Jackson, Dublin.

DUBLIN: National Museum of Ireland: Barrel-organ by Robert Woffington, William Street, Dublin. (fl. c. 1785-1819). Resemblance to Flight & Robson's work suggests he may have bought the organ from them for resale. Woffington was a pupil of J. Weber (*q.v.*).

DUNLEATH, Lord, Newtonards, Co. Down: Bevington: 4 stops: 3 barrels: 1 sacred and 2 secular.

ERSKINE, Mrs., Newry, Co. Down: Orchestrion by Imhof.

GUINNESS, Hon. A. E., Castle Knock, Co. Dublin. German barrel and finger organ acquired by Rooney & Coffey c. 1952. (Now defunct).

GUINNESS, Hon. Desmond, Leixlip Castle, Co. Kildare: Flight & Robson: 4 stops plus drum and triangle: 3 barrels x 10 tunes: 1 sacred, 2 secular.

HOBART, Lady Harriet, Dublin: Barrel-organ repaired by Weber in 1779.

JAMMET'S, Dublin: Orchestrion by Heller of Berne.

JOYCE, T. Kilternan Abbey, Co. Dublin: Orchestrion.

KILREA Church, Co. Londonderry: Barrel and finger organ by T. J. Robson. Presented in 1858: 16 stops: 2 barrels x 10 tunes: 2 manuals. The gift of the Mercers Company of London in whose Hall it is said to have been formerly. (Per Rev. E. Fleming, Portadown).

MAGUIRE, Mr., Bangor, Co. Down: Aeolian organ, 20 stops: 2 manuals: player attachment. In 1954 organ removed and dismantled.

MEATES, T., Organ-builder, Ranelagh, Dublin: Barrel-organ.

PERRY, Rt. Hon. Edmund Sexton, Dublin: Barrel-organ repaired by Weber in 1779.

RATHCOOLE Church of Ireland, Co. Dublin: Small T. C. Bates "Sacred Barrel-organ" No. 2483, in West gallery c. 1830: 3 stops: 20 notes: in poor condition: 1 barrel x 10.

ROTHWELL, Mrs. Helen, Kells: Barrel-organ.

TARTARAGHAN Church, Portadown, Co. Armagh: T. C. Bates: 2 barrels x 10: 5 stops: No. 2031: "The gift of the Hon. and Rev. J. N. Clements ..1849."

WILLIAMSON, Rev. A., Kesh, Co. Fermanagh: keys of barrel-organ and 4 stops in swell-box sold to Rev. A. Packenham, Crumlin, Co. Antrim, who replaced it in 1880, with a 2-manual organ.

WOODLANDS Convalescent Home, Finglas, Dublin: Small barrel-organ of Flight & Robson: 6 stops: 3 barrels each of 10 secular tunes. House closed c. 1956 and organ bought by Mr. G. F. Lockhart of Woodlands Gate Lodge, Finglas.

AUSTRALIA

PORT MACQUARRIE, New South Wales: Barrel and finger organ by J. W. Walker dated 1856. In St. Thomas' Church of England. 3 barrels each of 11 hymns and psalms. Used only as a manual organ but Dr. K. G. Pont of University of N.S.W. (1968) states that the barrel action is to be repaired. The tune-lists have vanished.

CANADA

ABBOTSFORD, Quebec: Church of England has a barrel-organ still in use. (Per Cleveland Fisher, Manassas, Va., U.S.A.).

ESQUIMAULT, B.C. : Bates, 1859, in Dallymore residence.

LUSTY, E. G., Rodney, Ontario: Chamber barrel-organ made c. 1830 by Richard Coates, owner's great-grandfather, who made three or four such organs including the church barrel-organ in Sharon Temple Museum. *Vide infra.*

ROUGEMONT, Quebec: St. Thomas' Anglican Church: J. Walker 1844: barrels only, no manual: 3 stops: 27 notes: pipes are replacements: 3 barrels each of 10 tunes. In excellent order—once broadcast on C.B.C.

SHARON TEMPLE MUSEUM, Ontario: Richard Coates, of Oakville, Ontario, 1820: 4 stops: 133 pipes: 2 barrels each of 10 hymns and psalms. Coates, a sawmill operator and amateur organ builder, was said to have been a bandmaster at the battle of Waterloo.

VANCOUVER, British Columbia. The first organ used here was a barrel-organ by T. C. Bates & Co., London, with 3 barrels each of 10 tunes. It was installed in Christ Church Cathedral, Victoria, B.C., in February 1859, three years after the erection of the church. In 1862 the barrel-organ was replaced by an organ by Bevington & Sons of Soho, London, and shipped around Cape Horn. In October 1869 the building was burned down but the barrel-organ was saved by two priests and purchased by one Wm. Seeley, who had also built a keyboard for the barrel-organ (and had installed the Bevington organ). Seeley rebuilt and erected the barrel-organ in a room adjoining a bar. No more is known. *Vide The Organ* No. 151, Jan. 1959.

YORK MILLS, Toronto, Ontario, St. John's Anglican Church. T. C. Bates & Son: brought from England at a cost of £81.10.0 incl. freight and installed in 1847. 5 stops: 3 barrels each of 10 tunes No manual. Crank works barrel and bellows. Still plays a pre-service voluntary each Sunday. (Per Rev. L. Gunsworthy, Willowdale, Ont.). *Vide Country Life,* 30 Sept. 1965.

FRANCE

PERROT, J. M., Paris: Large chamber barrel-organ by Flight (incomplete): a label inside reads " Daniel Grey, Organ Builder, No. 6 Ely Place, St. George's Road, Southwark," but this may relate to an extra set of bellows independent of the ordinary feeders and operated by a foot-lever.

GUIANA

DEMERARA—Barrel and finger organ by Robson was removed in 1868 from St. Michael's Church, Alnwick and sent to Demerara Bethel Chapel. 3 barrels of 10 tunes each.

NEW ZEALAND

WANGANUI MUSEUM: Barrel-organ (*ex* Brightling Church, Sussex) sent out in 1829: by A. Buckingham: 3 barrels each of 10 tunes: in working order since 1955. *Vide Sussex County Magazine,* Nov. 1955.

SWITZERLAND

MANGOLD, Karl, Zollikon, Zurich: Collection of automata includes serinettes, pionne and parisienne, roller-organ and a barrel-organ by John Kleyser & Co., London (1829-1870): *Vide Glareana,* 13 Jhg., No. 3/4, Dec. 1964.

UNITED STATES OF AMERICA

ALVIN, Texas. A concern known as Hobbs' Antiques restores barrel-organs and sells some.

BEDFORD, New York. A small barrel-organ is preserved in Jay Mansion, Route 22, Bedford, New York.

BUENA PARK, Calif. Barrel-organ at Knott's Berry Farm, said to be German c. 1835. In playing condition.

CARLYLE, Pennsylvania: Longman & Broderip, London, 1784, in library of Dickinson College. Restored by Pro Musica Inst. Co. of Annapolis.

ELLSWORTH, Maine. Small chamber barrel-organ in Black House: possibly by Pistor of London: 2 or 3 stops: unplayable.

GLOUCESTER, Mass. Barrel-organ by Longman & Co., London, in First Universalist Church. Taken from an English merchant ship in the Revolutionary War by Capt. John Somes who in 1780 gave it to the church in whose historical room it now stands since its use was discontinued in 1802. Unplayable for many years. 4 stops: originally 3 barrels each of 10 tunes, 2 secular barrels and 1 with 2 marches and 8 hymns and psalms. Only 2 barrels survive.

GUINNESS, Murtogh, New York: Barrel-organ by Dobson & Munro, London.

HEINTZ, Ralph M., Los Altos, Calif., John Langshaw, Lancaster, England: 3 barrels x 10 tunes. Also smaller barrel-organ, anonymous.

HERSHEY Museum, Pennsylvania. Two barrel-organs made by P. L. Dieffenbacher, Turbotville, Pa., in 1892 and 1899 respectively.

METHVEN, Mass. Small French barrel-organ, c. 1820, is owned by Robt. C. Newton.

NORTH BEVERLEY, Mass. The late E. G. Shaw had a collection, dispersed some years ago. It contained a small barrel-organ, the fate of which is unknown.

PHILADELPHIA: Independence National Historic Park: Geo. Astor & Co., London, c. 1810: Restored by Pro Musica Inst. Co., Annapolis.

PIERREPONT MANOR, New York. Zion Episcopal Church contains a barrel and finger organ by George Jardine, 1842. In regular use, the organ is well known.

TRENTON, New Jersey. Barrel-organ by Pistor, Swan Street, Minories, London, was purchased *ca.* 1767 by Sir George Houston, who later presented it to Aaron D. Woodruff, of Savannah, Georgia. The organ was among the effects of Woodruff's descendant Joseph F. Mayer and was sold in 1962.

TROY, Pennsylvania. Daniel F. Pomeroy, Jr., has a concert roller organ: a small Spanish street organ: cylinder-piano by ' G. Mina, 11 First Street, New York, No. 10,' formerly in use at New York Hippodrome.

WALTHAM, Mass. Charles P. Fisher residence. Small barrel-organ (or roller?), assumed to be French c. 1800: 3 or 4 stops: compass 22 notes. All secular music.

WINTERTHUR, Delaware: Anonymous: in Winterthur Museum. Restored by Pro Musica Inst. Co.. Annapolis.

YALE UNIVERSITY, New Haven, Conn. Clementi & Co., London: 6 stops including drum and triangle: 4 barrels—2 sacred, 2 secular. From the old Warner Tavern, Northampton, Mass. *Vide Belle Skinner Colln. Catal.,* No. 4, pp. 11-12. Also R. Wolf & Co., London (1837-1845).

Note: The author is indebted to the following for much of the foregoing overseas information: A. Laufman, Harrisville, N.H.; E. A. Boadway, Short Falls, N.H.; Miss Barbara Owen, Pigeon Cove, Mass.; John Holmes, Monasterevan, Eire.; Randal L. Henley, Dublin, 3, Eire; Rev. E. Fleming, Portadown, Co. Armagh.

PLATE 32

Winwick Church, Northants.
Barrel-organ by Wm. Prowse, London, 1864. 7 barrels each of 10 tunes, in removable shelves.
Completely restored in 1969 by K. G. Parrott and E. W. Timmins, both of Rugby.

APPENDIX I

SACRED TUNES: THEIR SOURCES OR COMPOSERS

In Chapter IV an attempt has been made to attribute each Hymn, Psalm or Chant to its composer, but this is not always possible for a number of reasons. Firstly: confusion arises where the same name is given to different tunes. Were the barrel-organs on which these tunes are listed in working order, the matter could be decided, but few are in working order, while, of others, only remnants survive with tune-lists. Secondly: the same tune had sometimes a different name in another part of the country or at an earlier or later date. Exceptionally, a Parish Church had its own Tune-Book, *e.g.* Milton Abbot (Devon) words and music, and Cardeston (Salop) words only—of both of which the author has a photocopy—and Stratfieldsaye (Hants). An extensive list, by counties, is given by the late Canon K. H. Mac-Dermott in his "The Old Church Gallery Minstrels" (1948) as Appendix II, with a list of tune-books for general use as Appendix III. A list of nearly a hundred Tune Books prior to 1900, forming Canon Boston's Collection was printed in the Proceedings of the Ancient Monuments Society 1964 pp. 210-214. The following list comprises the principal sources prior to 1846 from which the tunes in Chapter IV herein are taken.

1525	Old Strasbourg Psalter.	c. 1781	Wesley's Sacred Harmony.
1551	Genevan Psalter.	1780	R. Harrison's Sacred Harmony.
1561	Anglo-German Psalter.	c. 1786	Gardner's Psalms.
c. 1561	Archbishop Parker's "The whole Psalter translated . . ." to which are added nine tunes by Thomas Tallis.	1786	Dr Stephen Addington's "Collection of Psalm Tunes" (6th Edition).
1591	Damon's Psalter.	1789	Psalmodia Evangelica.
1592	Este's Psalter.	c. 1789	Hymns & Psalms used at the . . . Refuge for female Orphans.
1615	Scottish Psalter.	c. 1790	Isaac Smith's "Collection of Psalm Tunes in three parts".
1621	Prys's Psalter.		
1621	Ravenscroft's Psalter.	1791	Psalms of David . . . Music selected, adapted and composed by Dr Arnold assisted by J. W. Callcott.
1635	The Psalms of David . . . with their whole tunes &c. (Edinburgh).		
1671	Playford's Psalms and Hymns.	1791 & 1800	Rippon's Selection of Psalms & Hymns.
1708	Lyra Davidica.	1794	Tattersall's Psalter.
1718	Chetham's Psalmody.	1799	Peck's Collection of Hymn Tunes . . . (London).
c. 1723	The Divine Musick Scholar's Guide . . . collected by F. Timbrell.	c. 1800 & 1802	Miller's Sacred Music.
1735	Tans'ur's Harmony of Zion.	1800	Dr Watt's Psalms & Hymns.
1738	König's Choralbuch.	c. 1803	Miller's "David's Harp".
1749	Hymns & Sacred Poems, Dublin.	1806-25	Latrobe's Selection.
1760	Caleb Ashworth's Collection of Tunes.	c. 1810	Isaac Tucker's Sacred Music.
		1815	J. H. Walker's Collection.
1761	Arnold's Compleate Psalmodist 1741-1779 (7 editions).	1825	Wilson's Collection.
		1827	Burgoyne's Collection.
1762	Riley's Parochial Harmony.	1828	T. Clark's "Congregational Harmonist".
1769	Sixteen Hymns as they are sung at the . . . Countess of Huntingdon's Chapel in Bath; set to music by Benj. Milgrove.	1836	W. Hawes's Collection.
		1840	John Fawcett's "Melodia Divina".
1770	Williams's Psalmody.	1846	Gauntlett's "Comprehensive Tune Book".
1776	Herder's Collection.		

APPENDIX II

TUNE LISTS

Fifteen specimen tune-lists follow: some selected from barrel-organs still usable, others from barel-organs no longer in existence or reduced to manual.

Avington, Hampshire.
Bressingham, Norfolk.
Brightwell Baldwin, Oxon.
Cardeston, Salop.
Edgecott, Northants.
Fawsley, Northants.
Fobbing, Essex.
Hampton Gay, Oxon.

Helhoughton, Norfolk.
Letheringsett, Norfolk.
Mattishall Burgh Church, Norfolk.
Milton Abbot, Devon.
Shelland, Suffolk.
Wissington, Suffolk.
Garton-in-Holderness, Yorkshire.

AVINGTON, HAMPSHIRE. Barrel-organ by unknown maker c. 1849. Restored 1961. 3 stops. 2 barrels each of 15 tunes.

Barrel 1	Barrel 2
1. Morning Hymn.	1. German.
2. Evening Hymn.	2. New Sabbath.
3. 100th Psalm.	3. Carey's.
4. Hanover.	4. St. James.
5. Wareham.	5. Mount Sinai.
6. Portuguese.	6. Shore's Cottage.
7. St. Stephen's.	7. Moscow (Russian Vesper Hymn).
8. Cambridge New.	8. Luther's.
9. St. Ann's.	9. Missionary Hymn.
10. Shirland.	10. Lord Dismiss Us.
11. Sicilian.	11. My Rest is in Heaven.
12. Helmsley.	12. My God, My Father.
13. Chant—Soaper.	13. Chant—Mornington.
14. Chant—Jones.	14. Chant—Norris.
15. Chant—Trent.	15. Chant—not traced.

BRESSINGHAM, NORFOLK. Barrel-organ by (?) B. Flight. 6 stops of 28 notes. 2 barrels each of 12 tunes.

No. 1	No. 2
1. Morning Hymn.	1. Magdalen.
2. Shirland.	2. Mount Ephraim.
3. Sicilian Mariners.	3. Old Hundredth.
4. Oxford.	4. Austria.
5. Carey's.	5. Rockingham.
6. Hanover.	6. Sheffield.
7. Irish.	7. University.
8. Wareham.	8. Abingdon.
9. Warwick.	9. London New.
10. Mornington (Chant).	10. Dupuis (Chant).
11. Buck (Chant).	11. Crotch (Chant).
12. Beckwith (Chant).	12. Jones (Chant).

BRIGHTWELL BALDWIN CHURCH, OXON. Barrel-organ by Joseph Walker, London, 1843. Restored in 1960. 5 stops of 22 notes. 2 (of original 3) barrels each of 10 tunes.

No. 1	No. 2
1. Morning Hymn.	1. Evening Hymn.
2. Wareham.	2. Luther's Hymn.
3. Pastoral or Surrey.	3. Abridge.
4. Devizes.	4. Cambridge New.
5. Sheldon or New York.	5. Lansdown or Bath.
6. Portuguese Hymn.	6. Babylon.
7. Angels' Hymn.	7. Sicilian or Mariners.
8. Shirland.	8. Hanover Old 104th.
9. Eaton.	9. Easter Hymn.
10. Lord Mornington's Chant.	10. Robinson's Chant.

114

ST. MICHAEL'S CHURCH, CARDESTON, SHROPSHIRE. Barrel-organ by T. C. Bates, 6 Ludgate Hill, London, installed c. 1850. 2 barrels each of 10 tunes.

Barrel 1

1. New Sabbath (or Stockport).
2. Mount Ephraim.
3. Portugal New (Adeste Fideles).
4. Cambridge New.
5. Bedford.
6. Devizes.
7. Abingdon (or Heighington).
8. Magdalen (altered from Tallis' Canon).
9. Morning Hymn.
10. Old Hundredth.

Barrel 2

1. Sicilian Mariners.
2. Rousseau's Dream.
3. Montgomery.
4. London New.
5. Irish (or Dublin).
6. Harts.
7. German Hymn.
8. Easter Hymn.
9. Alma.
10. Abridge.

EDGECOTT, NORTHANTS. Barrel and finger-organ by G. M. Holdich, 1855. 9 stops and 3 combination pedals: Loud, Medium, Soft. 1 barrel of 12 tunes.

1. Morning Hymn.
2. Bedford.
3. Warwick.
4. Shirland.
5. Sicilian Hymn.
6. Easter Hymn.
7. Evening Hymn.
8. Portuguese Hymn.
9. Eaton.
10. Irish.
11. Carlisle.
12. St. Martin.

FAWSLEY, NORTHANTS. Barrel and finger-organ by Joseph Walker, London, 1839. 7 stops; pulldown pedals: 2 barrels each of 12 tunes

Barrel 1

1. St. George.
2. Abingdon.
3. Oxford.
4. Martin's Lane.
5. 113th Psalm.
6. Martyrdom.
7. Richmond.
8. Ranelagh.
9. 148th Psalm.
10. Burford.
11. Sheldon.
12. St. Stephens.

Barrel 2

1. Swiss Cottage.
2. Weston Favell.
3. Bromsgrove.
4. China.
5. Portsmouth.
6. New 148th.
7. Mount Ephraim.
8. St. James.
9. Gainsborough.
10. London New.
11. York.
12. ?

FOBBING, ESSEX. Barrel-organ by Bevington & Son, 48 Greek Street, Soho, c. 1830. 4 stops of 24 notes. 3 barrels each of 12 tunes.

Barrel 1

1. Old Hundredth.
2. Morning Hymn.
3. Wareham.
4. Harrington.
5. Bedford.
6. Abridge.
7. Cambridge New.
8. Devizes.
9. Mount Ephraim.
10. Sicilian Hymn.
11. Easter Hymn.
12. Carlisle.

Barrel 2

1. Evening Hymn.
2. Portuguese Hymn.
3. New Sabbath.
4. Warwick.
5. University.
6. Irish.
7. Tranquillity.
8. Shirland.
9. Surrey.
10. Vienna.
11. Advent Hymn.
12. Rousseau's Dream.

Barrel 3

1. St. Olave.
2. Rockingham.
3. Bishopthorpe.
4. Job.
5. Westminster.
6. Martyrdom.
7. Manchester.
8. Wakefield.
9. Eaton.
10. 148th Psalm.
11. Beethoven or Trinity Chapel.
12. Hanover.

HAMPTON GAY CHURCH, OXON. Barrel-organ by Bryceson, London, c. 1830. 5 stops of 22 pipes. 3 barrels each of 10 tunes. No. 3 list is indecipherable.

Barrel 1

1. Cambridge New.
2. Cranbrook.
3. 110th Psalm.
4. Easter Hymn.
5. 104th Psalm.
6. St. Anne's.
7. Carey's.
8. Sheffield.
9. Haughton.
10. Peckham.

Barrel 2

1. Davey's.
2. Angels' Hymn.
3. Adeste Fideles.
4. Mount Ephraim.
5. Bedford.
6. Evening Hymn.
7. St. James.
8. Sicilian Mariners.
9. Abridge.
10. New Eagle Street.

HELHOUGHTON CHURCH, NORFOLK. Barrel (& finger?) organ by H. Bryceson, London, 1852. Originally in West Raynham Church until 1890. Now manual only. 6 stops. Barrel 4 is spiral.

Barrel 1
1. National Anthem.
2. Easter Hymn, Salisbury.
3. The 100th Psalm, Savoy.
4. Vienna, double.
5. Islington.
6. Luther's Hymn.
7. Stockport.
8. Helmsley.
9. Monmouth, six lines.
10. Portugese Hymn.
11. Anniversary, six lines.
12. Creation, double.

Barrel 2
1. Devizes.
2. Sheldon.
3. Cambridge New.
4. Arabia.
5. Hanover Old 104th.
6. Oxford.
7. Oswestry.
8. Mount Ephraim.
9. Abingdon.
10. Abridge.
11. Evening hymn.
12. Lord Mornington's Chant.

Barrel 3
1. St. Ann's.
2. Warwick.
3. St. Stephens.
4. Falconstreet.
5. Irish.
6. Darwell's 148th.
7. Truro.
8. Shirland.
9. Sicilian Mariner's.
10. Jones, double chant.
11. Morris', double chant.
12. Grand, single chant.

Barrel 4—Spiral
1. Hotham, double—7.
2. Eaton, six lines—L.M.
3. Coronation Anthem—2¾ rounds.
4. March in the Occasional Overture — 2¼ rounds.
5. Hallelujah Choras—3¼ rounds.
6. Pastoral Symphony—2½ rounds.

LETHERINGSETT CHURCH, NORFOLK (Formerly in Hindringham Church). Barrel-organ by T. C. Bates, London (No. 2964) c. 1835. 6 stops. 3 barrels, each of 10 tunes.

Barrel 1
1. Luther's.
2. Islington.
3. Bedford.
4. Sheldon.
5. York.
6. Shirland.
7. Old 104th and 109th.
8. German Hymn.
9. Hanover.
10. Robinson Double Chant (twice).

Barrel 2
1. Evening Hymn.
2. Portuguese.
3. Rockingham.
4. Abridge.
5. Saint Anne.
6. Devizes.
7. Irish.
8. St. Bride's.
9. Haydn's Emperor.
10. Mornington (twice).

Barrel 3
1. Carey's " Surrey."
2. Morning Hymn.
3. London New.
4. Manchester.
5. St. James.
6. Mount Ephraim.
7. Sicilian Mariners.
8. Easter Hymn.
9. Tallis. Single Chant 3 times.
10. Battishill. Single Chant 3 times.

MATTISHALL BURGH CHURCH, NORFOLK. Barrel-organ by Walker, London, 1852. 3 barrels each of 10 tunes.

Barrel 1
1. Morning Hymn.
2. Luke's Hymn.
3. Wareham.
4. Abingdon.
5. Abridge.
6. Carlisle.
7. Haydn's Hymn, Vienna.
8. Advent Hymn, Helmsley.
9. Easter Hymn, Salisbury.
10. Chant, Robinson.

Barrel 2
1. Evening Hymn or Magdalen.
2. Carey's Surrey.
3. Rockingham.
4. Oxford or Lincoln.
5. St. Mary's.
6. St. David's.
7. Mount Ephraim.
8. Peckham.
9. German Hymn.
10. Chant, Crotch.

Barrel 3
1. Old Hundredth.
2. St. Olave's.
3. Montgomery.
4. Truro.
5. London New.
6. St. James.
7. Charmouth or Manchester.
8. Prague (this rather fast).
9. Hanover or Old 104th.
10. Worcester.

MILTON ABBOT PARISH CHURCH, DEVON. Barrel-organ by Flight & Robson, St. Martin's Lane, London: gift of His Grace The Duke of Bedford. 4 barrels. Incorporated in rebuilt organ c. 1890. No longer barrel-operated.

Barrel 1

1. St. Ann.
2. Sicilian Hymn.
3. Brunswick.
4. Sheffield.
5. St. James.
6. Surrey.
7. Morning Hymn.
8. Old 100th.
9. Portuguese.
10. Haydn's Hymn.

Barrel 2

1. Rockingham.
2. Manchester.
3. York.
4. Kent.
5. Lincoln.
6. St. Mary's.
7. Messiah.
8. Burford.
9. Broadworth.
10. Suffolk or Evening Hymn.

Barrel 3

1. Easter Hymn.
2. Windsor.
3. All Saints.
4. Bishopthorpe.
5. Hanover.
6. Bedford.
7. Emanuel.
8. Hatfield.
9. Salisbury.
10. Gallway.

Barrel 4

1. Psalm 47 N.V.
2. Psalm 66 N.V.
3. Psalm 8 O.V.
4. Psalm 121 N.V.
5. Hymn for Christmas Day.
6. Psalm 9 N.V.
7. Psalm 93 N.V.
8. Evening Hymn, and 92nd Psalm N.V.
9. Psalm 147 N.V.
10. Christmas Hymn.

SHELLAND, SUFFOLK. Barrel-organ by Bryceson Bros., London, c. 1810. 6 stops of 31 notes. 3 barrels each of 12 tunes.

1. Hotham, double.
2. Doncaster.
3. Easter Hymn.
4. Old 100th Psalm.
5. Haydn's Hymn; eight lines.
6. Islington.
7. Helmsley.
8. Sicilian Mariners.
9. Falcon Street.
10. Weston Favel.
11. New Sabbath.
12. "Creation", double.

1. Morning Hymn.
2. Kent.
3. Portugal.
4. Portuguese Hymn.
5. Burnham 148th.
6. Rockingham.
7. Hanover, proper 149th.
8. Manchester.
9. New York.
10. Wakefield.
11. Bedford.
12. Lincoln.

1. Evening Hymn.
2. University.
3. St. David's.
4. St. James's.
5. St. Anne's.
6. St. Stephen's.
7. Warwick.
8. Shirland.
9. Peckham
10. German Hymn.
11. Hymn (sic).
12. Glory be to Thee, O Lord.

WISSINGTON, SUFFOLK. Barrel-organ by John Gray, London (No. 32) c. 1840. 4 stops. 3 barrels each of 10 tunes.

1. Old 100th Psalm.
2. Job.
3. Easter Hymn.
4. St. Anne's.
5. Luther's Hymn.
6. Hanover.
7. London, New.
8. Surrey.
9. Weston Favel.
10. Bedford.

1. Woodside.
2. Sylvanus.
3. St. Bride's.
4. Irish.
6. St. Stephen's.
5. Cambridge New.
7. St. George's.
8. Burford.
9. Abridge.
10. Oxford.

1. Islington.
2. Mount Ephraim.
3. Devizes.
4. Vienna.
5. Martyrdom.
6. St. Olave.
7. University.
8. Wareham.
9. Helmsley.
10. New York.

YORK COUNTY MUSEUM. Barrel-organ from Garton-in-Holderness Church, by H. Bryceson, London, 1846. 5 stops of 28 keys. 4 barrels each of 11 tunes.

1. Hundredth Psalm.
2. Rockingham.
3. Luther's Hymn.
4. Easter.
5. Helmsley.
6. Hotham.
7. Portuguese Hymn.
8. Easter Hymn.
9. Christmas in Bristol.
10. Dr. Dupuis' Chant.
11. Russell's Chant.

1. Pastoral Symphony, Handel.
2. Arabia.
3. Wareham.
4. Monmouth.
5. Creation.
6. Devizes.
7. Lord Mornington's Chant.
8. James' Chant.
9. Humphries' Chant.
10. Nine Responses.
11. Glory be to thee, Lord.

1. Sheldon, New York.
2. Cambridge, New.
3. Manchester.
4. Abingdon.
5. Mount Ephraim.
6. Portugal.
7. Hanover.
8. Irish.
9. German Hymn.
10. Bedford.
11. Norris' Chant.

1. Morning Hymn.
2. London New.
3. Warwick.
4. Anniversary.
5. Truro.
6. St. Anne's.
7. Shirland.
8. Carlisle.
9. Darwall's.
10. Sicilian Hymn.
11. Evening Hymn.

APPENDIX III

It may surprise those readers interested in the Church Bands which preceded the Barrel-organs to learn that many relics of the former survive—often in the Church in which they were played. Occasional dates of reference in Churchwardens' Accounts afford evidence of instruments used and their cost. Time has removed those who could recall the Church Bands and yet many an interesting short account could still be written around the few facts which follow. Parish histories often contain references to the Church Bands but such sources are seldom sufficiently known or accessible.

"MacDermott" refers to the late Canon K. H. MacDermott's book, *The Old Church Gallery Minstrels* (London, 1948).

BEDS.: BIDDENHAM:—Clarinet in Church.
> BLUNHAM:—B flat clarinet (Cramer, London), in Peterborough Museum.
> BROMHAM:—Clarinet in 1823, cost £1.
> CADDINGTON:—Bassoon, 6-key. Anon., in Luton Museum. In 1786, churchwardens paid £2, 2s. for a hautboy and reeds.
> EATON BRAY:—1822/24: Repairs to clarinet and bassoon.
> EATON SOCON:—In 1791 flute and hautboy accompanied the psalm singing.
> FLITTON:—Gallery Orch.: 2 clarinets, violin and flute, *pre* 1843.
> FLITWICK:—Violin and flute introduced in 1834.
> MELCHBOURNE:—Cost of bass string charged to Parish.
> NORTHILL:—Violin used in the church now with a family at Caldecote.
> RAVENSDEN:—Bassoon: 7 keys: (J. Hart, Hatton Garden, London), with reed box; now in Modern School Museum, Bedford.
> TODDINGTON:—In church are: 1 flute; 1 6-key clarinet; 5-key bassoon (Parker, London). In the village: cornet (J. Pask, London); string bass; violin made by the Squire of Toddington. *Vide Beds. Mag.* 1951/52, Vol. 3, No. 19, p. 101.
> WESTONING:—A small orchestra only recently abandoned (1951). *Vide Beds. Mag. idem supra.*

BRECON: ABERDW:—In case in the church: Flute 8-keys (G. French, London), flute, keyless (Goulding & Co.); pitch-pipe.

BUCKS.: BOW BRICKHILL:—Reputed scene of Thomas Webster's "The Village Choir": clarinet, 'cello and bassoon in band.
> HAWRIDGE:—8-key bassoon (Astor, London), now in Bucks., County Museum, Aylesbury.
> MILTON KEYNES:—1843: "Strings, bass Voile 4 s" (*sic*).
> QUAINTON:—Key-bugle now in Bucks., County Museum, Aylesbury.

CAMBS.: BALSHAM:—4-key bassoon (Milhouse, Newark), copper bell instead of wood; 6-key clarinet (Goulding & Co., London); 6-key C clarinet (Anon.); pitch-pipe.

CHANNEL ISLES: GUERNSEY:—St. Martin's: C clarinet (H. Wrede, London, *pre* 1848). Forest Parish Church: Fife, 5-keys (Butler, London); Flageolet, 1-key (Metzler, London); 2 flutes (Anon.); 1 clarinet (C. Gerock, London).

CHESHIRE: ASTON BY SUTTON: The accounts of St. Peter's Church in 1797 record: "Repairing bassoon 12/6d." *Vide* Proc. Hist. Socy. of Lancs. and Cheshire, Vol. 102, p. 131.
> BUNBURY:—Bassoon bought in 1712 for 5 guineas. Oboe bought in 1801 for 14s.
> FARNDON:—Bassoon cost £6, 0s. 8d. and in 1785 two new clarinets and reeds cost £5, 12s. 9d. At same time, a new hautboy was bought for £1, 8s.
> CARRINGTON: The accounts of St. George's Church from 1803-1819 contain references to 4 reeds for bassoon 6/- in 1803; repairs to bassoon £1, 11s. 6d. in 1816; Strings for bass viol almost annually. *Vide* Proc. *idem. supra*, p. 144.

CORNWALL:—FEOCK—Said to have seven bassoons?

CUMBERLAND: WATERMILLOCK:—6-key bassoon (C. Gerock, London), now in Castle Museum, York.

DENBIGH: EFENECHTYD:—Oboe (Milhouse, London) is in the church.
GLEN CONWAY:—6-key bassoon (G. Astor & Co., London) in the church.

DERBYSHIRE: ASHOVER:—Memorial to David Wall (1739-1796), bassoonist.
CHURCH BROUGHTON:—6-key bassoon (much wormeaten) in church chest in 1913.
HARTSHORNE:—In 1789, a hautboy cost 19s.
HAYFIELD:—In 1793, a hautboy cost 21s.
MATLOCK:—St. Giles: In 1870, a small organ was accompanied by fiddles, clarinet and bassoon.
MORLEY:—c. 1820, Church bassoon, now in Derby Museum.
SOUTH WINGFIELD:—Violin in use in church recalled.
TISSINGTON:—Glass case contains the clarinet used to lead singing 1826-1840.
YOULGREAVE:—New reeds for bassoon in 1751 cost 3s. "Ben Jones to buy reeds for the bassoon," 3s.

DEVON: TAVISTOCK:—A serpent hangs in the church (in 1943).
TRENTISHOE:—West Gallery of c. 1770 has a hole cut in one panel to accommodate the 'bass viol'.
WHITESTONE:—In glass case in church are 2 clarinets, bassoon, violin and bow.

DORSET: BOURTON:—Flute (Astor, London) used till c. 1840 in Bourton Church, now in Dorchester Museum.
GILLINGHAM:—In church: 6-key bassoon (Cramer, London) (badly wormeaten): 6-key C clarinet (Astor, London).
POOLE:—Wesleyan Chapel had serpent in use till organ installed between 1865 and 1870.
PUDDLETOWN:—In the church are: 5-key clarinet (G. Astor (Unicorn)); 5-key clarinet (Goulding & Co.); 1-key Octave Flute (Bilton (Unicorn)); 3 flutes and part of another (Anon.).
SHAPWICK:—4/5-key clarinet (C. S. Barfoot, Blandford).
WINTERBOURNE ABBAS:—Clarinet, flute and 'cello were played till c. 1895 by a shepherd, a thatcher and a farm labourer in the West Gallery, dated 1701.

ESSEX: BOCKING:—Clarinet and keyed-bugle from the church now in Braintree Town Hall Museum.
BATTISFORD:—Serpent from church now in Christchurch Museum, Ipswich.
BROOMFIELD:—Clarinet stolen in November 1963 from glass case in bell-ringing chamber.
CHIPPING ONGAR:—'Bass Viol' played by the grandfather of the present owner of it.
FAIRSTEAD:—Clarinet (A. Macqueen, Colchester), now in Chelmsford Museum.
FINGRINGHOE:—Churchwardens' Accounts in 1823 record purchase of a bassoon and a reed-case £3, 5s. 6d.; baize for bag 1s.; 3 Ling's bassoon reeds 6s.; Introduction to the Bassoon 2s.; In 1832, Walk's Tunes cost 9s. 6d.; a flute, 'tipt' and with 4 brass keys, £1.
GOOD EASTER:—Glass case contains bassoon and flute of the Church Band.
HUTTON:—In 1837 an accordion was used to lead the singing.
INGRAVE:—A band of fiddles, flute, 'cello, bassoon and clarinet: the last played by the village blacksmith lacked F sharp.
STANFORD RIVERS:—In 1816 Vestry minutes refer to a bassoon.
TENDRING:—Churchwardens' Accounts in 1775 record payment for a 'bass-viol'.
UGLEY:—Churchwardens' Accounts for 1805-08 record purchase of a 'bass-viol'.
WHITE RODING:—An accordion used to lead the singing.

GLAMORGANSHIRE: CARDIFF:—St. John's Church: 12-keyed serpent (Key, London), now in National Museum of Wales.
YSTALYFERA:—In early 1930's a choir of 40 to 50 was accompanied by 1 or 2 violins, cornet, trombone and American organ.

GLOUCESTERSHIRE: AMPNEY CRUCIS:—In glass case in church: Flute (Phillips, London); Flute (Metzler, London); Oboe, 2-keys (A. Bland & Weller, London).
BISLEY:—In 1814, Joel Chew provided a new bassoon costing six guineas.
BREAM:—A serpent is in the Parish Church (1951).
FRAMPTON-ON-SEVERN:—In 1773 a singers' gallery was erected and reference is made to fiddle, 'bass-viol' and violoncello. (Could this mean double-bass and 'cello ?).
HINDLIP:—Flageolet and clarinet now in the late Canon Boston's Collection, Lamas Manor, Norwich.
LECKHAMPTON:—8-key clarinet (I. B. Cramer & Co., London), in Municipal Museum, Cheltenham.
LITTLE RISSINGTON:—Two bassoons c. 1840 (on sale June 1937), from the church: 5/6-keys (Denman, London) and 8-keys (Hasler, London).
ROCKHAMPTON:—Old diary of a former incumbent records in 1850: "Spoke to Woodward about not playing the ophicleide which obliged Farmer Pinnell to go out of church."

HANTS.: ALRESFORD OLD:—Clarinet. *Vide Hampshire Churches* by Margt. Green.
  BOLDRE:—6-key bassoon (G. Astor, London), formerly in Church went into dust.
  CRONDALL:—Pitchpipe of 1783. Church band was replaced by barrel-organ in 1842-1859.
  MATTINGLEY:—Clarinet, boxwood, 6 square brass keys, reed tied with string. Locked in a glass case.
  MILFORD-ON-SEA:—Accounts record purchases:—1776 bassoon bought for £4, 8s. 7d.; 1785 clarinet bought for 19s.; 1791 pitch-pipe bought for 5s.; 1793 violin bought for 18s.
  MINSTEAD:—A tombstone near the West door depicts a Serpent.
  OWSLEBURY:—Serpent in the church.
  ROMSEY:—Serpent (John Fusedale (1789-1816), London), played in the church, now in Rushworth & Dreaper's Collection, Liverpool.
  ROTHERWICK:—3 clarinets and a bassoon in use till 1870 have keen kept in the church since 1939.
  SPARSHOLT:—A bassoon is in a locked case in the Church.
  YATELEY:—In a West Gallery erected in 1755, a band of 3 clarinets and a bassoon played till replaced in 1836 by a barrel-organ. In the church there are:—1-key piccolo (E. G. Williams); 12-key clarinet (Key, London); 6-key clarinet (Astor, London); 6-key clarinet (Cahusac, London); 6-key bassoon (W. Milhouse, London). A fourth clarinet is preserved in the village.

HEREFS.: CLODOCK:—Musicians gallery c. 1715.
  CROFT:—St. Michael's: Musicians Gallery, 18th century.
  WESTON-UNDER-PENYARD:—In 1840 John Robbins, a string-bass player and bootmaker, made a new barrel for the Church barrel-organ.

HERTS.:—ALDBURY:—In 1813 Churchwardens' Accounts record: " Paid James Puddefoot for bassoon reeds, 10s. 6d."
  ST. PAUL'S WALDEN:—Bassoon (Proser, London), now in Luton Borough Museum. Also a flute (T. Stephens).
  WELWYN:—8-key bassoon (W. Milhouse, London), in Herts. County Museum.

HUNTS.: GLATTON:—'Cello from church band now in Peterborough Museum.

ISLE OF WIGHT: KINGSTON:—In Vestry is an 8-keyed bassoon (wormeaten) (Anon.), played in a small West Gallery before the restoration of the church in 1872.
  NORTHWOOD:—A clarinet is preserved in the Vestry.

KENT: ALDINGTON:—8-keyed bassoon (Denman, London), played by Wm. Slingsby in the 1880's.
  BIRCHINGTON:—8-keyed bassoon (J. Wood, London), now in Modern School Museum, Bedford.
  PENSHURST:—11-keyed ophicleide in use c. 1820, formerly in Canon K. H. Macdermott's Collection.
  SELLINGE:—6-keyed bassoon (G. Astor & Co., London), bought from a descendant of the player. Now in L. G. Langwill's Collection.
  WYE:—Bassoon (Anon.) in former Nettlefold Collection.

LANCS.: HEYSHAM: The churchwardens' accounts for the Parish Church record annually from 1853-1856 payments for " fiddle strings," usually 8d. to 1/- each.
  MELLING:—7-keyed serpent (No. 337 in Day's *Catal.* of Royal Military Exhib. 1890), now in Lancaster Museum.
  OVER WYRESDALE:—In Vestry in case containing a 'cello, flutes, clarinets and " a large bass flute though this is in pieces " (1965).
  STANDISH:—In 1789 a new French Horn, Clarinets, Bass Viol, Reeds and strings were purchased. *Vide History of the Parish of Standish* by T. C. Porteus, (1927), p. 79.

LEICS.: DESFORD:—Serpent from church now in Leicester Museum.
  NEWTON LINFORD:—Serpent from church now in Leicester Museum.

LINCS.: BASSINGHAM:—Bassoon (Milhouse, Newark), in parish chest (1934).
  CASTLE BYTHAM:—6-key clarinet by Preston, London, now in Stamford Public Museum.
  NAVENBY:—4-keyed bassoon (Milhouse, Newark), c. 1760. *Vide Galpin Society Jl,* X, p. 38 with illustration.
  WHAPLODE:—Bassoon in Church.
  WINTERTON:—In Parish Church are Bassoon (incomplete), Tenor Oboe and Flute by Milhouse and Clarinet by Metzler.

MONTGOMERYSHIRE: KERRY:—Bassoon (W. Milhouse, London), with clarinet-type mouth-piece (Key, London), and clarinet (Thomas Key, London); now in National Museum of Wales, Cardiff.
MONTGOMERY:—Bassoon in the church. *Vide Transactions of Ancient Monuments Socy.* New Series, Vol. I 1953).

NORFOLK: BARSHAM:—Double-bass and bow. *Vide Church Times* 11 July 1947.
BRISTON:—Metal 'cello is in the church (1967).
GRESSENHALL:—Clarinet (Metzler, London), and flute (I. B. Cramer & Co., London), now in St. Peter Hungate Church Museum, Norwich.
HINGHAM:—The church bassoon was said to survive in 1958.
MATTISHALL BURGH:—A metal-bodied 'cello used to be in the church. *Vide Church Times,* 11 July 1947.
SPORLE:—A clarinet is preserved in Canon Boston's Collection.
WRETHAM:—Flute from the village bears a label reading " John Leach, Shepherd, Wretham, 1710 ". *Vide Church Times,* 11 July 1947.
WYMONDHAM ABBEY CHURCH:—Flute used in the West Gallery Orchestra in 1830, now in Collection of Rev. Gordon Paget, Provost's House, Bury St. Edmunds.

NORTHANTS.: COURTEENHALL:—Choir and band of bugles, trombones, etc. in early 19th cent., declared to be too noisy. *Vide MacDermott, Old Church Gallery Minstrels,* p. 8.
EASTON-ON-THE-HILL:—6-keyed bassoon (C. Gerock, London), (unicorn), in the church. The west gallery was removed in 1848 and the last reference to the church band records sale of a clarinet in 1852. *Vide Galpin Socy. Jl.* XIV pp. 37-40 and Plate.
HARRINGWORTH:—Clarinet in the church.
NORTHAMPTON:—St. Giles' churchwardens in 1795 paid £4, 13s. 6d. to Bland of Holborn, for a bassoon: a balance of 5s. 9d. being reserved for " new reeds for the bassoon if wanted ". In the same year and for several years after, 10s. 6d. was paid to the bassoon-player. In 1799 his salary was raised to a guinea per annum. In 1806 two guineas was paid " to Roberts who plays the bassoon for one year to Michaelmas last ". *Vide* Dr. J. C. Cox,, *English Church Fittings,* p. 240, and Serjeantson's *History of St. Giles, Northampton,* p. 215.
ROCKINGHAM:—A violin from the church band now (1954) in possession of a parishioner at Easton-on-the-Hill.
RUSHTON:—Church band of over a dozen in 1851 recalled by the late O. F. Wainwright of Belton, Lincs., in 1934. *Vide MacDermott, loc. cit. ante,* p. 8.
WARMINGTON:—A serpent is in the church.

NORTHUMBERLAND:—KIRKWHELPINGTON:—A string band played in a gallery in the church according to *History of Northumberland* by Hodgson, at one time Vicar of the Parish.
SLALEY:—6-keyed bassoon (Cahusac, London), played in the church by a man Blackburn, was sold by his granddaughter in 1948. Now in L. G. Langwill's Collection.

NOTTS.:—WINKBURN:—Ophicleide in use c. 1850, now (1948) property of E. Bee. *Vide* MacDermott, *loc. cit. ante.* p. 31.

OXON:—GORING-ON-THAMES:—A bassoon last used in the Church c. 1810 is preserved in the building.

RADNORSHIRE:—ABEREDW:—A glass case in church contains 8-key flute (G. French, London); flute (Goulding & Co., London); pitch-pipe.
DISCOED:—A pitch-pipe is in the church in which W. H. Howse, F.S.A. of Presteigne led the singing with his violin in the 1940's.
KNIGHTON:—The church band c. 1835 consisted of a " violin, flageolet and bass viol," till the installation of a barrel-organ in 1844. This was replaced in 1869 by an organ by Gray & Davison.
LLANBADARN FAWR:—A violin and bow played in the church in the 18th c. were presented to the church in 1955 by A. J. Lewis, great-grandson of the player.
LLANBISTER:—A bassoon and remnants of other instruments are in a glass case in the church.
LLANFIHANGEL-NANT-MELAN:—The singing in the tiny church in the 1940's was led by W. H. Howse, F.S.A., of Presteigne on the violin.
PRESTEIGNE:—A frame in the church holds a 6-keyed B flat clarinet (Metzler, London); 4-keyed flute (Wood & Ivy, late George Wood, Soho, London). Presented by the grandson of the then choirmaster, S. Nicholas, who played the instruments.

RUTLAND:—LIDDINGTON:—A horn used in the church is now in Leicester Museum.
PRESTON:—Till 1846 the church band consisted of B flat and C clarinets, 'cello, bassoon and flute: *Vide* E. J. Sharpe, *History of Preston in Rutland*.
RIDLINGTON:—In the church are: 8-keyed bassoon (Astor, London), with copper bell (J. Kohler, London); 4-keyed B flat clarinet, 8-keyed A clarinet, (both R. Wolf & Co.); 4-keyed flute.

SALOP: CLUN:—A double-bass played in the church band survives. (Per W. H. Howse, F.S.A., Presteigne, 1957).
COCKSHUTT:—Extracts from the Churchwarden's Accounts 1796-1884 kindly made by the Vicar in 1934 record:

	£		
1796 Pd. for strings for the Bass Viol	—	12	9
1797 Pd. for strings for Bass Viol		12	9
„ oil for the clock 6d. & viol strings 4d.	—	—	10
„ To make the sum towards the Bass Viol		14	—
1800 Pd. Saml. Green for a New Clarinett	1	11	6
do. Do. Mr. Bickley for Hotboy Reeds	—	10	—
21st April 1802 At the above Vestry it was agreed to allow the sum of £2.2.0 for the encouragement of the Psalm Singers to be paid yearly by the Chapelwarden*			
1810 July 2nd for Violoncello strings		4	8
March 27th 1812. One third string for Viol		1	3
Pd. Mr. Rowe for Viol strings		6	6
1817 Mr. Bickley for 4 Hoboy Reeds		5	—
1818, 1819 Willm. Davies for a Bassoon for Cockshutt Chapel*	2	10	—
Six strings for the Bass Viol		7	—
1819 Reeds for church instruments		2	8
1820 Violoncello strings		6	6
Hotboy Reeds		2	—
1821 Mr. Bickley for Holboy Reeds		4	—
John Read for Bassoon do.		4	—
* Cockshutt Church is called " Chapel " here because it was a daughter-church to Ellsmere.			
Saml. Cartwright for Clarionet Reeds		1	—
1822 John Read two reeds for the bassoon		2	6
1823 New Boes for the Violoncello		7	—
Saml. Cartwright for Clarionett Reeds		1	—
1825 Saml. Cartwright for Reeds		1	—
4 Bassoon reeds		4	—
1828 Edwd. Cartwright for Bassoon Reeds		4	—
„ Clarionets Reeds		1	2
1829 Edwd. Cartwright for 3 Bassoon Reeds		3	—
„ Saml. Cartwright for 3 Clarionett do.		1	—
1831 Bassoon Reeds		1	—
1832 Saml. Cartwright for Reeds		1	—
„ do.		1	—
1834 Pd. Mr. Green for repairing the Clarionett		2	6
1837 Two Clarionett Reeds	—	—	6
„ Mr. Baugh's bill for new Clarionett	2	3	—
1840 Clarionett Reeds		1	—
1841, '42 „		1	—
1844, '46 „		1	—
1848/9 Psalm Singers salary	8	—	—
1848/50 Mr. Boucher in exchange of old instrument for D flute	7	—	—
1861-62 W. Hay—Key for Harmonium	1	—	—
1884 Tuning Harmonium	9	—	—

SALOP:—MAINSTONE:—In the church are: 6-keyed bassoon (W. Milhouse, London), 6-keyed clarinet (G. Miller, London, over a ' unicorn'). The instruments were purchased in 1828-29. (Per E. W. R. Newman, Churchwarden of St. John the Baptist Church, Mainstone (1957)).

SOMERSET:—KELSTONE:—Bassoon, (Goulding, London), and Serpent from the church in the late Percy Bull Collection.
LUCCOMBE:—Dr. J. C. Cox recollected well the church band of this parish of which his father was for some years Rector. The band ceased to exist in 1859.
PILTON:—In the church are a clarinet and a flageolet.
SELWORTHY:—The band continued to occupy the west gallery until after the death of " Old Sir Thomas Acland " in 1871.

STAFFS:—SHARESHILL:—4-keyed flute, (Cramer & Son), and 5-keyed clarinet (Cahusac, Strand, London), are in Birmingham Midland Institute Collection.

SUFFOLK: BARKING TYE:—In church is a serpent (Francis Pretty, Obelisk, London).
    BARSHAM:—The church double-bass is now in St. Peter Hungate Church Museum, Norwich.
    BLAXHALL:—The church band of violin, flute and 'cello was replaced as late as 1863.
    GREAT WALDINGFIELD:—A Kent-bugle, well polished, hangs on the wall of the church. (1952).
    POLSTEAD:—A bassoon played in the church band by the grandfather of the donor (H. G. Beatham of Belstead) is now in Christchurch Mansion Museum, Ipswich.
    WICKHAM MARKET:—Flute (Goulding & Co., London), and flute (Clementi & Co., London), formerly used in the church band are now in the Carlisle Museum.

SURREY: SHERE:—In the church are: Flageolet (Hollings); flute (Potter); and clarinet (Key).

SUSSEX: ALFRISTON:—Five bassoons said to have been in use. *Vide Sussex Church Music* . . . p. 91.
    BRIGHTLING:—Nine bassoons said to have been presented to the church by John Fuller M.P. (1757-1834).
    BUXTED:—In the church are: 9-keyed bassoon, (C. Gerock, London), and side-blown flageolet (Parker, Piccadilly, London). *Vide MacDermott, loc. cit. ante.* p. 23.
    FERRING, EAST:—Charles Street (1790-1868) played the 6-keyed bassoon in church. He stuffed some wool in the bell to soften the tone. The village boys nicknamed it " Father's Gun " from the way in which it was carried to and from church.
    HEATHFIELD:—In 1901 " four instruments that used to be played in the musicians' gallery " were extant: 2 bassoons, 1 bass-horn and 1 brass serpent in a case. *Vide* Percival Lucas, *Heathfield Memorials* (1901). By 1920, the whereabouts of the instruments could not be traced. The blacksmith played a bassoon which he called " a sacbut." *Vide* MacDermott, " Susex Church Music . . . p. 93.
    HENFIELD:—In the church are: oboe, 2 silver keys (Potter, Johnson's Court, Fleet St., London); clarinet in high F, 6 keys (1 missing), (Key, 2 Pall Mall, London).
    LAVANT, EAST:—In church Vestry is 1-key flute (Bland & Weller, London) played in 1824.
    LINDFIELD:—In 1837 a 9-keyed bassoon was played by John Wells (1812-1856). A silhouette portrait of Wells playing his bassoon appears on plate facing p. 36 in MacDermott's *Sussex Church Music*. In the church museum are two clarinets: one by Bilton, London, and one by Key, London.
    SIDLESHAM:—8-keyed bassoon (Metzler, London), and oboe (Longman & Broderip) with marks " Muraeus " and lion rampant. Presented to Lewes Museum by the late Canon MacDermott. *Vide Sussex Church Music* . . . p. 41.
    STEDHAM:—Bassoon played in church by George Faulkner (1816-1894) was in 1919 in possession of Walter Faulkner of Stedham.
    WEST TARRING:—In the church are: 7-keyed bassoon (Milhouse, London); 11-keyed bassoon (Anon.: oboe, dated 1791 (T. Collier, London): ivory clarinet (Anon.). *Vide Sussex Church Music* . . . pp. 40-41.

WARWICKSHIRE:—BERKSWELL:—An old 'cello hangs in the South Gallery.
    BRAILES:—Bassoon, 4 keys (Cahusac, London), dated 1769 formerly played in the Church, now in L. G. Langwill's Collection.
    CHADSHUNT:—Miss Fleming, whose grandfather walked two miles to church with his 'cello in a baize bag, has a flute (Preston, London); flute (Bland & Weller, London); recorder (Hallet); flageolet (Anon.).
    HAMPTON-IN-ARDEN:—Churchwardens' Accounts record:

1820 Reeds and mending bassoon	10/6
1821 2 reeds for the bassoon	5/-
1822 Mending the bassoon	5/6
1825 A new bassoon.	£5:4:0

    A barrel-organ was presented to the church in 1839. *Vide Hampton in Arden,* by J. C. Adams (1951).
    KNOWLE:—In 1824 at this daughter-church of Hampton-in-Arden, the church band consisted of " 1st clarionette, 2nd clarionette, German flute, basson (sic), 'cello, tramboon, trumpet, horn." *Vide Hampton-in-Arden,* by J. C. Adams (1951).

WESTMORLAND:—WARCOP:—In the church are: 5-keyed clarinet, boxwood with ivory rings; 7-keyed bassoon.
    KIRKBY LONSDALE:—Prior to the first organ in the church in 1799, a church band was in use. A 'cello from this is owned by Mrs. C. Maybery, Heysham, Lancs. *Vide Annals of Kirkby Lonsdale* by A. Pearson (1930), p. 49.

WILTS.:—Langley Burrell:—In Parish Registers is a note on 10 July 1796 by the Rev. Samuel Ashe, Rector, recording the gift of a bassoon for use in the Parish Church. *Vide N. & Q.* 15, Vol. CLXXII, 16 Jany. 1937. Nothing is known of the subsequent history of the bassoon.

Oaksey:—Basshorn (Key, London) from the church was lent by Canon Galpin to the Music Loan Exhibition, 1904.

Seend:—In Holy Cross Church is a keybugle. An ophicleide played c. 1830 at Seend was owned by F. Cox of Quemerford in 1934. *Vide* MacDermott, *loc. cit. ante,* p. 31.

YORKS.:—Clayton Heights (Old Dolphin) Wesleyan Chapel:—In 1835 a clarinet was bought for £1 and delivered to Edward Sharp. The organ was introduced in 1838. *Vide Hipperholme to Tong,* by J. Parker (1904), p. 455.

HALIFAX:—Illingworth Moor Methodist Chapel:—1829 Bass bow, 6s. 6d.; 1831 2 Bassoon Reeds, 3s.; 1832 Delivered the bassoon, with 2 new reeds, 3s.

Lightcliffe:—A unique seating plan of the church orchestra, pre-1787, survives. See Plate 33. Churchwardens' accounts in 1781 and 1787 record purchases of "2 Bass strings, 2s. 6d." *Vide Halifax Antiq. Socy. Trans.* 1909. (Per L. Morgan).

Ripponden:—In 1828 the church band instruments were dispersed. *Vide Halifax Anteq. Socy. Trans.,* 1958, p. 22.

Worsall:—A serpent from the church band is in the Castle Museum, York. *Vide Museum Guide* p. 9.

PLATE 33

Seating plan of the orchestra in Lightcliffe Church, Yorkshire. Undated but pre-1787. (By courtesy of Rev. Canon White and Mr Leslie Morgan.)